7.95

D0396857

Creative Dreaming

Patricia L. Garfield, Ph. D.

SIMON AND SCHUSTER • NEW YORK

2 3 4 5 6 7 8 9 10

Library of Congress Cataloging in Publication Data

Garfield, Patricia L
    Creative dreaming.

    1. Dreams.   I. Title.
BF1078.G17   615'.851   74-14978
ISBN 0-671-21903-0

To beloved Zal:
In my dreams he is
the strong one,
the wise one,
the loving one,
the giver of gifts
—just as in waking life.

Contents

Foreword

This book was put together with love, and care, and dreams. I did not discover the principles presented in it, I merely wove them together. The result is an intricate fabric designed by many dreamers from widely varied cultures and times. It is a product of mine—but also of those before me who reported their intimate dream lives and those who observed and wrote of the dream lives of others.

My mother's enthusiasm for Freud and Jung, when I was fourteen, probably marked the beginning of the book. Over the past twenty-five years the shapes and textures of my own early dream recordings have shifted dramatically. A special turning point occurred a few years ago, when Dr. Joe Kamiya of San Francisco, chatting at the XXth International Congress of Psychology in Tokyo in 1972, chanced to remark, "If you're going to Malaysia, why not visit the Senoi?" ("The *who*?" I replied.) Later, he generously provided his dream lab and several night hours of assistance to me and my sleepless students to help verify some of my experiences with the EEG.

Dr. Moti Lal, at the hospital for aborigines in Gombak, Malaysia, introduced me to some of the Senoi and translated our conversations for me. Dr. Ivan Polunin and Dr. Geoffrey Benjamin, both of the University of Singapore, gave generously of their knowledge of the Senoi. The excitement of the possibility of conscious control of dreams led me to the works of Kilton Stewart, Mary Arnold-Forster, the Marquis d'Hervey de Saint-Denys, and many others. My colleague Braulio Montalvo, in Philadelphia, shared his knowledge of Carlos Castaneda when he was still but slightly known, and of Giovanni Guareschi. Jack Leavitt of Berkeley made his extensive library collection available. Sidney Harman, a dear friend, helped me with my first tentative contacts with the publishing world of New York. Dr. Arthur McDonald, of Lame Deer, Montana, gave special assistance with the American Indian chapter. Thanks to each one.

Professional colleagues from the Association for the Psychophysiological Study of Sleep exchanged stimulating ideas with me. I'm grateful, too, to students in my dream seminars who shared their own dream experiences. Our children (Linda, Steven, Wendy, Cheryl), relatives, friends, and dreamers everywhere opened their personal dream lives, sharing their own patterns first with me . . . and now with you.

Still others smoothed out the finished product: Jeanne Perilman snipped loose ends, making all presentable, from the earliest version onward. Mary Nagle typed it again and again . . . and again. More, many more, helped, guided, encouraged, assisted.

And Zal, always and forever, Zal, since first I knew him, gave his support. Indeed, sometimes he kept the whole project from collapsing. Although constantly busy, he could always manage to listen to yet another dream, inspect the manuscript one more time, make a new useful suggestion.

I hope this dream-woven fabric pleases you. Examine it. Try it on. If you like it, style it to fit. May it give you much pleasure.

Patricia L. Garfield, Ph.D.

San Francisco, June 1, 1974

part one

How to Plan
Your Dreams

CHAPTER ONE

Learn to Control Your Dreams

In the cool quiet hours of early morning, a young man tosses and turns upon his bed. Still asleep, he kicks off his blanket; the sheet is a tangled mass; his hair falls damp on his forehead. Although his body lies limp for a few seconds, his fingers twitch and his face grimaces. His pulse speeds up, his cheeks are fiery, his breath comes in gasps. Beneath closed lids, his eyes dart rapidly back and forth. Now he moans softly, then louder. With a violent movement, he jerks awake. Sweating, shaking, shivering, he sits up in bed and fumbles for the light. We don't have to ask him what the trouble is, we need no brain machine to confirm the fact: he has surely had a nightmare. The same thing happens millions of times each night to millions of people. Bad dreams are common experiences in our society.

He does next what most of us do. He reassures himself, "It was just a dream"; he feels relieved at his escape from it. He tries to shake off his anxious feelings by going to the bathroom and splashing his face or getting a drink to get rid of the bad taste. If he knows some psychology, he will muse on the symbolic meanings of his dream images, and worry.

What was the frightening image in his dream? It could have been almost anything. Our frightening dream images take many forms: a ferocious tiger in pursuit, a grotesque monster looming up, a demanding father, a murderer after us, a rapist attacking. We have legs that will not move, a pounding heart, and clammy hands. Gigantic tidal waves engulf us, buildings crumble, a formless blob descends from the sky. Each of us can add many other scenes of our own dream making. The variations of nightmare forms are endless but the scenario is limited: We become aware of the frightening image; we respond with fear. It moves toward us; we move away. It chases; we run. It traps us; we "escape" to the waking world. What a pity! Most of us don't even know what an opportunity we have missed.

In "escaping," we leave the fear-producing images behind—to pursue us on another night. By confronting them, instead, we can conquer them. We can deal with our problems at their origin in our own minds. We can learn about ourselves and grow. We can unify our personalities. We can transform our fear-producing dream enemies into dream friends. It is true. We can build into our dream world friendly images that will help us not only in our dreams but in our waking life as well. We can make dream friends who will provide us with solutions to our problems and with marvelous creative products. Dream friends can show us how to solve a knotty problem at work, provide a theme for an advertising campaign, create an original dress design, compose an epic poem, or sing a new song. Whatever our problems are, dreams can provide novel ideas and sometimes magnificent resolutions.

Nightmares are not necessary to launch this adventure of changing dream life. Dreams are all we need. And we have them every night—four or five of them, to be exact. Research has clearly established that each one of us dreams four or five times a night. We spend about 20 percent of our total sleep time in a dream state. For most of us, this means we dream one and a half hours each night or, on the average, spend *four years* of our lifetime in a dream state.[1] Those of you who say you don't dream are simply not remembering your dreams, unless possibly you ingest large quantities of dream-suppressing drugs.[2] That's approximately *four years* you could be spending with full awareness in useful, creative growth. If you have trouble recalling your dreams, you will find Chapter 8, "How to Keep Your Dream Diary," helpful. You may want to read it before you go on with the rest of this book. Dream recall is, to a large extent, an acquired habit and can be learned.

Those of you who already remember a fair amount of your dreams can increase your recall until it is almost total. I've trained myself to recall almost every dream immediately after it occurs; several of my students in dream seminars have learned to do this as well. We'll deal with the techniques later in detail.

Let's assume that you recall your dreams moderately well or will use the suggestions given and learn to do so. Now, with your dreams in mind, you can begin to shape them. Like a sculptor with clay, you can mold them into a form that will actively serve you, replacing terror and puzzlement. You can produce a thing of beauty and usefulness that will sustain and enrich your life.

You don't believe it? Most people don't—at first. When I tell people about dream control, they say it can't be done. They quote authorities who say it can't be done. When someone denies the possibility of dream control, I present the evidence of cultures in which it clearly exists. I tell them about my visit to the Senoi tribe in Malaysia and how they teach their children, from the time they can talk, to dream in a particular pattern. Every member of the tribe learns to eliminate nightmares and produce artistic creations from his dreams. Eventually a person who at first denies that dream control is possible will concede that it may exist, but only in primitive tribes.

Then I tell them about my own experiences in controlling my dreams and experiences of my students in dream seminars. I tell them the rules of dream control and suggest that they try it. Even as they say it can't be done, they often find their own dreams changing. They are astonished and say, "OK, so you can control your dreams, and you can do it in our culture, but should you?"

Yes, you should . . . if you want to. If you are not ready to relate to your dreams in this way, your dream mind will reject the suggestions. It cannot hurt you to try. If your dream mind accepts the suggestions, you open the way to a whole new world within yourself. You will find that as-yet-undreamed-of riches become available to you in your dreams. Our dreams are already shaped without our awareness. It is difficult to know what our dreams would be like in a "pure, untampered" state. All that we have heard about dreams, all that we have read, all the opinions of the authorities we accept, all our beliefs and expectations shape our dreams. To a large extent, our dreams are *right now* what we make them. They are already tampered with. I suggest that we deliberately shape them in a way that is certain to be beneficial to us.

Some people in our culture have already noticed the "shapability" of dreams. Patients in therapy describe having Freudian-type dreams—that is, dreams with predominant sexual and aggressive symbolism—when they consult a Freudian analyst. The same patient, when he switches to a Jungian therapist, begins to have Jungian-type dreams of mandalas and archetypes. This change is not merely a shift of emphasis in interpretation but a shift in actual dream content. The patient has learned to shape his dreams according to the wishes and expectations of his therapist.

Therapists—a few wise ones who have noticed how consciousness can shape dreams—have helped their patients to improve by deliberately influencing their patients' dreams. Take the case of eleven-year-old Johnny. He had many problems, for which he was being treated, but one of the most troublesome was a terrifying nightmare of a monster pursuing and, sometimes, catching and hurting him. Two or three times a week for more than eighteen months, Johnny would awaken in a panic and come screaming to his weary parents' bedroom. He could not sleep at all without a light in his room.

Johnny's therapist, Dr. Leonard Handler,[3] sat the boy upon his knee. He told Johnny he could help him get rid of the monster. In the warm office, lined with books, held by the secure arms of the man he had grown to trust, Johnny was asked to close his eyes and imagine that the monster was there with them. Dr. Handler assured Johnny that he would protect him and help him get rid of the monster. When Johnny, eyes screwed tightly shut, nodded his head to indicate that he could see the monster, Dr. Handler held him firmly and pounded his outstretched hand loudly on the desk, shouting again and again, "Get out of here, you lousy monster, leave my friend John alone!" He repeated this over and over while holding the trembling boy. He added, "Get away and stay away—don't you ever come back or I'm going to get you! You leave my friend John alone!"

Soon Dr. Handler had Johnny jubilantly pounding and shouting with him, "Get away and leave me alone!" Next, Dr. Handler turned out the lights. Johnny gave a start and hesitated, but in a short while he was again yelling at the monster without fear. They practiced for about fifteen minutes. Before Johnny left Dr. Handler's office that day, he promised he would yell at the monster whenever he saw him and recalled the method. When Dr. Handler met with Johnny the following week and asked about the monster, Johnny reported that he had seen the monster once, he had yelled at it, and after a brief moment it vanished. Dr. Handler and Johnny practiced monster-yelling a few more minutes. In the subsequent six months Johnny had only two nightmares, neither of which was about the monster. Ordinarily, he would have had between forty-eight and seventy-two nightmares during this period of time. He certainly succeeded at scaring away the dream monster. Fortunately, most of us are not troubled by nightmares as often as Johnny, but we can learn techniques that are somewhat similar, yet far more sophisticated, to dispense with those nightmares we do have. You can use your conscious mind to confront and conquer your dream enemies just as Johnny did.

Then there is the case of Margherita. In his autobiography, the Italian author Giovanni Guareschi [4] has described his efforts to help his young wife, Margherita, during a period of severe disturbance. Margherita felt that she was a prisoner of her dreams. Her first complaint was of dragging her "unhappy feet" through endless streets in the "world of shadows, desires, and fears" (her dreams), where she dwelled all alone. Guareschi suggested, much to her disgust, that she get a bicycle. He insisted that she would feel much better if she would concentrate on traveling by bicycle instead of by foot in her dreams. He would have suggested a car if she had known how to drive. Several days later Margherita reported that she had obtained a bicycle in her dreams and was, indeed, less tired from her nightly wanderings. A week later, however, she fell into a deep depression. She told Guareschi that she had had to go back to walking in her dreams because she had had a blowout. Guareschi urged her to repair the blowout; if she could get a bicycle in her dreams, she could also get rubber, cement, or a bicycle repair shop. Margherita maintained that she had tried and it was hopeless; she was totally alone. Guareschi did an unusual thing at this point: He taught Margherita skills in her waking life to use in solving her dream problems. First, he led her by the hand to his garage workshop, where he took his own bicycle from the wall and showed her how to change a tire. After fumbling several attempts, she finally managed to change the tire successfully. He repeated the process a few days later, instructing her in how to change the bicycle tire over and over again. Recalling his experience in learning to operate a machine gun, Guareschi had Margherita repeat the operation blindfolded. She seemed preoccupied for the next two days, but on the third she cried triumphantly that she had fixed the bicycle of her dreams and it now worked perfectly. All was well for several months before Margherita spoke of her secret world again. One night she tearfully told Guareschi that while riding along a narrow mountain road in her dream world, the bicycle slipped from under her and she rolled to the bottom of a ravine, where she now lay, badly hurt. He asked her to call for help, but she felt it was hopeless. She was in total despair, believing that her end had come. Guareschi rushed out and bought manuals on mountain climbing which he persuaded Margherita to study with him. They found pictures of the type of rock formation in which she was imprisoned; they studied instructions on crucial movements to climb the steep mountain wall and learned them by heart. Margherita tried, but in her mind her hands were scratched and bloody, and she felt she had to resign herself to death. Guareschi, in an agony to help his patient-wife, begged her, "Cry out, cry out day and night. Try to call me. Don't stop calling me. Who knows, I may hear you." Later that evening, he felt he heard a distant cry. Speeding home, he found Margherita humming as she set the table. She confirmed that she had called him in her dream. At last he had heard her, she said. He had appeared at the edge of the ravine in her dreams, had thrown her a long rope, which she had tied around herself, and had pulled her up to safe ground. Margherita serenely declared, "... I'm not worried any more. I know that if I'm ever in danger and I call to you, you'll hear me and come."

Giovanni Guareschi probably did not know it, but he was applying (albeit not systematically) some of the basic principles of dream control in his attempts to help the emotionally disturbed Margherita. These are principles that can be applied not only to deeply disturbed patients but ordinary dreamers who wish to benefit from their dreams to the fullest extent. They are principles that you, yourself, can begin to apply tonight. They are ways of relating to your dreams that can help you when you are troubled; they are ways that can give you exquisite joy when you are untroubled.

The chapters that follow will tell you about these principles in detail, the "rules" I have derived from them, and how to use them. For the moment, let me simply point out the ones that are operating with Margherita. The most important principle is to *confront and conquer danger in dreams*. This is what Dr. Handler taught Johnny to do. This is what Guareschi taught Margherita to do. He did not permit Margherita to resign herself to endless lonely wanderings, nor to a broken bicycle, her means of self-propelled movement, nor to being entrapped, hurt, and dying in an inaccessible hole. Guareschi urged her repeatedly to take action, to confront, to resolve her difficulty. You will see how this principle is the basis of both the Senoi and the Yoga systems of dream control. The Senoi tribe and the Yogis of the dream state have developed fearlessness of dream images and positive resolutions of dream problems to a fine degree. We can learn a great deal from them.

Your conscious thoughts can profoundly affect your dream life. Guareschi apparently sensed this when he used his relationship with Margherita to convince her that she could change her suffering dream life. He urged her to use the skills she had, such as bicycle riding; he taught her new skills that she could incorporate as solutions to dream problems; he made her practice until they were an automatic part of her, until she could literally do them blindfolded. Guareschi helped Margherita start a positive growth cycle. Notice how each time Guareschi successfully persuaded Margherita to confront and conquer danger in her dream, she "carried over" the successful feeling to her waking state. The dream success generates a mood of capability in waking life. As you will see in later chapters, a feeling of ability to cope in waking life and a sense of happiness often result from positive dream experiences and increase the probability of success with waking life problems. As you practice and develop dream control skills, you will establish a similar growth cycle in yourself.

Notice also Guareschi's insistence that Margherita call for help with her dream problems. Although for a long time she felt it was hopeless to do so, Margherita was eventually able to evoke the helpful image of Guareschi in her dreams. The Senoi people call such helpful dream images their "dream friends." They have an ingenious technique (described in Chapter 5) for establishing innumerable dream friends. This helpful potential already exists within you; it needs only to be shaped and encouraged. You start by asking for help in dreams.

Dream friends begin by helping you solve dream problems and move to providing you with solutions to problems of your waking life. They can provide you with artistic creations beyond your present ability to imagine. They can become your helpers and guides for life.

Both Johnny with his fear of a dream monster, and Margherita, with her fear of lonely dream imprisonment, needed assistance. Dr. Handler and Giovanni Guareschi provided that assistance. Therapists everywhere may wish to use the principles of dream control to help their patients move in a positive direction. But the patients must make certain efforts for themselves. Within the private world of dreams, only the dreamer can choose his action. With guidance, he may choose wisely. This book can be your guide.

For the ordinary dreamer, therapeutic support is unnecessary. He may wish it, he may enjoy it, he may obtain it and use it to grow. But it is not essential for him to begin relating creatively to his dreams. You, on your own, can embark on the great adventure of creative dreaming once you understand the principles of dream control. With the manual of dream control to guide you, you can steer away from dangerous shoals. You can guide your dream vessel to exotic lands, to new and marvelous experiences.

All over the world, researchers in dream laboratories are beginning to notice the "shapability" of dreams. You are probably already familiar with the 1953 discovery that rapid eye movements (REMs) almost invariably accompany the dream state. Eugene Aserinsky, a young graduate student at the University of Chicago, was working under the direction of Dr. Nathaniel Kleitman, an expert in the field of sleep.[5] They were studying sleep patterns in newborn infants and were puzzled by the jerky movements of each baby's eyes that seemed to appear at periodic intervals. In order to check whether these same movements occurred during the sleep of adults Aserinsky and Kleitman made careful all-night records of adult volunteers' sleep, using the electroencephalograph (EEG) machine, a machine that "writes" brain waves.

Minute changes of electric potential within the brain are detected by metal contacts pasted to specific spots on the outside of the subject's head and carried to the EEG machine, where they are amplified. The EEG machine transmits the continuous electrical changes to ink-filled pens, which translate the changing brain rhythms into tracings on a moving graph paper. The resulting record appears as wavy lines: brain waves. One or more pens record changes in electric potential in the brain, another pen records changes in muscle tension, and two pens record movements of the eyes. Although the EEG machine had been in use for many years, even in studying sleep, researchers had only used it to sample a twenty- or thirty-minute period of sleep; all-night records, considered to be expensive and unnecessary, had never been made. We had no idea what we were missing.

Aserinsky and Kleitman were astounded to discover that adults show a period of rapid eye movement, just as the infants had shown. They were able to awaken their adult subjects during a REM period and ask them what they were experiencing. Almost invariably, the sleepy subject would say he had been in the middle of a dream. This discovery had immediate impact. At last dreams could be scientifically observed and measured. What further unlocking of the secret of dreams might not be possible? Dream and sleep labs sprang up throughout the world. Today, twenty years later, more than two dozen dream labs exist in the United States alone. The study of dreams has become a significant and respectable scientific exploration, one that can directly benefit you.

Researchers in every corner of the earth confirmed the

discovery by Aserinsky and Kleitman that humans have a cyclical pattern of sleep. The average adult, during an average night's sleep, has four or five REM periods, which emerge from deeper stages of sleep. These periods typically occur every ninety minutes during sleep and last a specified amount of time, beginning with a short ten-minute REM and ending with a thirty- to forty-five-minute REM toward morning. Every person measured was found to have periodic REM. For the first time, scientists learned that *dreaming is a universal nightly experience*. People differ in their ability to *recall* dreams, not in the act of dreaming. As I commented earlier, you have four or five chances, totaling about one and a half hours, in which to practice dream control each night.

Researchers discovered more and more physiological changes that accompany REM periods: The pulse rate quickens and becomes irregular; the breathing rate becomes faster and irregular; the blood pressure becomes irregular; males have full or partial penile erections (the female equivalent has not yet been observed); large muscles become limp, while small muscles in the face or fingers twitch sporadically. Researchers confirmed what pet owners watching their sleeping pets twitch have long known, that REM sleep occurs in dogs and cats as well. In fact, all species of mammals, and even some birds, experience REM sleep. Whether REM sleep is accompanied by dreams in animals is uncertain, yet many laboratory studies [6] suggest that animals dream as well.

So far researchers in dream labs have been more interested in the form of dreaming, rather than the content or meaning of dreams. By now the dreamer in the laboratory has been exposed to endless kinds of stimulation to examine his dream response to them. From the viewpoint of dream control, researchers have noticed some extraordinarily important happenings. Two very common dream experiences have never occurred in the dream lab (or, if they have, so rarely as to be currently unreported to my knowledge). Nightmares are common phenomena among civilized peoples, yet dream researchers have not observed them in the laboratory.[7] "Wet" dreams, technically known as nocturnal emissions, in which the male ejaculates semen during a dream, are common, too, especially among the young male college students who serve as frequent subjects in dream labs, yet they remain unobserved. It is as though the subject is unwilling to be watched during this activity. He exercises a kind of control, with or without awareness, that will not permit certain of his personal activities to be scrutinized. This is a tiny hint of the control that is possible.

In other cases, dreamers are willing to go along with the experimenter and learn to discriminate between sounds while sleeping, listen to information while asleep that they can repeat while awake, signal to the experimenter by pushing a button when their dreams start, or follow instructions given to them while asleep. Several dreamers have learned to sense their internal level of consciousness while asleep and turn specified brain waves on and off at will. Thus, the dreaming subjects are exercising control that is suggested to them by the experimenter. On the other hand, sometimes they have stubbornly refused to dream altogether, or if they dream, they refuse to reveal the content.

People used to believe that bodily activities were clearly divided into voluntary and involuntary actions. We can move our arms, but we cannot affect our digestion. Today we are discovering that processes previously conceived of as impossible to control actually can be controlled. Modern science is beginning to discover what Yogis have been doing for centuries. People in the lab have learned to regulate their blood pressure, control the amount of acid secretion in their stomachs, or increase the alpha wave frequency of their brains by feedback techniques.

Similarly, people can learn to control their own dreams in a way that is helpful for them. They need only train themselves to correctly observe themselves and they can provide themselves with the feedback information to shape their dreams to their own benefit. This book is designed to explain this vital process.

You may have already sensed a hint of the possibilities that exist. Many ordinary dreamers have experienced a rudimentary kind of dream control. If you have ever had a frightening dream in the midst of which you said to yourself, "I don't need to be afraid, this is just a dream; I can wake up if I want to," you have had a few seconds of dream control. Some dreamers use this awareness of the dream state to escape the fearful dream by awakening; other dreamers use awareness of the dream state to change the theme of the dream so that they are no longer frightened, or even if the action continues as before, they become interested rather than remaining afraid. The tiger that is ferociously chasing the dreamer turns into a playful kitten; a helicopter appears to rescue the dreamer from the cold water engulfing his sinking ship, and so forth.

Many dreamers experience a fleeting moment of consciousness. They usually have no idea that dream consciousness can be expanded from a single thread of thought to the entire fabric of the dream. The dreamer who becomes totally aware of his dream state and can hold on to this awareness—a tricky business, but one that can be learned—becomes capable of experiencing his heart's deepest desire in his dreams. He can "consciously" choose to make love with the partner of his choice; he can travel in his dreams to distant lands; he can converse with any figures he wishes, real or fictional, dead or alive;

he can find solutions to his waking life problems; he can discover artistic creations. The dreamer who can become "conscious" in his dream state opens for himself an exciting personal adventure. Both the lucid dreamers and the Yogis of the dream state have developed to a high degree the skill of becoming aware of dreaming while in the dream state. You will see how you can apply their techniques to your own dream life to open for yourself the door to this enchanting experience.

But there is more than adventure. The creative dreamer's greatest advantage over the ordinary dreamer is his continuous opportunity to unify his personality. The fearlessness of dream images that the creative dreamer learns from the Senoi, Yoga and lucid dream control systems produces a mood of capability that carries over into waking life, providing a foundation for confident, capable action. By applying principles of dream control, you can shape your dream state into a supportive and helpful level of consciousness; by using the solutions to problems and artistic creations your dream life provides, you will enrich your waking life. As this positive growth cycle continues, you will function more and more as a whole, as a unit of humanity, part of which operates while awake and part while dreaming, with each supporting and promoting growth of the other part.[8]

The creative dreamer develops specific skills to achieve a level of attention and ability to concentrate as he practices dream control. The creative dreamer learns to sustain dream images for long periods of time. As you acquire this skill, you will find that your memory for dreams increases and becomes vivid. You will be able to focus your attention on aspects of your dreams that interest you and retain clear visual images of them. The skills of attention, focused concentration, and memory may generalize to waking behaviors as well.

The creative dreamer greatly increases his productivity of

solutions to problems and artistic creations because he has greater access to his full range of accumulated memories and skills than the ordinary dreamer. You have recorded within you, in a way that is not yet clear to scientists, every experience of your lifetime. Whatever events have been seen, heard, touched, tasted, smelled, or sensed in any way by the receptors of your body since you were conceived have traveled through your nervous system and been recorded in your brain. Researchers believe this "storage" exists because, under certain conditions, people can recall these previous observations and they can be verified by outside sources.

People under hypnosis have been able to recall forgotten details of the babyhood experiences. People who have been unconscious during operations have later been hypnotized and were able to describe verbatim conversations held between the doctors and nurses while the operation was performed. People [9] who have performed the complex task of bricklaying years before they were hypnotized were able to report under hypnosis amazingly accurate, minute details about specific bricks, which could then be verified by checking the *actual* brick. Everything we are exposed to is recorded.

Our brains seem to file away in minute and accurate detail every aspect of our experiencing. Ordinarily, this detail is of no particular use and our minds focus only on items necessary for daily operation. We concentrate on today's market list without cluttering our thoughts with the thousands of lists that may have come before it.

Yet, these infinitesimal memories constitute a vast, rich storehouse, a lifetime's supply of creative food, ours to draw upon as we wish. We can ask for the memory intact; we can request it to combine with other memories to present itself in a new form.

Many of these memory details appear unbidden as images in our dreams; others will only materialize in our dreams if they are called. You can deliberately use your dreams to communicate with your storehouse of limitless memories that can be put together in a combination that is uniquely yours. The principles of dream control in this book will give you a map on which to chart the beginning of your exploration.

A word of caution: Like any adventurous journey, the exploration of the land of dreams has its risks, though they are minimal in this case. The person who does not accept creative dreaming as a good way to relate to his dreams will simply not attempt it. As I mentioned earlier, the person who tries creative dreaming and is not ready for it will not obtain the desired responses; it cannot hurt to try. A person who is deeply troubled may or may not find creative dreaming helpful. Any person, however, who is continuously disturbed by nightmares or who is usually a heavy dream recaller and suddenly appears to stop dreaming should seek professional help from a clinic or practitioner. Local hospitals and university departments of psychology or counselling can give recommendations. Everyone experiences occasional nightmares or periods of no apparent dreaming, yet if they persist, they are danger signals requiring attention.

Creative dreaming may provide us with a safer path for the inward journey to expanded consciousness than the rough road of drugs followed by many modern people. The creative dreamer can experience several times a night the same expanded and limitless personal power sought by drug users without the same risk.

The dreamer who is ready to try creative dreaming and learns the principles of dream control may find he progresses in spurts. Certain concepts are incorporated rapidly. Others *seem* to be undigested for months yet later emerge unexpectedly in vivid detail. Perseverance is important.

Our brains may be capable of far more than their fantastic storage capacity. Individuals have long reported, and researchers are just beginning to confirm, brain capabilities (at least in some individuals) to receive and send sensory information without known sensory organs.[10] We presently have no idea how extensive these skills may be or what may lie beyond them.

As you succeed in establishing creative dreaming, you will be achieving a lifetime victory. You will increase your capacity for concentration and recall. You will build a capacity for coping with fear-producing dream situations that carries over into the waking state. You will experience pleasurable adventures in your dreams. You will understand yourself better. You will help define and unify the unique personality that is you. You will find support and help for waking problems. You will be able to produce things of usefulness and beauty that both express yourself and enrich the world. And all this may be just the beginning . . .

CHAPTER TWO

Learn From Ancient Dreamers

You can start dreaming creatively tonight. You can begin at the simplest level of dream control in which you, the dreamer, plan the general content of your dreams. The advanced techniques described in later chapters will eventually be most helpful, but you can begin valuable practice now. Dreamers in ancient times used their dreams in a special way to gain answers to their questions or to obtain cures from sickness.

Pretend for a moment that you are a Greek in ancient times, and you'll see how it worked:

> You are trudging along a dusty road. You are a pilgrim on your way to the temple of healing at Epidaurus. You have a few things in a sack: A bit of food and some gifts for Asclepius, the god. You don't need much, for when you reach the sanctuary you will fast or eat little, especially avoiding foods that prevent dreams—wine, meat, certain fish, "broad beans." You've had no sexual intercourse since your journey began and will not until you finish your stay at the temple. When you arrive, you will bathe in the cold water of the fountains to wash off the dust from the road and to make yourself even more pure. You will try to make your mind as clean as your body, for above the entrance gate is written: "Pure must be he who enters the fragrant temple; Purity means to think nothing but holy thoughts." [1]
>
> Surely your long journey will be worth the trouble.

You've been anxious and worried lately; your system has been out of sorts. Your mind must have unawaredly allowed some disease to pass into your body. You must attack the disturbance quickly or it will grow.

Now ahead you can see the sacred groves of the valley of the temple. You hear the birds, feel the fresh breezes, smell the sweet fragrance of flowers. Perhaps you will take the baths and engage in athletic games or in dancing at the gymnasium; these help restore the inner rhythms of the body. You will be refreshed by the beauty of the art, the concerts, and the plays. So many have been helped before you! The wondrous cures of the god are inscribed on stone tablets all around the sanctuary.

Now you round a bend in the road and can see the tip of the rotunda coming into view above the trees. Beyond it are the stone seats of the theater. Soon you will be in the main temple, kneeling at the foot of the giant ivory and gold statue of Asclepius, the god of health; soon the temple incense will fill your nostrils, the hymns and incantations of the priests will ring in your ears. Perhaps you will feel so well from doing all the prescribed things that you will not have to endure Enkoimisis (sleeping in the forbidden dormitory, the "abaton"). You can enter the forbidden dormitory to seek a dream of the god's personal visit to cure you only if you have first been invited by the god in a dream. Now, you get out your wheat cakes from your sack, to offer to the god. You hasten your steps, feeling a lift of spirit already . . .

It is several days later. Now you are in front of the temple at dusk, the "hour of the sacred lamps." You have fulfilled all the preliminary requirements, been purified, made your offering, listened to the teachings of the priests. You have improved in health yet still do not feel total harmony. Last night in a dream you saw a misty figure beckon to you. Although the dream was dark, it seemed to be a bearded man wrapped in a cloak, carrying a staff, motioning you to come.

And then you woke. You know it was the god inviting you; the priests have given permission; tonight you go to the forbidden dormitory. In the flickering torchlight you and the other pilgrims beseech the god to grant all of you the curing dreams you seek so eagerly. Now you walk into the slender dormitory buildings, mysterious in the torchlight. You lie down upon a sheepskin, still flecked with blood from the sacrifice. In the dim light, you watch the movements of the large yellow serpents that writhe across the floor. They are nonpoisonous, you know, but so many and so enormous. You remind yourself they were nurtured by the god. You lay your head on the fluffy sheepskin, the air heavy with incense. Now the temple servant walks through the porticos extinguishing the torches and telling the pilgrims it is time for sleep. In the quiet blackness, you hear only the echo of the hymns in your mind and the soft swish-swish of the slithering snakes.

You will not be surprised to hear that many thousands of pilgrims had the predicted dream under these circumstances. The pilgrims were impressed by the rituals, they wanted to please the priests; and their friends gave them a lot of attention when they had the "proper" dream. Just as they had been told would happen, and just as they *expected* to happen, most pilgrims had vivid dreams in which the god Asclepius appeared. Often he looked like his statue, sometimes like a boy, or he even appeared as an animal. Whatever his form, he touched the afflicted pilgrims and cured them, or advised them what to do to be cured, and told them what further offerings might be required. When the pilgrims awoke in the morning, feeling refreshed and well, they shared their dream experiences.

This special way of relating to dreams is referred to as "dream incubation." The description is representative of dream incubation in ancient Greece, but actual practice varied from country to country, temple to temple, and time to time. Researchers believe that 300 to 400 or more temples [2] in honor of the god Asclepius existed in the ancient world. These temples were in active use for nearly 1,000 years (from the end of the sixth century B.C. until the end of the fifth century A.D.). We can extract techniques to help us relate to our own dreams from the dream incubation methods used by ancient dreamers.

Ancient dreamers performed many actions unnecessary to induce dreams. Since dream incubation was defined as the practice of going to a sacred place to sleep for the purpose of obtaining a useful dream from a god, they believed that they needed holy places and gods. Researchers [3] suspect that the practice of incubation originally had the cure of sterility as its chief purpose. Many of the priests assumed that some sort of sexual union with a god or goddess occurred while the pilgrim slept at the temple; sometimes literal sexual union occurred in the form of sacred prostitution. The numerous healing cults of the ancient world are believed to have evolved from the treatment of sexual inadequacy. (If this is so, the sacred snake of Asclepius may take on additional symbolic meaning, as it does in psychoanalysis, as the male sex organ, in this case a part of the god.) Later, dreamers practiced incubation in more general ways: (1) to obtain advice on problems or (2) to become healed from a variety of afflictions. Modern therapists' efforts to use dreams therapeutically probably descended from these ancient practices.

You will see that you need neither believe in a specific god nor go to a sacred place to employ dream incubation. What, then, are the essential elements of inducing a desired dream?

The first essential is to *place yourself where you will not be distracted from the subject of your desired dream.* The ancient Greeks found such a place in their dream induction temples and sanctuaries, buildings of great physical beauty, usually in magnificent natural settings far from the bustle of busy lives. When I visited sanctuaries more than fifteen centuries after they were actively used, they were still serene and tranquil amid olive groves and great plane trees. Ancient Assyrians, Egyptians, and Chinese, too, built their dream incubation temples in similar peaceful country settings. Even primitive people are believed to have descended into their own private caves and to have slept on the ground, either on the tombs of their ancestors or on the skins of sacrificed animals, in hopes of receiving healing dreams.[4]

Any place where it is easy for you to feel peaceful and rested will do: your favorite mountain path, an isolated beach, or a quiet garden. Even your backyard, living room, or bedroom (if you can arrange to be uninterrupted) can serve the purpose. Most forms of intense concentration require that the practitioner withdraw from busy daily activity and keep external distraction low. Modern therapists frequently attempt to provide a similar serene setting.

A peaceful place can be generated in many ways. The Yogis who withdraw their attention and turn it inward to meditate in the midst of great distraction create for themselves a private place. Religious devotees sometimes accomplish this with internal prayer amid noisy surroundings. You may find it easier, at least initially, to go to a place that is externally peaceful rather than create an internally peaceful one. If you can manage both external and internal peacefulness, so much the better.

After you have obtained your own peaceful place, the next step is to *clearly formulate your intended dream.* The priests of Asclepius described to the pilgrim what he could expect when he slept in the forbidden dormitory. Stelae (upright stone slabs with inscriptions) were placed around the temple grounds.[5] These stelae described previous pilgrims, their diseases, and the curing dreams they had received at the temple. The pilgrim also heard other pilgrims tell about their curing dreams on the morning after having them, so he had a clear idea of what he could expect to experience. Madison Avenue did not create advertising, nor latter-day hypnotists the notion of suggestion.

The element of expectation is important. Thousands of pilgrims reportedly experienced the predicted healing or advising dreams. This phenomenon could be dismissed as a result of external suggestion—the purification rites, the sacrifices, the ceremonies, the beauty, the activities, the influence of the priests, the music, the incense, the experiences of friends, the mysterious atmosphere. However, the same effect can be produced when a modern dreamer anticipates having a particular dream—when he formulates a clear intention and proceeds to have the predicted dream—so there is a basis for suspecting that *self-induced suggestion* may be fully as powerful, if not more so, than outside influence. As a man believes, so shall he dream.

The ancient Greeks were not the only groups to experience miraculous cures in dreams. The ancient Hebrews, Egyptians, Indians, Chinese, Japanese, and Muslims all practiced dream incubation. Christians of today see their own saints in curing dreams; Japanese of today may see Yakushi (the master of healing) as a monk in curing dreams. Each faith expects to see its own god. One theorist [6] suggests that the often-blurred image in a curing dream is a Jungian archetype of the healer, the savior, the doctor-god. He thinks that one of man's deepest desires is to find an omnipotent force capable of helping and curing. The dreamer who sees his god merely borrows the face of a specific saint or a god of current belief; identification as Asclepius or Saint Michael does not occur until after the person awakes—a recognition looking back on what has taken place.

I suggest instead that the form of the god is *predetermined* (rather than being a recognition following the dream), that it is shaped by the expectation of the dreamer. As you formulate clearly your intended dream you will shape your future dream experience even more directly.

Now, dreamers can either formulate intended dreams for themselves or have dream images imposed on them from an outside source. The hypnotist who gives a subject some clear, authoritative, convincing suggestions about what to dream is deliberately imposing his intention. Present-day psychoanalysts often shape the dreams of their patients (as noted in Chapter 1) without deliberately intending to do so. Most people's dreams are unawaredly shaped by the culture and ideas that surround them.

The human mind is highly suggestible. When I describe to students how they can induce their own desired dreams and they succeed in so doing, they are often responding to *my* suggestions rather than their own. They do not know that the mind can formulate its own suggestions and carry them out with remarkable efficiency. This step is crucial for inducing dreams: Clearly decide on one desired dream. By doing this, you narrow your field of consciousness and shut out distracting dream possibilities. Pick any topic you would like to dream about. For example: "I want a dream to tell me what to do about ——" (a particular situation), or "I want a dream to tell me how to feel better," or "I want a dream of flying." *Choose a specific dream topic*.

You can choose to induce any dream image you wish.

Hopefully, you will select an image that will have a beneficial effect on you. Hippocrates, the ancient Greek physician (c. 460–360 B.C.), believed that the sun, moon, and stars appearing in dreams represent the dreamer's organic state. If the dream stars shine brightly and follow their natural orbit, the dreamer's body is functioning normally. If dream stars become clouded or fall from their orbit or a cosmic catastrophe occurs, some disease is taking shape in the body. For example, as he stated in *Treatise on Dreams:*

> It is a sign of sickness if the (dream) star appears dim and moves either westwards or down into the earth or sea, or upwards. Upward movement indicates fluxes [an abnormal discharge of liquid] in the head; movement into the sea, disease of the bowels; eastward movement, the growing of tumors in the flesh . . .[7]

Dreams in which symptoms of illness seem to appear prior to awareness of them in a waking state are called "prodromic" [8] (from the Greek word *prodromos,* meaning "running before").

Hippocrates reasoned that if certain dream symbols foretell illness, other dream images symbolic of health (such as radiant sunshine, bright stars, mighty rivers, or dazzling white clothing) can be used for therapeutic purposes.

Certain modern therapists, such as the Frenchman Robert Desoille with his "guided daydream" therapy, treat patients using a similar technique. They suggest dream symbols believed to be beneficial to a deeply relaxed yet awake patient who is "guided" through a health-producing daydream. Other modern therapists employ methodology in which a deeply relaxed yet awake patient is asked to visualize a series of scenes that are designed in a special way to be "curative images." Therapists do not, to my knowledge, ordinarily suggest that their patients *induce healthful images in their dreams.* Here is one of many areas in which we can learn from the ancients.

You do not need to wait until you are sick to enlist the aid of your total self (including your so-called subconscious) to reinforce your health. You can suggest to yourself dream images believed to be reflective of good health and thereby encourage well-being in yourself. Changes in your dreams can change your attitude, which affects your actual physical health. The ability to change your dreams gives you great power over your internal states and eventually over your external behavior.

So far, you have obtained a peaceful place where you can concentrate on inducing a specific dream. Next, *put your intention into a concise positive phrase.* To simply state to yourself, for example, "I think I'll try to have a flying dream tonight," is not strong enough. Say instead, "Tonight I fly in my dream." This phrase establishes a clear-cut pattern. The dream state part of the mind can be thought of as an unruly, hard to reach child; it is lovable, emotional, and highly imaginative but difficult. Make the message definite, brief, and positive.

Dreamers from earliest times have attempted to induce dreams by some kind of ritualistic formula: dream incubation formulas are found in written records that date from approximately 3000 B.C. The first four civilizations—the Middle East,[9] the Egyptian, the Indian, and the Chinese—all left some record [10] of their views on dreams and their methods of inducing them.

The ancient Assyrians, for example, had a special prayer for invoking good dreams and preventing evil ones. Clay tablets found in the royal library of Assyrian Emperor Ashurbanipal, who reigned from 668–626 B.C. in Nineveh, contain this ritual:

> My gracious god stand by my side
> . . . My friendly god will listen to me:
> God Mamu of my dreams,
> My God, send me a favorable message.[11]

The people of Islam, too, had a prayer ritual that many researchers believe was a kind of dream incubation even though it does not involve sleeping in a sacred place. The practice, called *istiqâra*,[12] consists of the recital of a special prayer before sleep with the expectation of an answer to a difficult problem in a dream of that night. In addition, people in Kurdistan (a mountainous and plateau region in Iran) and the Dervishes (a Muslim ascetic order) employed a drug mixed with wine (mang) to induce visionary sleep. Drugs, however, are *not* essential to inducing dreams.

You need neither drugs nor religion to obtain dream answers. You can easily adapt the *istiqâra* form of dream incubation to your own benefit by using the elements that are crucial to obtain a desired dream: (1) clearly formulate the desired dream, (2) accept the fact that it is possible to induce dreams, and (3) concentrate your attention patiently and persistently on the desired dream. Instead of a prayer, you can substitute a simple, clear request to yourself for a specific dream. Using the same words, or a similar phrase, repeat it many times, concentrating your thoughts upon it. The possible advantage of dream answers obtained in this way over answers achieved by ordinary thought processes is that they draw upon the full range of your mental and emotional resources.

Your body should be in a deeply relaxed state when you present yourself with suggestions for the intended dream. Many methods of relaxing will produce a desirable body state. This step is particularly important because the mind is more receptive and you can also concentrate your thoughts better when the body is relaxed. Sometimes relaxation is imposed from the outside by suggestions of a hypnotist or by ingestion of drugs. This is generally to be avoided in dream induction because most drugs, including alcohol, suppress REM during sleep and, accordingly, there are fewer dreams to recall. Sometimes relaxation is directed by a therapist. In "systematic desensitization therapy" the patient is instructed in "progressive relaxation" before therapy begins and stays in a relaxed state during treatment sessions. In "autogenic therapy" the patient is taught six standard exercises to help him "experience the body as a resting mass which is heavy and warm" [13] before he proceeds to a graded set of meditative exercises.

You can learn to accomplish deep muscle relaxation for yourself (a preferable approach in my view, since it is then yours and always available). A basic exercise in Yoga is savasana, or "dead man's pose," in which the practitioner achieves complete relaxation. The practitioner lies flat on his back on the floor with his eyes closed, allowing his body to become totally limp from toes upward. He first tenses and then relaxes each set of muscles systematically until the entire body appears lifeless. The pose is employed between other exercises (referred to as postures) to ensure return of blood circulation to normal, as well as after exercising has been completed, and also prior to meditation. This Yogic posture predates other forms of relaxation techniques by approximately 4,000 years. Teachers of self-hypnosis [14] always recommend that relaxation be associated with a specific symbol in the practitioner's mind (for example, a specific number, or code word, or pleasant scene such as lying on the beach). For some people, relaxing in bed just before going to sleep provides the desired drowsy state.

While in a relaxed, drowsy state, repeat to yourself your intended dream phrase several times. Once you have clearly formulated your desired pattern (and sometimes even if you have merely been exposed to a clear pattern), internal responses begin. Best results may be obtained by repetition of the message. Some practitioners recommend repeating it "over and over again as a lullaby." [15] Mary Arnold-Forster, one of the most successful modern inducers of dreams, reminded herself of her desired dream several times during the day, as well as prior to sleep. For example, she would say to herself several times a day, "Tonight I fly in my dream. Tonight I fly. Tonight I fly." Your dream state mind will accept ideas that are repeated more readily than unrepeated ones.

Another helpful practice in inducing dreams is to *visualize the desired dream as though it is happening.* See it as though it is happening right now. Picture it. Feel as though it is already real. After you have pictured the dream, picture its results. As William James, the father of American psychology, said, "Act as if . . ." Try running a kind of mental movie of yourself seen as you will be and as you will feel when you have the advice or health you seek from your dreams.

The theory that *all* diseases originate in the mind, as the ancient Greeks claimed, is debatable; that *most* diseases originate in the mind is certain. Hypnotists can produce in a subject any disease symptom by suggesting it. It is reported that Yogis can both produce and remove disease symptoms by self-suggestion. Even modern-day physicians claim that 60 to 80 percent of all hospital beds are filled by patients whose diseases are not *purely* physical in origin. Knowledge of psychosomatic medicine is crucial in modern treatment. Ideas in your mind powerfully affect the state of your body.

External conditions alone are not what cause problems; the way we *think about* external conditions causes problems to ourselves. We in our own minds can make a "heaven out of hell or a hell out of heaven." We choose by what we choose to think.[16] Adopting a positive attitude, visualizing yourself in the desired condition can only be helpful. Relax and picture clearly the desired condition as a reality. Feel the pleasure associated with it. Do not negate the possible benefit with negative thoughts or arguments. William James said that the subconscious mind will bring to pass any picture held in the mind and backed by faith. Which brings us to the final step: Belief.

As has already been mentioned, you need not believe in a god to derive benefits from dream incubation; you need only believe. *The belief can be in anything.* Answers to problems and cures to illness have been received in dreams in every culture and in every faith in every time. The power to advise or heal actually comes from within the dreamer, not from a specific god outside him. *Belief* is what makes dream induction possible.

The faith that I am urging is really a faith in yourself. You can mobilize and utilize the resources within you by processes described in this book. If you believe in a particular god, you can formulate requests to him; if you believe in the wisdom of your subconscious mind or your dream state, you can pose your questions to it. We need to believe we can obtain answers in dreams, and we will.

Once the induced dream has been obtained, you should always review its message and consider its wisdom and applicability.

So far, we have been considering how to induce future dreams. You can do several things with the dreams you now have that will help you to be more successful in inducing future dreams. One of these helpful practices is to *carry on a conversation with the characters that have already appeared in your dream*. This is not as far-fetched as it may sound. While you are still in bed in the morning, in a drowsy state, you can think about your dream images. Choose any one that puzzles you, conjure up its image, and directly question it. You may be surprised to find how quickly an answer pops into your mind. For example, in one dream a strange doglike animal scratches my hand. This imagery puzzled me for it occurred during a time when such a dream event was rare. In a drowsy state I pictured the animal of my dreams. "Why did you scratch me?" I asked. "I didn't mean to hurt you. I just wanted you to pay attention to me" was the response that came to mind. This reply led to further thinking about the image and eventual self-insight. You can ask your dream images any type of question, such as "Who are you?" or "Why do you do so and so?" The answers that come to mind are often both unexpected and informative.

You may also question the dream as a whole, rather than a specific image. For instance, at one point I felt overwhelmed with the great outpouring of dream material I was experiencing. While awake, I questioned myself, "Dreams, why do you overwhelm me?" The mental response was quick and unexpected: "We want you to know how important we are!" This technique is a unique manner of *you* talking to *you*. Remember, all your dream images and dream actions are you.

Many dreamers find that when they lie down to sleep at night, recent dream images well up in their thoughts. These dreamers can use the drowsy state *before* sleep comes to question their previous dream images, rather than do so in the morning.

As you become skilled at questioning your dream images, you may find yourself posing questions to them or receiving answers *during* the dream. The image of a high school girl-friend once said to me in a dream, "Do you know that I always represent sex to you?" "Uh . . . no," I replied. "Haven't you noticed that I always wear shorts in your dreams?" she said in a tone that implied it was really rather foolish of me to have overlooked that fact. When I awoke, I realized how correct the statement was. Whether you question the dream as a whole or individual dream images, or whether you pose questions before dreaming, after dreaming, or during dreaming does not matter. The important point is to start communicating with your dream state.

Gestalt therapists suggest that you go even further than posing questions to dream characters. They suggest that you play the role of each element in your dream, be it person or thing. The role playing is based on the assumption that each image in the dream is a part of you. Many writers have described the Gestalt approach in detail,[17] so I will merely summarize it here. The dreamer puts himself in the place of each image of his dreams in turn by imagining or by elaborately acting out the dream in a group setting with the dreamer sitting in a different chair each time he speaks for a different character. The dreamer imagines or acts out how his dream characters *would* interact until two conflicting roles clearly emerge. Of these, one will be a domineering role, called "top-dog," in which the character is telling other dream images what they should or should not do. The conflicting role will be another character who is basically apologetic and defensive, called "underdog." The nature of the conflict between "topdog" and "underdog" represents the conflict within the dreamer. His task in Gestalt therapy is to make the "underdog" stand up to the "topdog" and state his needs clearly and convincingly. When the dreamer makes the "underdog" part of himself fully assertive, he fills the "hole" in his personality and completes himself. He forms a gestalt (a "whole"). You will find many interesting insights as you try this with your own dreams.

Gestalt therapists stress the importance of reexperiencing a dream as it is told. The dreamer is required to tell or write his dream in present tense, as though it is happening at the moment. Therefore, most of the dreams in this book are expressed in present tense. You will sense the difference this makes when you *record your own dreams as current action.* (More about dream recording in Chapter 8.)

As you work with your dreams, think about them, question them, induce them, you will find that certain positive elements emerge in your dreams: a friendly dragon may appear, a strong man with great muscled arms, a wise goddess, a fantastic ornament, a strange flying bird-animal—all sorts of unusual and interesting images will come to you. They represent emerging positive aspects of yourself.[18] (We shall return to this concept in Chapter 9.) By attending to your unusual and positive images, you increase the probability of their recurrence or of other equally positive symbols occurring. Try to use them in some way during your waking state—paint them, draw them, sculpt them, embroider them. You will be increasing your ability to positively influence future dreams.

Sharing your current dreams with others will also help to shape future ones. Mohammed is said to have had great regard for dreams. Each morning he asked his disciples to tell their dreams; he gave interpretations and shared his own dreams with them. This practice, as will be seen in Chapter 5, is similar to the Senoi practice of dream sharing at breakfast. My own seminars in creative dreaming convince me of the powerful effect that sharing dreams has on shaping them.

Another waking procedure that will increase your ability to induce future dreams is to *make observations or involve yourself in activities that are relevant to your desired dream.* You recall how Dr. Handler had Johnny practice monster chasing while he was awake and how Guareschi taught Margherita to change bike tires and mountain climb in order to help her solve her dream problems. Both these activities increased the probability that Johnny and Margherita would have the dreams that their therapists desired. One of the most successful recent dream inducers, Mary Arnold-Forster, regularly made waking observations on subjects she wished to dream about. For instance, she found that observing birds in flight while awake helped her to achieve the flying dreams that she wished to have. (We shall return to Mary Arnold-Forster's remarkable methods.)

You will find that most people need time to develop the ability to induce their own dreams. Inducing dreams is a learned skill; it takes practice. One researcher [19] made an unusual attempt to measure how much time was required for children to successfully self-induce a desired dream. He found that the median time for the self-suggested dream to appear was *five weeks;* the shortest time was two weeks. Children are believed to be more suggestible than adults, so we may require even longer. Patient persistence is essential. Other techniques, such as the ones that the Senoi use, seem to be incorporated more rapidly.

We have seen that you can influence your future dreams by behaviors prior to the dream (forming an intention, for example) and by behaviors subsequent to your present dreams (such as questioning the images). My own experience in applying these methods has been exciting and growth-producing. Almost every dream I have wished to produce has sooner or later appeared. The induced dream does not always contain all the elements I intended, but it often does. Sometimes it contains other more interesting elements as well. I have had particular success with inducing flying dreams, lucid dreams, and confrontation dreams. Specific techniques for inducing these types of dreams are described in the following chapters.

My approach has been to seek a peaceful place, usually my bedroom before sleeping. I put my body into a deeply relaxed state. I am familiar with several relaxation techniques: As a therapist-in-training I learned "progressive relaxation" in order to teach it to patients; as a beginning Yoga practitioner I learned savasana ("dead man's pose"); recently, I have experimented with Transcendental Meditation. While in one of these relaxed states, I have at times given myself "healthful suggestions" (such as "I feel relaxed," "I feel well," "I feel refreshed and rested"). I have not, however, attempted a healing dream per se.

Nevertheless, in the healing mode, I did on one occasion, when I was seventeen, see my own image of God in a dream. He was a great figure in the sky formed of pink- and blue-tinged clouds, his arms were held above his head with hands locked, his torso rose from a swirl of clouds, his body was muscular, he was bearded, and he wore a crown. Unfortunately, I recorded no more than a sketch of this image. It contrasts sharply with the ones more often described in healing dreams: The usual images are reportedly blurred, indistinct in character. Dreamers who have a clear conception of what to expect of a god or saint in a dream are likely to see their dream image distinctly. When religious figures appear in my dreams these days they are usually gods or, more often, goddesses of a uniquely idiosyncratic origin, rather than a stereotyped or archetypal image.

My own dream record has numerous dreams depicting my physical condition. For instance, in one dream I am taking a pullover sweater off a baby. It catches on the back of the neck and I have to tug at it. I wake with a severe pain in my neck from a strained muscle that I did not have prior to sleep. This dream depicted a physical event that seemed to occur simultaneously with the dream. It is impossible to tell whether the pain caused the dream or the action of the dream caused the pain, or the action of the dream predicted the pain that immediately followed.

In another instance, I give myself medical advice during a dream. This time I have a pain in a back muscle that I was vaguely aware of prior to sleep. During my dream I am suffering with this pain. I see a team of doctors consulting about the case and they conclude with a recommendation to apply heat. Of course, it proved to be the only helpful thing for the severe strain that developed and lasted several days.

Generally, my health is excellent. When it is not, however, I will almost invariably find it portrayed in my dreams. A recent symbol, since I took up plant growing in waking life, involves the condition of my dream plants. If my dream plants are droopy or infected, my waking condition corresponds; if they are blooming and sprouting new growth, my waking condition is likewise healthy. Recording and working with your own dreams will reveal the ways in which you symbolize your physical condition. Knowing this, it becomes possible to take prompt preventive or other appropriate action.

As you learn to induce dreams, you can consult your

dream state about your current physical condition and carry out recommendations if they seem wise. You may even be able to draw on the power of your own body to naturally heal itself, as ancient dreamers did.

In addition to promoting your physical health by dream induction, you can draw upon the vast untapped resources of your own mind to help solve your daily problems. I have already spoken of the huge internal recording of life experiences each person carries within him. The more positive events you can expose yourself to, the better: books, pictures, music, interesting people, new activities, travel to foreign lands. It will all be recorded. It can become available to you in your dreams. You can recall it in its original form or recombine it into totally new forms. As you gain skill in dream induction you can pose questions to your dreams and receive answers unknown to you in a waking state. You can draw upon *all* your knowledge. All levels of your mind become available for problem solving and creative production. You will become a fully functioning person rather than just a fraction of what you can be.

We can begin by applying principles extracted from the methods of dream induction used by ancient dreamers. A summary of the crucial elements for dream induction follows.

SUMMARY OF WHAT WE CAN LEARN FROM ANCIENT DREAMERS

1. Find a place (external or internal) where you feel peaceful and undistracted.
2. Clearly formulate your intention for a desired dream.
3. Put your intention into a concise, clear, positive phrase (a dream task).

4. Deeply relax your body.

5. While in a drowsy, relaxed state, repeat your desired dream phrase several times, to yourself or aloud (and occasionally during the day, if possible). Concentrate your thoughts on it.

6. Visualize your desired dream as though it is happening, and picture yourself after having had the desired dream.

7. Believe that your subconscious can provide the desired dream.

8. Work with your current dreams.

a. Question your dream characters or the dream in general while in a drowsy state.

b. Question dream images *during* the dream when possible.

c. Try to determine "topdog" and "underdog" characters in your dreams, and state the needs of "underdog" clearly and convincingly.

d. Record or tell your dreams in the present tense.

e. Attend especially to positive idiosyncratic dream images.

f. Produce positive dream images in some form in waking life.

g. Share your dreams with other people interested in creative dreaming.

9. Make observations or engage in activities relevant to your desired dream, especially just before sleeping.

10. Inducing dreams is a learned skill; it takes time and practice. Don't give up if you don't have immediate success. Keep trying.

CHAPTER THREE

Learn From Creative Dreamers

*There are rhythms in the world waiting for
words to be written to them.*[1]

You can discover creative products within your own
dreams. In a manner roughly similar to the way ancients incu-
bated dreams, you can deliberately induce dreams of artistic
creations or dreams that solve your problems. You can use a
technique in which you plan the general content of your
dreams, but in this case you are seeking a creative product
rather than advice or healing. Your dreams can become your
own muse, your own source of inspiration.

Most creative workers of the past have hit upon dream
inspiration by accident. Often, the dreamer is consciously
working on a product when his dream life suddenly provides
him with a crucial element that he is able to recognize and use.
Some of these dream products are famous—for example,
Coleridge's poem "Kubla Khan." Occasionally, the creative
dream image simply appears, without the dreamer being occupied at all with the idea in his waking life. Most creative
workers don't know that it is possible to deliberately evoke
creative dreams.

We can learn a great deal about producing our own
creative work in dreams by examining the process as it has
occurred in past creative dreamers. The process is the same for

us. We are able, as will be seen, to present our dream mind with a request for a creative product, draw upon the vast resource of material in our mind that was recorded in our past life, recombine it into original forms, and finally present it to ourself in a dream. Will it be this year's best seller? A latter-day Rembrandt? A new Moonlight Sonata? Obviously, the more varied and interesting the material we have previously put into our mind (just as in programming a computer), and the greater the conscious skills we have already built into our system, the greater chance we have of coming up with a worth-while product. But the possibility is always lurking there. As we start the creative dreaming process we greatly increase the probability of tonight's production.

Ordinary dreamers—those of us who are not already poets, novelists, scientists—can use the same techniques as great creative workers to come up with creative products that use our full resources. We need not be poets or artists. Whatever our work is, we can find creative solutions in our dreams. These products will be far more original, in most cases, than the products that can be devised simply by using thought process in waking life. In addition to the benefit of greater originality in our products, we can gain the value of greater unity of self, of our waking and dream lives. The more we use symbols from our dream life, the more we will be able to develop and express our own unique personality, at its integrated best.

Creative dreaming happens in two ways: In the first, dreamers observe the creative product in its totality in the dream. At other times, the dream provides the mood or idea from which the creative product evolves in a waking state. These creative products from dreams can be the result of deliberately planned creative dreaming as well as the result of unplanned creative dreaming. They can "just happen" to you or you can induce them.

The dreams of the first two writers to be discussed were influenced by opium addiction. This does not mean, however, that opium *caused* the creative dreams. On the contrary, in these cases, opium led eventually to terror-dominated dreams and *in*ability to work effectively. The power to have interesting dreams comes from the personality of the dreamer. Interesting material must exist in the dreamer before interesting dreams can occur. Creative dreams are quite accessible to the dreamer, as will be seen in later examples, without drugs. In fact, recent experimenters [2] found that writers and scholars who were given LSD produced work far below their normal standard while under the influence of the drug. We are concerned here with the *process* of creative dreaming. Drug abuse is incidental to the creative dreams, if not to the dreamer.

An important principle for inducing creative dreams is that the would-be creative dreamer occupies himself with the subject he wishes to dream about, often up until the last few seconds before he falls asleep. We shall encounter this principle again and again. Observe it as the English poet Samuel Taylor Coleridge (1772–1834) experienced his famous dream inspiration: One lazy summer afternoon in 1798 [3] the young poet whiled away the hours in his thatch-roof cottage in the western countryside of England. He idly turned the pages of a history book called *Purchas His Pilgrimmage*. His newly found opium habit nipped his gut so he drained the nearby glass of laudanum he had ready. He yawned as he read the words "Here the Khan Kubla commanded a palace to be built . . ." Flipping the page, he closed his eyes, his head tipped forward. His dark curls fell across his face and moved gently with his breath as he dozed. The golden rays of the afternoon sun lit his cheek. When he awoke three hours later the stately passages of

"Kubla Khan" were firmly in his mind, with their "caverns measureless to man" and "sunless sea."

In this case, the creative product occurred in its totality in the dream. Coleridge estimated that his original poem was 200 to 300 lines. He said that "all the images rose up before him as *things*" [4] along with descriptions of them without any sense of effort. Imagine his frustration when, in the midst of recording it, he was interrupted at the fifty-fourth line by someone on business. When he returned an hour later the remainder of the poem had melted away, leaving just the recorded fragment.

Although Coleridge's "Kubla Khan" is marked by characteristics of drug imagery—extraordinary mutations of space, the ebb and flow of images—his masterpiece cannot be dismissed as simply a drug experience. Many people have had opium-induced dozes; few have waked with great poems. Coleridge had the necessary conscious skill. Small beginnings of the final poem are found in his notebooks of the previous years. Yet, it was Coleridge's dream state that provided the special misty images and wove them into a unified whole.[5]

When Coleridge's biographer [6] was making an intensive study of Coleridge's works, he, too, experienced a dream of the "pleasure-dome" of "Kubla Khan." Intense occupation with any subject is likely to induce dreams of it. It may happen to you as you read this book.

Another English writer, Thomas De Quincey (1785–1859), provides a negative example of what can happen when a person does not know how to positively influence the content of his dreams. In *Confessions of an English Opium Eater*, De Quincey described changes in his dream life as he became addicted to opium. His dreams became progressively more painful. At the beginning of his serious addiction he found an increase in hypnagogic visions as he drifted off to sleep. Whatever he voluntarily pictured in the darkness prior to sleep was likely to transfer to his dreams, so that he feared to imagine anything. His dreams became accompanied by a "deep-seated anxiety and gloomy melancholy" inexpressible in words. He felt himself "descend, into chasms and sunless abysses, depths below depths, from which it seemed hopeless that I could ever reascend. Nor did I, by waking, feel that I *had* reascended." [7] De Quincey found that his sense of space and, later, his sense of time became distorted: "I sometimes seemed to have lived for 70 or 100 years in one night . . ." The content of his dreams shifted from palaces and cities to water and then to human faces, "imploring, wrathful, despairing," by the thousands. De Quincey's dreams became increasingly paranoid, with a Malay as his pursuing enemy and the Orient as the setting for his tortures, accompanied by sensations of tropical heat and beating sunlight. Moral, spiritual, and physical terrors beset him repeatedly in his dreams, and over all brooded a sense of eternity and infinity that oppressed him so much he declared, ". . . I awoke in struggles, and cried aloud—'I will sleep no more!' " [8]

Obviously, these are not changes we would wish to induce in our own dream lives. Much of De Quincey's dream suffering was directly attributable to his drug intake. Yet, he could have combatted the effects of it had he been skilled in dream control. Dream suffering can be eliminated as you learn to control your dreams. The power to will changes in dream content is a skill that can be acquired and is the secret to mastering nightmares. Both the Senoi (Chapter 5) and the Yogis of the dream state (Chapter 7) develop this skill to a high degree. Their methods would have helped De Quincey deal with his horrific dreams. They can help you deal with frightening dreams now.

Creative workers can obtain the mood and general content of their writing from their dreams, as De Quincey did, or they can receive the creative product itself in their dreams, as Coleridge did. In addition, creative workers sometimes receive imperatives to write in their dreams. Socrates,[9] the great Greek philosopher (c. 470–399 B.C.), for example, reported such dreams on the day he carried out his death sentence by drinking the hemlock poison. Many other writers' work was influenced by unplanned creative dreams.[10]

Creative dreams are by no means limited to the field of writing. William Blake (1757–1827),[11] the English artist-engraver-poet, produced many works of art with a dreamlike quality. He related that while searching for a less expensive means to engrave his illustrated songs, he dreamed that his dead younger brother, Robert, appeared to him and indicated a process of copper engraving, which he immediately verified and used. Believers in psychic phenomena suggest the possibility of the deceased Robert's actual visit during this dream, while others prefer an explanation based on the workings of the subconscious. Whatever the explanation, the fact is that Blake hit upon a unique solution in his dream. Notice, again, that he was consciously occupied with a search when the solution appeared in his dreams.

The field of music, too, owes some of its famous pieces to unplanned creative dreams. Giuseppe Tartini (1692–1770), the Italian violinist and composer, had such a dream. Tartini related that at the age of twenty-one he had a dream in which he sold his soul to the Devil. In the dream he handed his fiddle to the Devil:

> But how great was my astonishment when I heard him play with consummate skill a sonata of such exquisite beauty

as surpassed the boldest flights of my imagination. I felt enraptured, transported, enchanted; my breath was taken away, and I awoke. Seizing my violin I tried to retain the sounds I had heard. But it was in vain. The piece I then composed, the "Devil's Sonata," was the best I ever wrote, but how far below the one I had heard in my dream![12]

In Tartini's dream the creative product (*Trillo del Diavolo*, or *The Devil's Trill*) is present, yet he cannot recapture its exact form to his satisfaction. Notice his immediate attempt to hold on to it, an action that will be observed in many of these examples. If you roll over to return to sleep thinking you'll record your dream in the morning, you and posterity may be the loser.

In the field of anthropology, an astounding dream discovery was made by Hermann V. Hilprecht, professor of Assyrian at the University of Pennsylvania.

Hilprecht was working late one evening in 1893 trying to decipher the cuneiform characters [13] on drawings of two small fragments of agate that he thought were Babylonian finger rings found in temple ruins. He tentatively assigned one fragment to a particular period (that of the Cassite period, c. 1700 B.C.) but he was unable to classify the other. He went to bed about midnight, feeling uncertain about his classification and had this dream:

A tall, thin priest of the old pre-Christian Nippur, about forty years of age and clad in a simple abba, led me to the treasure chamber of the temple, on its southeast side. He went with me into a small, low-ceiled room without windows, in which there was a large wooden chest, while scraps of agate and lapis lazuli lay scattered on the floor. Here he addressed me as follows: "The two fragments which you have published separately on pages 22 and 26, belong together, are not finger rings and their history is as follows: King Kurigalzu (Ca. 1300 B.C.) once sent to the temple of Bel, among other articles of agate and lapis lazuli, an inscribed votive cylinder of agate. Then we priests suddenly received the command to make for the statue of the god of Ninib a pair of earrings of agate. We were in great dismay, since there was no agate as raw material at hand. In order to execute the command there was nothing for us to do but cut the votive cylinder into three parts, thus making three rings, each of which contained a portion of the original inscription. The first two rings served as earrings for the statue of the god; the two fragments which have given you so much trouble are portions of them. If you will put the two together you will have confirmation of my words. But the third ring you have not found in the course of your excavations and you will never find it." With this the priest disappeared . . . I woke at once and immediately told my wife the dream that I might not forget it. Next morning—Sunday—I examined the fragments once more in the light of these disclosures, and to my astonishment found all the details of the dream precisely verified in so far as the means of verification were in my hands. The original inscription on the votive cylinder reads: "To the god Ninib, son of Bel, his lord, has Kurigalzu, pontifex of Bel, presented this." [14]

Hilprecht had been working with drawings of the fragments at the time of his dream. As soon as he was able he went to the museum in Constantinople, where the actual fragments were. They were kept in separate cases since it was not known that they went together. Hilprecht found that they fit together perfectly. In all respects they confirmed the information in his dream. Clairvoyance? Prescience? Magic? Or the vivid assembly in a dream theater of the deductions of a brilliant mind immersed in the ancient riddle?

This unusual dream was first published in 1896 in *Pro-*

ceedings of the Society for Psychical Research because of the possibilities of a psychic element raised by the accuracy of the dream details. Either conclusion is possible. Whatever the essential verity, the combination that unlocked the 3,000-year-old secret occurred in the dream state. And the dreamer who unlocked it was deep in his subject up until minutes before he fell asleep.

We see the principle of subject immersion again in the creative dreams of two scientists that had powerful impact in their respective fields. The German chemist Friedrich A. Kekulé had tried for many years to find the molecular structure of benzene. He reported dreaming as he dozed in front of a crackling fire one cold night in 1865:

> Again the atoms were juggling before my eyes . . . my mind's eye, sharpened by repeated sights of a similar kind, could now distinguish larger structures of different forms and in long chains, many of them close together; everything was moving in a snake-like and twisting manner. Suddenly, what was this? One of the snakes got hold of its own tail and the whole structure was mockingly twisting in front of my eyes. As if struck by lightning, I awoke . . .[15]

This dream led Kekulé to the realization that the structure of benzene is a closed carbon ring, a discovery that revolutionized modern chemistry. When he reported it to his colleagues at a scientific convention in 1890, Kekulé concluded with the remark "Let us learn to dream, gentlemen, and then we may perhaps find the truth." [16] Suppose he had simply dismissed his dream of snakes as Freudian symbolism! Note once more that Kekulé implied he had had similar dreams for some time before the dramatic realization of their meaning struck him.

Some decades later, Otto Loewi, the German-born physiologist who came to the United States, reported a dream inspiration that won him the 1936 Nobel Prize in Physiology and Medicine. Prior to this time it was assumed that nervous impulses in the body were transmitted by an electrical wave. Loewi, in a conversation with a colleague in 1903, got the idea that there might be a chemical transmission of the nervous impulse, rather than an electrical one, but he saw no way to prove his hunch and it slipped from his conscious memory. It emerged again in 1920:

> The night before Easter Sunday of that year I awoke, turned on the light, and jotted down a few notes on a tiny slip of thin paper. Then I fell asleep again. It occurred to me at six o'clock in the morning that during the night I had written down something most important, but I was unable to decipher the scrawl. The next night, at three o'clock, the idea returned. It was the design of an experiment to determine whether or not the hypothesis of chemical transmission that I had uttered seventeen years ago was correct. I got up immediately, went to the laboratory, and performed a simple experiment on a frog's heart according to the nocturnal design . . . its results became the foundation of the theory of chemical transmission of the nervous impulse.[17]

The fact that Loewi dreamed of the experiment on the frog's heart on two successive nights may be an instance of recent laboratory findings [18] referred to as "lateral homology." In this circumstance, a particular dream element tends to occur and recur at a particular time. Note Loewi's first loss of the dream idea by unclear recording. On its second occurrence, Loewi took no chance on forgetting, and like Tartini seizing his violin, Loewi leapt from bed and dashed to the lab to test his dream idea. My method of dream recording, described in Chapter 8, will help you to retain vital nighttime ideas.

It has been noted [19] that Loewi performed a similar experiment for a totally different purpose two years prior to the dream. This similar experiment probably provided a crucial element that was later combined in the dream state with the hunch he had had seventeen years before his hypothesis-testing dream. What is noticeable in these discoveries of the dream state is the apparently special capacity of this state to combine thoughts or events separated across the geography of a lifetime into a unique gestalt discovery.

You have seen how consistently the element of subject immersion occurs prior to an unplanned creative dream. In planned creative dreaming this immersion is practiced deliberately.

Let's turn now from "lucky" dreamers whose creative products occurred spontaneously to dreamers who have deliberately induced their dreams of creative products. You will find their procedures even more applicable to your own dreams.

You recall the development of Thomas De Quincey's opium-influenced dreams from dreams of pleasure to dreams of horror. British author Robert Louis Stevenson (1850–1894) described a development of his dream life in the opposite direction: As a child, he was tormented by nightmares; as an adult he nightly entertained himself with fascinating dreams. This happy change appears to have come about as he gained control over his dreams.

Stevenson [20] traced the evolution of his dream life in his memoirs. He related his childhood struggles to keep from falling asleep and having to face his horrendous dreams. He would awake in terror from such dreams, "clinging to the curtain-rod with his knees to his chin." [21] As he grew older, his dreams became somewhat less terrifying but were still miserable. Later, as a medical student in Edinburgh, he was plagued by nightmares so much that he was driven to consult a doctor about them, after which his dreams became more commonplace.

Ultimately, Stevenson was able to induce a dramatic change in his dream life. He had been accustomed to setting himself to sleep with tales of his own concoction, purely for personal pleasure, dropping or changing the stories at whim. As he turned his amusement of storytelling into professional writing, he consciously sought profitable and printable tales. He found that his nightmares vanished. Whether he was awake or asleep, he, or what he called the "little people" of his dreams, were occupied in making stories for the market. Especially when he was pressed for money, he found that:

> . . . at once the little people begin to bestir themselves in the same quest, and labour all night long, and all night long set before him truncheons of tales upon their lighted theatre. No fear of his being frightened now; the flying heart and the frozen scalp are things bygone; applause, growing applause, growing interest, growing exultation in his own cleverness (for he takes all the credit), and at last a jubilant leap to wakefulness, with the cry, "I have it, that'll do!" upon his lips.[22]

How different is Stevenson's cry on awakening from De Quincey's, "I will sleep no more!" [23]

Stevenson stated that sometimes he was disappointed on examining the story in a waking state, finding it unmarketable. Often, however, he said his sleepless little "Brownies" did him honest service and gave him "better tales than he could fashion for himself." He comments that "they can tell him a story piece by piece, like a serial, and keep him all the while in ignorance of where they aim." [24] Stevenson's Brownies were his dream state at its integrated best.

The Strange Case of Dr. Jekyll and Mr. Hyde is a famous example of the tales partially produced by Stevenson's Brownies. Stevenson explains:

> I had long been trying to write a story on this subject, to find a body, a vehicle, for that strong sense of man's double being, which must at times come in upon and overwhelm the mind of every thinking creature.[25]

He had written an earlier manuscript on this topic but, dissatisfied with it, destroyed it. Then, pressed for money, he resumed thinking about the theme:

> For two days I went about racking my brains for a plot of any sort; and on the second night I dreamed the scene at the window, and a scene afterwards split in two, in which Hyde, pursued for some crime, took the powder and underwent the change in the presence of his pursuers. All the rest was made awake, and consciously, although I think I can trace in much of it the manner of my Brownies.[26]

Stevenson related that he did the mechanical work of setting tales down in the best words and sentences he could make, held the pen, and did the sitting at the table, "which is about the worst of it," mailed the manuscripts and paid for the postage, all of which entitled him to some share in the enterprise, but he gave his Brownies credit for the bulk of his writing.

There are many important points for prospective creative dreamers to notice in the evolution of Stevenson's dream life. In the first place, he was able to successfully confront his fear-producing dream images and transform them into cooperative "little people," his dream friends. You will see in Chapter 5 how the Senoi accomplish this transformation in a systematic manner. Apparently, Stevenson hit upon this technique himself, as others have occasionally done. You, too, can evolve your own dream friends who will work for you.

Stevenson, like so many of his creatively dreaming colleagues, thoroughly immersed himself in his subject: "For two days I went about racking my brains for a plot . . ." Note the timing: two days. You will see how this two days seems crucial. Perhaps there is a minimum time interval during which the dreamer must immerse himself in his subject. I have often observed both in myself and in students in dream seminars that certain rules of dream control take time to "sink in."

Stevenson's regular success in producing dreams of marketable tales is only partly a result of being deeply involved in his subject. He deliberately planned to have such dreams. He gave himself specific dream assignments. As Stevenson developed skill in dream control, the desired marketable tales became habitual dream responses. The British author Aldous Huxley [27] expressed envy of Stevenson's Brownies, yet every one of us can set up our dreams to serve us. Of course, we need to exercise our conscious skills. As you develop dream control, you will induce creative dreams well beyond what you now believe possible.

Artists, too, have produced many works based on their dreams. Some artists have deliberately induced dreams of paintings. An anthropologist [28] specializing in eastern Asia suspects that most of the fabulous monsters painted in Oriental art originate in dreams. He cites examples of well-known ancient Chinese paintings [29] that were inspired by planned dreams.

You, too, can call upon your dream state to provide you

with unusual images. As you develop skill in creative dreaming, you can occupy yourself with the subject you wish to dream about, present your dream mind with a request for a specific dream, receive it, and hold it vividly in your waking mind until you record it in some form. The Senoi tribe (see Chapter 5) develop the production of creative images in dreams to a high degree. You will see how it is possible to consistently have creative dreams.

Ordinary dreamers are able to train themselves to have creative dreams in the area of their work. The poet dreams poems, the violinist hears violin music, the mathematician dreams equations. The poet does *not* dream equations (at least not often!). Just as almost all of the dream-inspired inventions and discoveries described above, planned or unplanned, were made by the dreamer in the very area in which he was consciously occupied, the ordinary dreamer can evoke creative dreams in *his* area of work. You can, by the same processes, hit upon a dream idea for a research project at the office, a new arrangement for the baby's room, a new advertising slogan, or a new dress design. When an idea is original, it is creative, whatever its field of application. You can evoke creative dreams in your own field of interest, whatever it is.

However, ordinary dreamers sometimes have "artistic" dreams. When this occurs, the dream product has special personal meaning. My own lengthy dream record contains many examples of creative products, most of which were unplanned. Some of these products were astonishing to me for their surprising appearance and unusual character.

I am by no means a poet; the nearest I have come to this occupation is devising an occasional rhyme for a relative's birthday card. Yet, on a few rare occasions, poems have appeared in my dreams that, so far as I know, are quite original. I am not able to judge their merit (although I readily recognize they do not approach "Kubla Khan"), for the emotional response they evoke in me is exceedingly strong. For example, on one occasion, I was in a melancholy state of mind over a personal crisis. A driving rainstorm outside matched my miserable internal mood. Unhappy, I went to bed. At that moment, I received a telephone call from my beloved man that comforted me as I fell asleep. This is the record of the dream that followed:

A rather strange and lovely dream. I am trying to get some medicine at a drug store, but all the stores seem to be closed. Then I am in the kitchen in my mother's house (where I spent my teenage years). Everything is coated with a thick layer of dust. I wipe my finger on a plant and am horrified at how dirty it is. I hear someone coming up the cellar stairs. The door opens and it is my man. He has a silver-gray beard (which he did not at the time). He wears a silver-gray silk suit and looks all marvelously silvery-gray. In his hands he has a beautiful Persian cat with shiny, brushed hair. He comes close to me and I have the impression of height. He begins to tell me about a lovely painting he has seen with a girl and a cat like the one he holds. He begins to recite a poem. It seems exquisitely beautiful and as I try hard to remember it, I wake with some of the lines still in my head. I am amazed that midst all the dirt and ugliness and confusion of that house, from the cellar—the worst part of all—came all that beauty:

> *Through the inundated city,*
> *Hear my call;*
> *Through the knife-sharp pain,*
> *Hear my call;*
> *Through the strife-torn jungle,*
> *Hear my call;*
> *I am your mountain . . .*
> *Montevideo.*　　　　　　　　*("Montevideo")*

This poem reaches a level of my emotions so deep it moves me even years after its dreaming. Yet it is probably not the beauty of the poem (as I said, I am incapable of judging), it is a beauty of the relationship, of a need answered from without, of a strength felt from within. What a poet or a potential poet beyond my talents might have done in the same dream with the same feeling is impossible to say.

This dream closely fits the Senoi system (Chapter 5), as will be seen, long before my knowledge of it. In it, possible ugliness from the cellar is faced. The cellar, where dirt, disorder, and cold are at their greatest—the cellar, inhabited by cat-size rats that gnaw holes in the door and creep through in the kitchen at night to steal our food. The dream image emerging from the cellar of that house could be horrendous. But it is faced and found to be beautiful and it bears gifts of still greater beauty. I did not even need to ask, as the Senoi do, for a gift from my dream lover. It is a deeply satisfying dream. Note that, in this case, I was not focused on creating a dream poem, but I was intensely occupied with the emotion out of which the poem took shape.

On another occasion, at the end of a story, I dreamed:

> *I am with my youngest daughter buying food in a grocery store. We stand in the check-out line and we find that the male clerk is cheating us by charging us extra for things we've already paid for. This happened because the person behind us got their order mixed up with ours and we had to move things to a different grocery cart. The clerk is charging us $2.00 and $3.00 an item. I become furious and complain. Then, I grab him and tell him we will tie him up in the bathroom and tickle his naked body with feathers. Finally I pick him up and fly to the top of the room which has become like a large ballroom type of place. I can see the*

*fancy decorations on the ceiling. I swing the guy around by
the arm and drop him to the floor from the great height. He
splatters into pieces. From my position in the air, I announce:*
>*Thus be:*
>*Splat!*
>*Squashed flat ...*
>*Anyone who troubles me.*
>>*("Thus be," 7/10/70)*

The source of my anger and complaint was immediately
obvious to me upon awakening and, I felt, was quite justified.
The verse expressed my feeling of the moment succinctly. Interestingly, I had made a note in my record that I had just read
about a verse Dorothy Parker dreamed (quoted later). This
may well have triggered the idea to compose my own dream
verse without my consciously planning to do so.

There are other dream rhymes in my record, sometimes
accompanied by music as well. Now, I am even less a musician
than a poet, yet in dreams I sometimes hear singing of such un-
surpassed beauty that my dream characters are moved to tears.
It is, perhaps, memories of the many operas I have enjoyed. I
have no way to know for certain, since I have not the means to
hold on to the notes when I wake. They evaporate and are
gone with the morning light. Once in a dream, I sang a magnificent aria I never heard of before, "Celia Delwa Fawcett."
Only the echoes remained on awakening. Undoubtedly, if I
developed the conscious skill of musical notation I would be
able to retain my vanishing dream melodies.

I am not suggesting that the ordinary dreamer induce
dream poems and songs (unless, of course, he wishes to), but
those poems and songs that spontaneously occur in dreams have
special personal value and deserve special attention. Dream
songs, as we shall see in the next chapter, were particularly im-

portant in American Indian life. The dream songs received during the all-important adolescent vision quest became the dreamer's personal refrain. They were used throughout his life at stressful times (for example, war parties) and were also used to evoke the power of his own personal spirit. This is readily understandable as a function of the dream song's strong emotional power for the dreamer. *Give special attention to any poems or songs that appear in your dreams.* They may help you get in touch with your own internal source of strength.

One of my musically talented students became able to capture her previously elusive dream melodies as she participated in a creative dreaming seminar. Although she still dreamed of discovering an empty staff or of a complete song becoming a forgotten score, she was for the first time able to catch some of the tunes and even compose lyrics. She found that the music in her dreams indicated her various moods; the melodies were often minor (associated with despair), agitated (associated with anger), or nostalgic (associated with longing). In some of her dreams, she became the music while the notes "bounced above me like beads of wine and sweat." Her songs, recorded to the accompaniment of a guitar and shared with the group, were lovely with a wisp of the strange dreamlike quality of their origin. As your own personal dream songs or verses come to you, you will feel their extraordinary emotional power.

Students in my seminars also create marvelous writing based on their dreams, rather than the dream providing finished creative products. This seems to be an easier accomplishment, yet the work is original and of high quality.

Artistically talented students, especially, were able to reproduce visual imagery from their dreams. Some students reported walking in a dream through art galleries filled with marvelous paintings; they reproduced these dream paintings when awake. Others planned the general content of such dreams—for example, "Tonight I will dream something creative" or ". . . something artistic" or ". . . an unusual design." They frequently found that the desired element appeared as part of the ongoing dream; these, too, were reproduced on awakening.

My own dream record is filled with unusual artistic forms —I see dream paintings, dream sculptures, illustrated dream books, and strange shapes and symbols impossible to classify. I do possess some small artistic skill, so this subject of my dreams is not surprising, yet the topic is far in excess of my waking attention to art. I should give more waking time to art according to its consistent appearance in my dreams.

Again, the ordinary dreamer may not wish to induce artistic images. Yet, he is likely to find that unusual, idiosyncratic images appear in his dreams without intention. Such images have great personal value, as will be discussed in Chapter 9.

Problem solving was not reported by students so often as artistic creations were. Perhaps the student who elects a course in creative dreaming is one who is more likely to produce an artistic creation. A few students have reported solving mathematical problems in a dream that they were unable to do while awake. Others have reported increased skills as a result of dream "practice." For example, one student who practiced her tennis stroke in a dream found her actual ability considerably improved in her game the following day. Similarly, professional golfer Jack Nicklaus is reported [30] to have improved his golf swing after a slump on the basis of a dream in which he was hitting the ball well by holding his club differently. By changing his grip according to the dream, his "swing" returned. Thus, dreams can provide very practical creative solutions as well as products of fine art.

In the area of personal relationships, solving problems was

frequently reported by students, especially with application of the Senoi system (see Chapter 5, where examples are given).

As a clinical psychologist interested in the effect of consciousness on dreams, I have planned to have specific types of dreams. Whether this effort has been successful can be judged in the chapters of Part II, "*How to Become Conscious During Your Dreams.*" To me, it has been a great adventure and a great help.

Students applying the principles presented in this book report similar experiences—a kind of opening of a new world; one that was vaguely known before but not so fully participated in, a world less and less frightening and more and more beautiful; the "acres of diamonds" in one's own backyard, the "bluebird" in one's own tree: the fantastic world within.

As you train yourself to remember and record your dreams you, too, make the first step toward being able to use your full range of creative ability. As you learn skills in inducing your desired dreams, you will more and more be able to utilize the talent that lies within every one of us.

The elements of creative products are around us everywhere, especially within us. The material is all there. All we need do is recombine it, find a *new* combination. What prevents us is our habit of seeing things in the same old familiar way.

While we are children, this ability to see things differently is often squeezed out of us. We learn to behave and to respond in the "proper" way to the extent that our thinking becomes relegated to *acceptable* categories only; the fluidity needed to make new combinations of ideas becomes solidified. If we are lucky, we keep a few drops.

Creative thinking is still available to us, however, in our dreams. Here, images often and easily combine familiar elements in strange ways (and strange images are accepted as familiar). This is the essence of creativity if we but recognize it and use it. The creativity that has been unlearned or suppressed can be relearned and unsuppressed.

In many ways, the principles of dream control we have extracted from past creative dreamers resemble the well-known steps of the creative process,[31] as indeed they should. The dreamer who is intensely occupied with a subject of interest will already have satisfied the first three steps: (1) he will be motivated for a creative act; (2) he will have gathered relevant information; and (3) he will have made initial attempts to synthesize his material. His dream state mind continues to wrestle with the problem; he feels he is about to solve the problem; and the illuminating solution comes—either during the dream or immediately after awakening (steps 4, 5, and 6).

The fact alone that a dreamer has a "super-dream"[32] does not imply that it will be a *correct* solution. Dreamers have been sharply disappointed to read their midsleep revelations in the morning light, as Dorothy Parker was after having dreamed that she had the answer to the world's problems, scribbled it on a pad, and, in the morning, found she had written: "Hoggimous, higgimous, men are polygamous, Higgimous, hoggimous, women monogamous." All "super-dreams" need the final step of verification.

The wider and more varied the field of the creative person's experience, the greater is his chance of hitting upon a new combination. In our dreams, as you recall, we have access to the great collection of recording of our life experiences. Our dreams can draw upon the full range of our experience rather than just a portion of it. We should continue to widen our experience, but what we have already within us is infinitely vaster than is usually recognized. From the chaos of our recorded experiences, remembered images, and feelings, we can link together elements that are uniquely ours. Researchers have defined creativity in many ways, but they basically agree that creativity is "the process by which original patterns are formed and expressed." [33] Your dreams can aid you in this creative process in any field of interest you wish.

Thus, the probability of devising creative products (artistic creations or problem solutions) becomes greatly increased as you draw upon your dream life. As you develop advanced skills in creative dreaming, especially those described in Part Two, you will more consistently have creative dreams. As you produce and use your dream symbols in a waking state, you will do more than create a product. You will also help to integrate yourself. In a very real sense, the greatest creative product of your life may be the creation of your whole, unique self.

Summary of What We Can Learn From Creative Dreamers

1. Eliminate fear-producing dream images by building positive dream images that work for you.

2. Build general experiences of the variation that exists in the world—travel, read, see art, hear music, study, work, experience the external, feel the internal. Absorb all of it. It will be recorded.

3. Immerse yourself in your area of special interest. Expose yourself to all relevant material—books, movies, lectures, direct observation. Try to make your subject make sense to you. Get the necessary material for your product. Deep interest in a subject or intense emotional involvement will lead to saturating yourself in it. Soak up your interest.

4. Build specific conscious skills in your chosen field. Get the necessary ability to produce a creative product, waking or sleeping. All the elements necessary for problem solution need to exist in your repertoire of knowledge. Your dreams will help recombine these elements into a new order.

5. Intensely focus your attention in your area of special interest for several days at a time (at least two or three). Work on your subject up until time to sleep. This serves as a kind of suggestion to dream about it. You may also wish to give yourself a specific dream assignment as well.

6. After you have your creative dream, clearly visualize it and record it in some form as soon as possible: write it, paint it, play it, make it. Visualize it while you translate it into a concrete form.

7. Give special attention to your recurrent dreams and idiosyncratic dream products.

8. Also helpful:

    a. Practice creative process skills. See familiar things in strange ways; see similarities between dissimilar things; get free from rigid thinking.

    b. Provide yourself with time, opportunity, and privacy for creative work.

    c. Produce first; judge later. Don't evaluate ideas at the same time you're generating them.

    d. Persist in producing and using symbols from your dreams, especially positive symbols and helpful figures. You will both help to integrate your personality and increase the probability of products.

    e. Develop advanced skills in creative dreaming (see Part II).

CHAPTER FOUR

Learn From American Indian Dreamers

You can develop your own powers by appropriate use of
your dreams. Your existing capabilities can be encouraged to
grow by relating to your dreams in special ways. Let's see what
we can learn from American Indian dreamers about developing our existing abilities in dreams.

All American Indian tribes * assigned special importance
to dreams in their lives. The nearly 1,000,000 Indians [1] that
white men found when they arrived in North America lived in
different areas of a vast land, in very different climates, in very
different ways. Explorers and settlers first encountered Indians
of the eastern forests. Some of these, such as the Iroquois, lived
by farming corn and hunting deer; some, such as the Ojibwa,
survived by hunting caribou and elk in the frozen northeast;
others farther south, such as the Cherokee, cultivated tobacco
and built mounds. After the Spanish arrived with their horses
in the 1600s, settlers encountered Indians like the Cheyenne,
who had moved to the plains with their newly acquired animals to hunt the roaming herds of buffalo. Settlers in the dry
southwest encountered Pueblo Indians, who lived in great ter-
raced villages of adobe; they farmed and raised sheep. Some
Indians lived simply by gathering wild plants; and others, like
the Navajo, wove blankets and made silver jewelry. As the set-

* All references to Indians throughout this chapter will be to the
American Indian peoples as a group.

76

tlers went farther west, they found Indian tribes like the Sho-
shone, who lived mainly on acorns and other seeds, and a few
who subsisted on roasted grasshoppers. Reaching the wet, mild
northwest coast, settlers found rich Indians like the Kwakiutl,
who fished plentiful salmon from the cold streams, even hunted
whales, collected berries, produced beautiful cedar woodcarv-
ing. These Indians were quite different from one another in
language and custom, as well as life style, as they are to this
day. Yet, one of their few shared beliefs was the great importance of dream life.

The ways that Indian cultures used dreams varied. Dreams
were often a part of the religious system. They provided a way
for the dreamer to contact supernatural spirits and gain power
from them. Dreams were often a part of the social system, with
special status and role assigned to the dream interpreter.
Dreams were almost universally used to predict the future,
with rituals to get rid of bad dreams or to encourage good ones.
Dreams were sometimes used to manage psychological problems, a kind of primitive psychotherapy, in which dreams re-
vealed wishes or indicated that certain curing rituals should be
applied. Each tribe thought its own way of using dreams was
the most important.

The study of the intricately complex American Indian
cultures' use of dreams is a lifetime work that deserves attention. I can only extract here a few central points that are
directly applicable to our own dream lives. Many of the practices American Indians engaged in were unnecessary to produce their desired dreams and, as you will see, in some cases
were actually detrimental to emotional and physical health. We
will want to avoid these harmful practices and exercise the
beneficial ones.

The first principle is this: *Dreamers who regard dreams as*

*important and even vital to success in life will receive and re-
member helpful dreams.* Indians, unlike current Westerners,
so regarded them. Let me tell you about an imaginary Ojibwa
boy,[2] Footprints-of-a-Bear, so you can see what I mean.

Footprints-of-a-Bear, "Footprints" for short, is about thirteen years old. Since early childhood, his parents have been
urging him to dream. When it is dark in the rush-covered
lodge and mother tucks the soft doeskin cover around Footprints, she brushes her warm cheek against his in goodnight
and never fails to remind him to lie still, to think of something
nice so he will have good dreams. Father has already commanded silence in the lodge and prayed for "thick" (deep)
sleep so the boy will not awake before his dream is over.

Both of his parents are anxious, for soon it will be time
for Footprints to find out what to do with his life. He will go
to seek his vision and he must be prepared. A great dream is
more to be desired than any material thing in life. Without it,
Footprints' life will be a failure. With it, he will gain the right
to any important career in the tribe—a hunter, a fisherman, a
medicine man, a conjurer, or even a warrior. Other powers
come in the great dream, too—the ability to tell the future or
to be successful in love.

For all the years of his life Footprints has been urged to
dream, to prepare himself for his *great* dream. For the past several months he has been fasting many mornings and even entire
days. He knows that his aching stomach is helping him make
ready for his guardian spirit (*manido*). Any day now, when
his soul is awake enough, it will visit him. If Footprints does
not succeed in his upcoming test, he will have no personal
guardian spirit to supply him with supernatural power. He
must have a great dream!

Up until now, Footprints has been living on "borrowed"

supernatural power. His parents had no naming dreams of their own so they invited a friend who had the right to bestow names to become godfather to their son. Godfather chose a name from some incident in his own adolescent great dream, phrasing it carefully, cryptically, so as not to reveal the plot of his dream. Then he presented the infant Footprints with a bear paw. Mother hung it on the brace of his cradleboard, where Footprints' baby hands set it swinging. When he learned to walk, his bear paw memento was placed in a woven bag with other treasures, from which he now pulls it when he needs to feel a bit of godfather's strength. Footprints and his "namesake" have exchanged gifts over the years. Now he must earn his own power.

In the spring, an elder of the village council dreams that the time for the puberty fast has come. Everyone makes preparations. Footprints is to be included. He must go while he is "pure" (without sexual intercourse). His parents accompany him to a lonely spot in the mountainous forest, near the edge of the timber line. Here they construct a "nest" in a high tree. By laying poles across branches about fifteen feet above the ground, they construct a kind of stage. Footprints is to remain here, day and night, for the next several days—as long as ten— or until the vision comes. He may descend only to urinate or defecate. He may have a few sips of water from the pouch or a few dried beans but he well knows it is scarcely enough to stay alive. He watches his parents vanish into the green forest, and alone on his perch, trembling with excitement and fear, he waits.

Footprints concentrates hard on his special wish, to become a conjurer. He thinks about it, plans how he will help people when he is part of the Great Medicine Society (*Midewiwin*). Hours pass. He can hear the soft steps of the animals hidden by the fragrant pine trees. Warm spots of sunlight dance on his face; soft breezes stir the fringe on his shirt. Now it grows darker and he begins to worry.

What if the spirit never comes? What if there is no hope for him? He knows he must suffer if the spirit is to appear. The ache in his belly is strong already. Perhaps he will have to chop off a little finger joint, as some of the other boys have done, before the spirit will come to him. Oh, let it come soon! A flood of fear descends with the black night. Weeping and praying, he cries until his strength is exhausted, and he falls asleep on the scratchy poles.

Footprints hears a twig snap and opens his tear-crusted eyes to look down into the worried face of his mother the next morning. She asks gently for his dreams. He remembers none. He is weak but the dawning light and his mother's closeness refresh him. He will be strong. No matter what, even if his mother offers, he must not take food from her. It would ruin his chance of success and he would despise her for it. Now his father appears beside her. His father reminds him to guard against a dream visit from an evil spirit; he must look for a powerful guardian like an animal or bird. Footprints has heard all this many times. If he is very blessed he will receive the sun or thunder as a guardian spirit; even the moon is greater than an animal spirit guardian. He knows, too, that his father can cancel out an unfavorable dream by scraping Footprints' tongue with a cedar knife and throwing it into the fire. He knows the danger a strong guardian, especially one offering doctoring power, can bring: He will have a shorter life, obligations, and restricted freedom. Yet, he will be powerful.

And so Footprints' second day of isolation begins. Now lightheaded and dizzy, he recommences his prayers and entreaties; he sobs and sleeps and tries again . . . and again . . .

By the end of the third day, Footprints is in a strange state. He feels more than lightheaded, almost floating. He is only occasionally aware of the pangs of hunger, for his mind seems strangely occupied with sights and sounds around and within him. Images appear and vanish. We might wonder if he is asleep and dreaming or awake and hallucinating, but he does not, for the Indians do not discriminate; the only label is "vision."

Lying on his nest, softly weeping, Footprints suddenly stops. His neck prickles with fear. Someone is there. He spins his head to look. An old man! Right beside him. But how strangely tender is his gaze. He has the look of great wisdom. Ever so gently he touches Footprints' hot brow and says, "My grandchild, I come to pity you. What do you want?" In a tremulous voice, Footprints replies, "Oh, master, I want to enter your lodge. Grant me that honor." "Then come . . ." The old man turns and with swirling robes floats down into a small tent. Footprints shakily scrambles down after him. It is dark in the tiny tent, barely big enough to cover their bodies, but Footprints can feel the heavy presence of a third person. And now the winds begin to blow, strongly shaking the whole tent, flapping, rapping. Shrieking loudly, the winds lift the whole tent, carrying it off to the other world. The old man presses a root into Footprints' fist. "Keep this for twenty-one moons," he says. Then he moves slowly in a circle with Footprints following, round and round and round the three figures move, the old man uttering a strange rhythmic tune, a grunt, then "Sky, sky," over and over. Then with a great shout the old man thrusts his arms upward, "Open the sky from the center!" he cries. And everything spins, the winds whirl, and Footprints is swept up and around, blown farther until with a start he finds himself lying on his back in his nest looking at the sky through the leafy branches. He has come, the master of conjuring has truly come. Footprints' life will never be the same.

Footprints knows what his future holds. Three more times the master of conjuring will appear to him in a dream. He will always have the third figure with him; this is the spirit of *Miki-nak*, the great turtle. The next two dreams will be in the Western Region, but the last will be on earth, where the master will teach him how to construct the conjuring tent. Footprints must follow every sign and instruction with great care. When twenty-one moons have passed, he may begin to conjure, not before. He will find the root left by the master near the foot of his tree nest. He will carry this root and use it with the song of his dreams to call the master back to him or to summon his power in times of danger. He must not use his new power too often or he will wear it out.

Footprints will not tell this dream to his parents. It is his own dream, his great dream, his private source of power. They will see the results of it when he begins to conjure; they will get clues of it when he later dreams permission to grant names and he uses bits of this great dream for names. They will see other clues in the new designs he puts on his clothes. They may even overhear him mumbling his dream song when he calls on his power, but he will slur the words so they cannot hear it too clearly. He will never reveal the secrets of his dream, for that would threaten his power and his life. His parents will respect this and only suggest he concentrate on it, dream more about it, and try to talk with his *manido* (perhaps a kind of primitive gestalt conversation with the dream image).

You can observe many similarities between the ancient dreamers and the Indian dreamers. Both have learned well the importance of dreams and the kinds of dreams that must be obtained for success. Both are exposed to strong cultural pressures to produce what is called a "cultural pattern dream,"[3] a dream required by their society. Modern psychologists would say that the appropriate dream is "reinforced," that is, it is followed by strong rewards so the probability the dreamer will have it is increased. Both ancient dreamers and Indian dreamers were offered powerful rewards for the right dream. Produce the right response—the right dream—and health or wealth or power follows. When position in society and prestige depend upon proper dreams, they are likely to occur. In our society there are no cultural pattern dreams required, nor, indeed, much societal reward for dreaming. Only you, the individual dreamer, can encourage your own desired dreams by the pleasure they bring you.

Your reward for creative dreams can come from your pleasure in the dream, from the creative product, or from increased skill in waking life: One successful confrontation with a fearful dream enemy that leaves you feeling capable to deal with waking life problems will encourage you to have more such dreams. *You can provide yourself with the rewards for dreaming that our society does not give. Regard your own dreams as important and they will aid you.*

When Indian dreamers became exposed to our culture, their culture pattern dreams began to break down. Researchers[4] studying the manifest content of dreams in Indians exposed to our culture found fewer and fewer cultural pattern dreams and more and more dreams dealing only with personal problems. Thus, another principle we can extract from Indian dreamers is continuous encouragement to dream actively. Indian dreamers, like ancient dreamers, are exposed to endless suggestions to dream that begin in childhood. *You can provide yourself with continuous encouragement to dream of a desired subject and obtain that dream.*

Any dreamer who regards dreams as important and worthwhile is likely to remember and utilize his dreams. In fact, one researcher [5] finds that people in cultures that give dreams importance have dreams that are more consistent with consciously held ideals rather than dreams unacceptable to the self. Dream events in such societies tend to be relevant to waking life events. Thus, if you regard your dreams as nonsense, they are likely to remain so, if recalled at all; if you regard your dreams as valuable, they are likely to become more and more so. You can develop existing skills and potential skills by relating to your dreams in special ways. *As you regard your dreams as important they will become more relevant for waking life.*

Indian dreamers achieved this goal beyond what we have seen so far. Ancient dreamers and past creative dreamers were planning only the general content of their dreams. Indians were required to plan dream content, as you saw in the case of Footprints, in *elaborate detail.* A would-be conjurer must have *four* dreams with specific characters, in a specific setting, in a specific order. A would-be warrior must dream the right to organize a war party. Every step of the campaign must come to him in a series of dreams depicting the path to take, where camp should be set, where food will be found, how many enemies will die, how many of their own men will be killed, and so on. Applicants for the announced forthcoming campaign had to submit their dreams for judgment before being allowed to participate. Researchers [6] are convinced that most of the elaborately required dreams actually occurred rather than being fabricated. Indians believed that attempts to conjure without the required dream series, for example, brought mental or physical illness upon the faker or his family. Unsuccessful conjurers were suspected of being charlatans. Some Indians never achieved the desired dreams. Perhaps they were unwilling to risk society's test of the power of their dreams.

To not have the required elaborate dreams was safer than to be exposed as a charlatan.

You will see in later chapters that other groupings, too, induce elaborate dream content. You are able to do more than plan a general desired dream. As you gain creative dreaming skills, *you will be able to induce very specific elements in your own dreams* that will enable you to use your own dream life even more fully.

We have already spoken about the value of obtaining dream friends. The spirit guardian (*manido*) who comes to the Indian in a dream offers a special type of friendship. By saying, "My grandchild, I come to pity you," the spirit in Footprints' dream is offering to adopt the dreamer and to care for him as a grandparent cares for a child. He is binding himself to his child protégé with the strongest ties of loyalty the tribe can offer.[7] Calvin Hall, the contemporary American psychologist who has devised a system for classifying the manifest content of dreams, regards the offer of a long-term relationship, such as this one, as the ultimate gesture of dream friendliness. It is equivalent in his system to becoming engaged or married in a dream. You should accept and appreciate all friendly gestures in your dreams. Dream friends can be as real as the friends you can touch while awake. You can think of the dream state as another, albeit very special, level of reality. In it, as in waking life, *the more friends you have, the better, and the better friends they are to you, the better it is for you.*

The Senoi obtain their dream friends in a different way, as you will see, and their friends have a different relationship to the dreamer. The Ojibwa give great importance to appeals to pity. There may be some semantic confusion here. Perhaps pity to the Ojibwa is not the same as it is to us. However, the Ojibwa seem to deliberately place themselves in a servile relationship to their spirits. In contrast, the Senoi dream friends may well be said to "come to serve" the dreamer, who relates more as a master-father. More of this in the next chapter. Meantime, *prefer service to pity from your dream friends.*

We have spoken, too, of the potent emotional force for the dreamer that songs have when obtained in a dream. Footprints heard his song from the "master of conjuring." Other dreamers obtained their dream songs [8] from an object or animal in the dream. For example, one Indian "sang a song he heard the trees singing," and another "repeated the song which the crows sang." Indians who were persuaded by researchers to tell their dream songs reported simple, repeated phrases such as "Straight-horned one, buck," or "The heavens go with me." Obscure wording ensured privacy of the dream contents. By singing the song softly in times of danger or serious undertaking, the dreamer believed that the supernatural power granted in his great dream was strengthened. Yet dreamers who have no belief in supernatural beings have powerful responses to their own dream song. Why dream songs hold such emotional force for their dreamer has not been studied. These songs seem to encapsulate a piece of the dreamer's deepest sense of self. *Catch hold of any dream song of your own. Treasure it.*

Perhaps a person in a dream state may be in a state of consciousness particularly fertile to musical composition. Or, it may be that fasting and isolation are elements in the production of vivid imagery and dream songs. One researcher of Indian dream songs [9] believes that lack of food creates a condition of abnormal activity in the brain that is similar to one produced by narcotics. She observed song composition during or immediately after altered states of consciousness in many Indian tribes. Since the digestive system is scarcely active during fasting, perhaps productive elements are more available to the central nervous system. Certainly there is a change in brain chemistry during fasting that can result in a changed state of consciousness. Dreamers have often composed dream songs without fasting, but lack of food may, in some unknown way, enhance the mysterious process. Perhaps thin air found in the high mountains or rocks preferred by Indians as fasting places also influences dreaming.

Recent experimental studies [10] have clearly established that when a person engages in singular quiet daily activities, he or she actually has *more* dreams (increased amount of REM) than when engaged in busy social activities. Subjects who studied, read, wrote, and so on in a room alone all day showed lengthened REM cycles at night (as much as 60 percent more REM). Relative isolation increases dreaming (and *total* isolation can produce hallucinations in normal people [11]). *Awareness* of dreaming is no doubt increased when there are no social distractions. My own lengthy dream record [12] shows many peaks of dream recall when life is relatively peaceful. Perhaps dreaming is greater in isolation as a compensation for a quiet life. Or, perhaps physical inactivity is responsible for increased dreaming. Another possibility is that the increased dreaming in relative isolation is a result of new learning. A person who is relatively isolated is bound to be more introspective. Reading, writing, and thinking are likely to lead to learning. Researchers have frequently observed increased REM following new learning.[13] Regardless of explanation, if you have trouble getting in touch with your dream life, *a good time to begin is on a peaceful holiday when life is unhurried and you are unpressured by people around you. You will dream more and be more aware of it.*

Another principle we can extract from Indians' use of dreams is their practice of representing elements from their dreams in waking life. We commented earlier on the value of giving form and substance to your own imaginative dream symbols. Indians carried out this principle to an elaborate extent. Many of the products of Indian culture are believed to be directly derived from dreams. Several Indian songs are known to be songs obtained by warriors in their vision quests. Prior to their death the songs became community property. Some Indian tribes share dream songs from the outset. Many Indian dances originated in dreams. All sorts of cultural artifacts— drums, pipes, headdresses—are thought to be dream derived. Many decorative patterns on pottery, jewelry, paintings, blankets, and clothing are likewise from dreams. At the very least, using symbols from your dreams will enrich your environment. Using personal dream symbols can add beauty and interest to our culture generally, but it may also have an integrative personality effect for you, the dreamer. The dream symbols I have produced in waking life—poems, art, or abstract designs— are deeply satisfying. More about this in Chapter 9. *Meantime, give your dream symbols some waking form*—sketch the strange figure you saw in your dream last night, embroider the unusual design on a piece of clothing, weave the dream pattern into a rug, play the dream music, write the dream poem, use your creative dream ideas.

Certain practices of the Ojibwa Indians appear to be unnecessary for inducing their desired elaborate dreams. Other practices are essential to dream induction—the belief in importance of dreaming, reward for dreaming, external suggestion to dream, self-suggestion to dream, intense concentration on the desired dream, thinking about dreams, relating to dream images, and using symbols from dreams (and possibly enhancement of dreaming by fasting and isolation). We are able to follow these practices. Giving dreams an important role in our lives may accomplish more than we realize.

Relating to dreams in special ways may actually *help to build the dreamer's independence.* Admittedly, this is a speculative leap from current evidence. Roy D'Andrade,[14] an American anthropologist, attempted to find out why some societies use dreams extensively but other societies do not. Using a sample of sixty-three societies (including several American Indian tribes) chosen from the largest collection of anthropological data available (the Human Relations Area Files), D'Andrade researched the presence or absence of several uses of dreams in these societies. He found that the following traits often occurred together:

1. Supernatural figures appear in dreams and give important powers, aid, ritual, and information.

2. Religious experts (priests, shamans) expect to use their own dreams in performance of their role (for example, curing, divination).

3. Culture pattern dreams are required before some roles may be assumed (for example, the four dreams Footprints needed before he could become a conjurer).

4. Dreams are induced by special techniques (such as fasting, drugs, sleeping alone).

D'Andrade regards these four traits as a general characteristic of attempting to seek and control supernatural powers by the use of dreams. He hypothesizes that the effort to seek and control supernatural powers through dreams arises out of anxiety. He reasons that societies in which the sons live separately from their parents after marriage will be more anxious and therefore exhibit more use of dreams than societies whose sons live with their parents. Here, D'Andrade assumes that isolation of sons from parents and independent living at marriage produce anxiety. He further reasons that societies that obtain their food by individual efforts and skills (hunting and fishing societies) will be more anxious and therefore show more use of dreams than societies that obtain food by group efforts (agricultural and animal-raising societies). Parents in societies that live by farming and breeding animals train their children to be obedient and responsible, rather than independent. D'Andrade reasonably assumes that pressure to become independent produces anxiety. There are obvious parallels with our society, which I will discuss shortly.

D'Andrade finds support for both of his hypotheses. The societies in which sons move away from their parents' residence show more use of dreams than societies in which sons remain living with their parents. In fact, *the farther the son moves away from his parents, the more likely his society is to use dreams to control supernatural powers.* The same relationship did not hold for daughters (presumably because men are dominant in these societies). The hypothesis about hunting and fishing societies' greater use of dreams was supported even more strongly: 80 percent of the hunting and fishing societies use dreams to seek and control supernatural powers, while only 20 percent of agricultural and animal-raising societies use dreams this way. Thus, *the more a society required independence* (hunting and fishing societies) *the more likely they were to use dreams extensively* to contact and control supernatural powers. These relationships held with a single society as well as when groups of societies were compared.

D'Andrade interprets his findings to mean that the use of dreams to seek and control supernatural power is caused by anxiety about being alone and the need to be self-reliant. I think we can go further. I suggest that the extensive use of dreams is an attempt by the dreamer to deal with his problems. I believe that the proper use of dreams produces and increases self-reliance. Perhaps dreams are originally used because of anxiety, but I believe they are more probably used as an active attempt to solve problems facing the dreamer. Our own society is certainly one in which married sons almost without exception live apart from their parents. We are also a society that requires assertiveness and independence for success. Ours is not a cooperative, compliant culture. According to D'Andrade's hypothesis, our society should show an extensive use of dreams to seek and control supernatural powers. Obviously, we do not. It is also obvious that there are many differences between our complex, time-pressured society and the primitive ones D'Andrade studied. Yet, perhaps we are missing out on a crucial element that could help us cope with our anxiety-ridden society. Perhaps, like the primitive hunting and fishing societies, we can deal with our anxieties by seeking and controlling not supernatural powers but the powers within ourselves through extensive use of dreams. *You may actually be able to develop your own independence by appropriate uses of your dreams.*

We, as a society, may well benefit by developing the extensive use of dreams, by organizing our internal power to work for us. We can paraphrase D'Andrade's traits to read:

1. Friendly figures appear in dreams and give important help and information.
2. Experts (teachers, therapists) expect to use their own dreams in performing their roles (teaching, curing).
3. Creative dream patterns provide material helpful in the dreamer's life role (the artist dreams paintings; the poet dreams poems).
4. Dreams are induced more readily by special knowledge of dream induction techniques.

If we each develop our own abilities by proper use of our

dreams, we may well be benefiting and improving our society as well as our own selves.

Evidence supporting my conjecture that you can develop independent abilities by appropriate use of dreams is emerging from hospital delivery rooms. A pair of American researchers, Carolyn Winget and Frederic Kapp,[15] recently investigated the relationship of dreams to childbirth. They studied seventy women about to give birth to their first child and analyzed the women's manifest dream content (that is, the images as they appeared in the dreams). When these women subsequently gave birth to their babies, thirty-one of them delivered in less than ten hours, thirty-one delivered in between ten and twenty hours, and eight women took more than twenty hours to deliver. Average labor for a woman with her first child is eighteen hours from onset of regular uterine contractions to emergence of the infant. The average length of labor in this group was somewhat less (13.36 hours). Winget and Kapp found that the things a woman had dreamed about while she was pregnant were directly related to the length of her labor!

Women who delivered in less than average time, in less than ten hours, had anxiety in more than 80 percent of their dream reports. Women who took longer than average to birth their babies, more than twenty hours, showed anxiety in only 25 percent of their dream reports. Women intermediate in their reports of anxiety in dreams were also intermediate in length of labor. The more the woman had anxious dreams of labor, the more likely she was to efficiently deliver her first-born.

A woman, heavy with child, skin and belly stretched to the utmost, resting her weighted stomach somewhat uncomfortably by lying on her side and dreaming uneasily of her ordeal to come is actually preparing herself to cope with it successfully. Winget and Kapp believe that the function of the dream is an attempt to master in fantasy an anticipated stress in waking life. They believe that the women they studied were attempting to cope with the anticipated crisis of childbirth. Those women who did not face the stressful situation by preparing for it in their dreams (by denying and repressing, to use psychoanalytic terms) endured prolonged labor. Winget and Kapp found that the women who endured long labor gave much *briefer* dream reports than those who delivered their babies efficiently. They believe that the women with long labor were too fearful to allow even symbolic dream expression of childbirth. Tension led to abnormal levels of various chemicals and hormones in the blood, prolonging labor. The pregnant women who reported long dreams with anxious themes of childbirth were "psychologically immunizing" themselves in their dreams. *After dealing with crisis in their dreams they could deal with it better in waking life.* We shall observe this carry-over effect many times. *Dreams can be crucial learning experiences.*

My personal experience confirms this finding. During pregnancy I often dreamed of the upcoming experience. I undertook training in natural childbirth, so my intense conscious occupation was naturally reflected, as we have come to expect, in my dream life. Subsequently, my total labor was only six hours, a remarkably swift and comfortable anesthetic-free delivery for a first child. At the time, I attributed this marvelous experience to breathing and exercise techniques learned in childbirth training classes. Retrospectively, I believe that my dream preparation was a major contributor to the easy delivery.

My dreams during pregnancy also often dealt anxiously with my plans to nurse. For example, in a dream I would find dozens of tiny starving kittens and wonder desperately how I could feed them. Later, I successfully nursed my baby daughter for over one year. Nursing is especially susceptible to the emotional state of the woman. A woman's psychological state is reflected in the amount of her milk production, turning off or "letting down" the flow of her milk. I speculate that anxious dreams of nursing may also help prepare a woman to cope effectively with this life situation.

Ojibwa women dealt with the concerns of childbearing in their dreams, too.[16] Since Ojibwa men believed that women's discharge during childbirth contained dangerous magical pollutions, midwifery was left almost entirely in the hands of women. The medicine man (*midi*) made only a brief appearance in cases of extremely difficult labor, to quickly give a prescription and leave before he became poisoned. Females were generally downgraded in this society, menstruating women being considered blights to every young living thing. The evil power of their first blood discharge necessitated confinement to an isolated lodge in the woods. Here the young girl was left dressed poorly, soot smeared about her eyes, instructed to gaze downward, to not look at any living thing, and to strew leaves in her path to warn others of her evil presence. She was provided with a body scratcher to avoid touching and thus poisoning herself. Even if raped by adventurous youths, her first duty was to protect *them* from her lethal gaze. Imagine fending off rape while covering the eyes! Obsessed and saddened with the terror of herself, she, like the young boy Footprints and his peers, could seek a vision. Small wonder that few women did, and those who succeeded had little chance to use their power.

A contemporary expert in Indian affairs, an Indian himself,[17] informs me that anthropologists do not understand the role of women in Indian society. He asserts that the role of females is better defined than the male role, that they have their own ceremonies, responsibilities, and creative outlets. He believes that Indian women are subjugated into less prestigious positions only in interaction with the mainstream society.

In any case, the Indian woman had a special opportunity to gain the prestigious role of midwife in Ojibwa society. A potential midwife should be over thirty-five, have calm temperament, and have had a few easy childbirths of her own. She attended other childbirths and learned the essential brews and massages. Some of these skills she was freely taught; she had to pay to learn other skills even if the teacher was her own mother. A skillful midwife could become wealthy from payments of grateful patients. The most important requirement for the role of midwife was probably her favorable dreams.

A favorable dream could bless a woman with childbirth powers. The required cultural pattern was a dream of an animal who has easy deliveries, such as a bitch, a mare, or a cow. Ojibwa women believed that a she-dog has the easiest time. One popular midwife reported a dream of a she-wolf that looked like a human person, with the voice of a wolf. The dream animal told her that she would have five children (which she did). The she-wolf licked the dreamer's hand and told her she would help her in childbirth.

Those of you who are pregnant may want to induce dreams dealing with childbirth and nursing. All of *you can develop your abilities to cope with your life situations by inducing dreams of them.* These dreams need not necessarily be accompanied by anxiety. Anxious dreams, however, may actually arise from a healthy concern about waking life problems. The concern extends to the dream state where the dreamer "practices" coping with the problem. We saw how concern about the need to perform in an independent, self-reliant way evokes extensive use of dreaming in primitive societies. As the dreamer practices dealing with problems in his dreams he is able to perform more independently in waking life. We saw how pregnant women who dealt extensively with childbearing in their dreams were able to give birth more efficiently than those who did not. It is the same for us. You can develop your waking independence by dealing with your problems in your dream life. You can prepare to deal with life crises by first preparing yourself in your dreams. *Successful problem solving in dream life carries over into waking life.* More of this soon.

Several of the principles we have extracted from American Indian dreamers have already been noted in ancient dreamers and past creative dreamers. We have noted elements to avoid. Other elements are both useful and beneficial. By representing our dream symbols in waking life, we enrich our environment and help integrate our personality. By using our dreams as an arena for practice in solving our life problems, we may develop our independence and ability to cope. We can encourage our existing capabilities to grow in our dreams. Proper use of individual dreams may contribute to better adjustment of our society as a whole. In the next chapter, we shall see how well adjusted a society can become through dream use. Principles we can learn from American Indians are summarized below.

Summary of What We Can Learn From American Indian Dreamers

1. Regard your dreams as important in your life and you will receive and remember valuable dreams.

2. You can reward yourself for dreaming, as the Indians' society rewarded them.

3. You can provide yourself with encouragement to dream.

4. Your dreams will become more relevant to your waking life as you value and use them.

5. You can induce elaborate detail, very specific elements, in your dreams.

6. The more dream friends you have, the better.

7. The more your dream friends serve you, the better.

8. Treasure any of your dream songs.

9. Peaceful, unpressured surroundings will help you recall your dreams, and you will dream more.

10. Give your dream symbols waking form.

11. Dreaming can develop skills of independence.

12. Dreaming can develop skills of problem solving.

13. Successful problem solving in dreams carries over into waking life.

part two

How to Become Conscious During Your Dreams

CHAPTER FIVE

Learn From Senoi Dreamers

It is morning in the Senoi household in Malaysia. Mother prepares fruit for breakfast. Outside, palm trees rustle with the cool morning breezes; the monkeys chatter; occasionally an elephant trumpets from the nearby steamy jungle; parakeets warble softly in the pomegranate tree; a brilliant butterfly flits past the open window. Inside, aunts, uncles, cousins, and visiting second cousins stir in the neighboring rooms of the communal longhouse, making ready their own breakfast. Sister has already wrapped on her decorated loincloth and placed fresh fragrant flowers in her long, dark, wavy hair. She sets out the leaf plates and bamboo cups. Grandma chews contentedly on her betel nut. The eight-year-old son rubs his sleepy eyes; he drifts into his spot at the breakfast setting. The family coconut-gathering monkey begs for his share. The durians, jackfruit, and bananas are passed around. As each family member helps himself, the father asks the most important question of the day: "Well, what did you dream last night?"

The question "What did you dream last night?" is actually the most important question of Senoi life. It will become an extremely important question in your life, too (if it is not already), as you apply Senoi concepts. You can apply the essential elements of the Senoi technique to your own dream life to eliminate nightmares and devise creative products as well as many other benefits.

Every morning at breakfast each family member, youngest to oldest, relates his or her dreams. No one will say, "I don't know," or "I don't remember," for dreams are the most central aspect of Senoi life, and everyone *does* remember. All activities from birth to death are largely determined by individual dreams. Children begin to report their dreams at breakfast as soon as they can talk. The authority figures—father, mother, grandparents, older brothers and sisters—all praise the child for having and reporting a dream. They ask the child about his behavior in the dream; they tell him what he did wrong in it, according to their system; they congratulate him on his correct behavior; they question him on past events relevant to the dream; they give him suggestions on how to change his behavior and attitude in future dreams; and, finally, they recommend social actions based on events in the dream.

When the process of dream sharing at breakfast is concluded, many of the family members go off to village council. Here the serious work of dream discussion continues. The men, adolescent boys, and some of the women share their dreams with the larger group. They discuss the significance of each dream symbol and situation. Each council member expresses his opinion of its meaning. Those of the tribe who agree on the meaning of a dream will adopt it as a group project. The Senoi people determine most activities of daily life from the interpretations and decisions that arise out of their council discussions: Friendships are formed; tribe members organize dream-depicted projects; tribe members even agree on when to move the compound based on dream discussions. Adults help the children to make artistic or mechanical things seen in their dreams. Some members work together to create costumes and paintings, perform dances, and sing songs they've seen or heard in dreams. The day is largely spent in these dream-inspired activities; at night, all the people retire to sleep, to dream, to live another dream-directed day. Obviously the Senoi, even more than the American Indians, regard dreams as important and so receive helpful dreams.

The Senoi people [1] are a large primitive tribe, now estimated to consist of approximately 12,000 individuals, living in the mountainous jungles of Malaysia. They are one of three large groupings of aborigines, called *Orang-Asli* in Malay, who live on the peninsula. They are not so primitive as the Negrito group, nor as civilized as the Proto-Malays group. All three groups are more primitive than, and relatively isolated from, the modern Malaysian and Chinese population of the peninsula.

Physically, the Senoi are tall, slim, light-brown people with fine, wavy hair. They live in extended family units in communal longhouses that are built to last five or six years. Each family has its own living compartments and cooks separately. The members of a longhouse interact like a village (*kampong*), with the central floor area as a street. Together with other extended families, they work a cleared area of the jungle (*ladang*), growing such crops as pumpkins, yams, bananas, rice, and tapioca. The soil is rich, so it is easy to produce food. They stay as long as the land is fertile, then move on.

The jungle is so dense with trees, shrubs, bushes, underground creepers, climbing plants, vines, ferns, ropelike trailers, rattan, and mosses in some areas that it is impossible to get through without a knife. Even the animals must use well-worn tracks in some spots. Researchers find it necessary to approach the Senoi by riverboat or helicopter. Once into the jungle, thick with animals and insect life, they are exposed to the constant threat of malaria, to which the Senoi are naturally immune. One field researcher reported to me when I visited Malaysia in 1972 that his malaria was "well worth a night of jungle music and dancing." I did not quite agree for myself.

The Senoi are mostly vegetarian but hunt some jungle animals with blowpipes. They catch fish by crushing on a rock at the stream's edge a fruit whose juice flows into the water, drugging the fish so that it floats to the surface and can be easily caught.

They decorate their bamboo vessels with patterns traced by fire. They are a musical people, using lutes, gongs, nose flutes, and drums to accompany group singing. Their numerical concepts are simple, with only four quantities: one, two, three, and "many"; some communities have the numerals four and five. Senoi who live on the fringe of the jungle have acquired some civilized customs from Malays living nearby, but they remain an uncivilized people by our intellectual, scientific, and material terms.

"Civilized" is a relative word, however. Although we are far beyond the Senoi in every material sense, they are more advanced than we are in other ways. They have achieved things we have vainly struggled for. The Senoi are a peaceful culture; violence of any sort is extremely rare. Staff members of the hospital for aborigines at Gombak reported to me, when I visited in 1972, that they could not remember ever having observed fighting among the Senoi themselves or with outsiders during the twelve years the most senior member had been at the hospital. The Senoi maintain this peacefulness despite warlike tribes near them; the other tribes are fearful of what they regard as the magic power of the Senoi.

The Senoi are a highly cooperative people. A basic Senoi exhortation is "Cooperate with your fellows—if you must oppose their wishes, oppose them with goodwill." [2] There is a feeling of shared responsibility. Food is shared, land is shared, life is shared.

Although cooperative, the Senoi are also individualistic and creative. Each person evolves his own unique personality and creative products. Solutions to social and domestic problems are varied and flexible—both polygamy and polyandry are tolerated, in addition to the usual monogamy.

Perhaps the most striking characteristic of the Senoi is their extraordinary psychological adjustment. Neuroses and psychoses as we know them are reported to be nonexistent among the Senoi. Western therapists find this statement hard to believe, yet it is documented by researchers who spent considerable time directly observing the Senoi. The Senoi show remarkable emotional maturity. Desire for possession of things and people seems extraordinarily slight, perhaps as a result of their advanced psychological development. They efficiently use a small amount of time to provide the material necessities of life—it takes, for instance, about one week for the group to build a house lasting five or six years; another week or so is needed to clear land for planting; cooperative food gathering requires only a couple of hours each day. They use the remaining time for large dream projects.

There are no well-controlled scientific studies to prove that peacefulness, cooperativeness, creativeness, mental health, and emotional maturity are the result of the Senoi's unique use of dream material. However, there is much to strongly suggest that, at the very least, their use of dreams is a basic element in developing these characteristics.

When Senoi children first begin to report dreams, their descriptions are very much like dreams of all children, in which, for example, frightening animals or monsters chase them. By the time they are adolescents, they have eliminated nightmares and consistently produce creative products from their dreams. How do the Senoi accomplish the remarkable change in their dream life?

I have studied Senoi dream practices by personally interviewing some members of the tribe (in English translated to Malay to Senoi who spoke both their aboriginal language and Malay). The Senoi I spoke with were employed at a hospital for aborigines at Gombak, on the fringe of the jungle. Their life style was already affected by their contact with outside cultures. I also interviewed contemporary researchers of these people who have spent considerable time living with them in the jungle in their natural state, and I researched the available literature. The chief source of written material is the work of Kilton Stewart. Stewart was an American trained in both anthropology and psychoanalysis who spent several years in Malaysia observing the Senoi use of dreams with Herbert Noone, the British anthropologist, who gathered the basic data on these people.[3] Material in this section especially draws on Stewart's writings.

Summarizing my findings, I have abstracted three general rules that are applied to a variety of specific dream situations. The first general rule is what I call *confront and conquer danger* in a dream. Suppose, for example, that a Senoi child reports to his parents at breakfast: "I dreamed I was chased by a tiger last night." The conversation might go something like this:

"Oh, what did you do?" inquires the father.

"I ran as fast as ever I could. He kept getting closer and closer. My legs couldn't move any faster. I woke up very frightened."

"It was good you had that dream, son, but you made a big mistake in it!" comments the father. "Tigers you see in the jungle in the daytime can hurt you, and you may need to run, but the tigers you see in your dreams at night can only hurt you if you run from them. They will continue to chase you only so long as you are afraid of them. The next time you have this dream, and you will have it again soon, you must turn around and face the tiger. If it continues to attack you, you must attack it."

"But what if it's too strong for me?"

"Call on your dream friends to help you, but fight alone until they get there. Always attack a dream image which attacks you. Do you understand? Never let something attack you in a dream and run from it. Always confront the danger."

This first general rule, to *confront and conquer danger*, is the most important rule in the Senoi system of dream control. We will see it in another form in the Yoga system of dream control (Chapter 7). You recall Stevenson's dream life, which evolved from a fear-ridden state to a creative one served by his helpful Brownies. You will see how Mary Arnold-Forster accomplished a similar change from fearful dreams to delightful dream adventures. Both of these creative dreamers appear to have hit upon the concept of confront and conquer dream danger on their own. You will experience dramatic change in your own dream life as you confront and conquer dream dangers. This rule, indeed, may be the basis of the well-adjusted personality for which the Senoi people are known.

Dreamers commonly encounter danger in their dreams, as any dream recaller will readily attest. Calvin Hall, an American psychologist who has gathered data on the frequency of various dream experiences, reports that aggression occurs in 50 percent or more of the dreams of young adult Americans.[4] The aggressive images are usually accompanied by anxiety, or fear, or even terror.

Not only is dream aggression common, but also the aggression appears in a specific way: The dreamer usually sees himself in the role of victim. According to Hall:

> . . . the dreamer sees himself as the victim about two-thirds of the time, on the average. Navajo dreamers are victims 89% of the time whereas their neighbors, the Hopi, are victims only 60% of the time. There are, of course, differences among individual dreamers, and in some dream series the dreamer is more often the aggressor than the victim. Children especially see themselves in their dreams as victims of attack either by adults or by animals. Women dream slightly more often of being victims than men do.[5]

Hall goes on to state that aggressive encounters are more often with male characters than female characters; he finds that animals are the most frequent enemy of the dreamer, with the male stranger the next most frequent enemy.

Since the dreamer so often finds himself the victim of aggression in his dreams, there are unlimited opportunities to practice the Senoi rule to *confront and conquer danger.* You, as a dreamer, can change the form of your dreams with wide repercussions if you apply this rule to your own dreams. Just as the Senoi do, civilized Western dreamers can evolve their dreams to eliminate nightmares. Specific suggestions for applying this rule will be given shortly.

The second general rule of the Senoi is a parallel of the first, except that it is directed at a different stimulus: *Advance toward pleasure in a dream.* The child is encouraged to move toward pleasurable sexual experience in a dream, to enjoy the sensations, to extend them to the ultimate. The child is also urged to enjoy the pleasurable sensations of flying in a dream, to relax and experience them fully.

The third general rule I call the rule to *achieve a positive outcome*. Suppose the Senoi child reports: "I dreamed I was falling from a great cliff." The conversation might continue in this manner: [6]

The father (or mother) says, "That's a wonderful dream! What did you do?"

"I didn't do anything. I just fell. It wasn't wonderful, it was terrible. I woke up scared before I hit the ground."

"Oh, that was a mistake. The earth spirits love you. They were calling you because they have something to show you. You must stay asleep, even if you're frightened. Try to relax and let yourself fall and land, to see what interesting things you will find. The next time you have this dream, try to fly, not just fall. Let yourself feel how marvelous it is to fly. Fly around to an interesting place." The child is thus urged to convert fear of falling into joy of flying.

Even the negative experience of being wounded or killed in a dream is to be converted into a positive experience. If the child is wounded in a dream, he is told that he has reduced the power of the attacker by using up some of the attacker's strength. If he is killed in his dream, he has permanently exhausted the adversary's power. He must immediately become reborn in a better form. This is surely a sophisticated "power of positive thinking" approach from these "primitive" people. That it is extraordinarily powerful will be seen.

The ultimate positive outcome, however, is the ending of the dream with a gift to the dreamer from one of the dream images. The dreamer must extract a beautiful or useful gift from a dream image to bring back to share with his family, friends, and tribe in general.

The dreamer should not allow his dream to end without completing a positive action. He should fall or fly someplace, make love to orgasm, fight to the death (or be killed), and always obtain a creative product.

Let us see how these general rules apply to specific dream situations. In any dream in which you find yourself the victim —that is, the recipient of any aggressive action—you are to become, as Hall would term it, "reciprocally aggressive." You should attack your dream enemy and fight to the death. If necessary, you can call on your dream friends to help you, but you must fight by yourself until they arrive.

The Senoi see the death of a dream enemy as a good thing. It causes the enemy's spirit to emerge as a servant or ally to the dreamer. According to Stewart, the death of a dream enemy releases a positive force from the part of the dreamer that has formed the antagonist dream image. The essence of the dream enemy then emerges as a helpful, positive figure.

Any dream character that is aggressive to you or simply refuses to help you is to be considered an enemy. Dream images that appear to be friends but attack or refuse to help are merely disguised as friends. Dream images are enemies only so long as you fear them.

I wish to note at this point that there is some disagreement as to the wisdom of "killing" a dream image (destroying it in a dream). Some theorists [7] take the view that a dream image should only be confronted, not destroyed. They suggest several techniques such as staring into the eyes of the frightful dream creature, overfeeding the dream creature thus rendering it helpless, forcing it to perform an activity that exhausts it, or making friends with the hostile dream figure by petting it. In my opinion, "killing" a dream image in Senoi terms is not harmful, since the effort is made to produce a positive figure in its stead—the servant, friend, ally. This is a "killing" only of the negative part of the image. You can either confront a negative dream image in some manner or "kill" it and produce a positive image in its stead.

Once the dream enemy has been confronted and conquered, the Senoi say its spirit should be forced to give the dreamer a gift. Only if necessary, the dreamer may bargain to obtain this gift. In the case of an amorphous threat, rather than a specific dream attacker, the dreamer advances into the vague threatening presence (for example, smoke) and *finds* the gift. This gift can be a poem, a story, a song, a dance, a design, a painting, or some other beautiful thing. Or it can be something useful, such as an invention or a solution to a problem. The value of the gift should be such that the dreamer obtains social consensus of its worth in a waking state.

The authority figures in the Senoi tribe suggest that certain actions be carried out in a waking state after aggressive interaction has occurred in dreams: If a dreamer sees the image of a friend act aggressively to him in a dream, he should advise the friend when awake, so that the friend has a chance to repair his damaged image; if the dreamer did not fight back in the dream, he should determine to do so in future dreams.

If the dreamer himself has been aggressive or refused to cooperate with a friend in a dream and this is a person he knows, the dreamer should make friendly gestures to him while awake.

If the dreamer observes someone being attacked and this is a person he knows, he should advise him of this while awake, to warn him. The dreamer himself should determine in future dreams to kill the aggressive object before it has a chance to attack.

Perhaps these deliberate behaviors of carrying actions over to waking life help solidify the peaceful, cooperative culture of the Senoi. Dreamers of the Western world would not be able to apply these concepts wholesale. However, these actions, applied to a limited group of understanding friends, might well enhance the relationships. A recent researcher [8] taught Senoi dream techniques to a small group of college students who applied them with good results on a two-week camping trip in the Santa Cruz mountains. The students achieved a smoother cooperative working relationship than any of them had previously experienced. One student experienced a prophetic dream while another had a lucid dream. Westerners can obviously apply Senoi concepts.

Turning from aggressive dream interaction to sexual interaction, the Senoi say that if pleasurable sexual contact at any level (for example, kissing or petting) is occurring in a dream, the dreamer should allow it to continue into intercourse and intensify the pleasurable sensations. Once the dreamer is engaged in intercourse in a dream, he or she should allow it to proceed through orgasm. The Senoi believe that the dreamer cannot have too much love in a dream. He should not be fearful of what appears to be improper or incestuous love in a dream; all dream images are parts of the dreamer's self that need to be integrated.[9]

Whenever the dreamer has a dream lover and proceeds through orgasm in the manner suggested, he should then ask the dream lover for a gift to remember him or her by. The gift should be a beautiful or useful thing of the type described above. Thus, confronted with a fear-producing image, you approach, confront, conquer, and *demand* a gift; confronted with a loving image, you approach, enjoy, climax, and *ask* for a gift. You always take something positive away from every experience.

In the case of falling dreams, the Senoi urge the dreamer ·to convert falling (a common fear-evoking dream) into joy of flying. If the dreamer is falling in a dream, he should allow himself to remain asleep, relax, and land. He should determine, however, that in future dreams he will try to fly rather than fall. If he is flying in a dream, he should allow himself to continue to do it, experiencing fully the pleasant sensations. Whether he is falling or flying, the dreamer should allow himself to arrive at some interesting place. The dreamer should observe this place, the people there, the costumes they wear, the dances they do, the music they sing and play, the designs they have; ideally, he remembers all of it and brings it back to share with the tribe. In this case, you *find* your gift (or more appropriately, treasure), rather than demanding or asking for it.

In any type of dream, if the dreamer encounters a friendly dream image (either by chance or by request), the Senoi say he should accept the dream friend's help; he should show appreciation to it for its friendliness; he should ask it for a gift; he should share and use the things given to him. If the dream image is especially friendly, the dreamer should ask it to become his guide (the ultimate friendly act in Hall's categories of manifest dream content). A contemporary researcher, specializing in the religious system of the Senoi,[10] told me that the ordinary Senoi acquires in his dream one or several "spirit guides" of some natural thing, such as a flower or rock. The rare Senoi considered to be a great shaman may have many spirit guides, including those of a different quality, such as a tiger. These spirit guides appear in dreams and call the dreamer "father." Each spirit guide becomes a child-friend who tells the dreamer things—about dances, songs, religion, and so on. Information from the spirit guide leads to changes in the religious structure. Religion thus varies from village to village, depending on personal revelation in dreams.

Notice the dramatic contrast between American Indian dream concepts (Chapter 4) and the Senoi on this point. To the American Indian, the dreamer is the suffering *child* who is helped out of pity by the grandfather spirit; to the Senoi, the dreamer is the *father* who is helped out of friendship by the child spirit guide.

What a psychological difference! The American Indian child must suffer fasting, exposure to the elements, prolonged weeping, and even self-mutilation in order to become a pitiable object so that the grandfather spirits will be moved to help him. The Senoi child must conquer his dream images in order to make friends, to become a father of the many child-spirits who can help him in his life. The difference in the dreamer's degree of confidence, in his ability to cope, in his degree of independence, and in his overall positive self-concept is remarkable. A dreamer who regards himself as a suffering Indian child pitied by one grandfather spirit will surely relate differently to people in waking life than a dreamer who sees himself as a father with many child-spirit friends. As you develop your own dream friends, you will sense the feeling of confidence their support generates. You will be providing yourself with a solid support.

In any type of dream, if the dreamer has images of food, the Senoi say he should always share it with other dream characters. This reflects the Senoi characteristic of communal responsibility.

The effect of applying the Senoi system of dream control, according to Stewart (and the evidence of my own experience), is to reorganize the dreamer's internal experience in such a way that his personality becomes unified. The results of unpleasant experience in waking life are at first neutralized in his dreams, then reversed. Negative images, if they occur at all, are no longer frightening; tension is reduced. The energy that went into forming negative images is transformed into a positive creative product. You will find many benefits as you apply this system.

Psychologists in the Western world are well aware of the power of attention in shaping behavior.[11] If a mother gives in to her child's temper tantrums, she is likely to have many more of them to deal with. Any child who receives recognition and praise for dreaming will certainly learn to recall more dreams as he is rewarded for doing so. We in the West are told that dreams are nonsense, or amusing, or psychologically revealing; accordingly, we forget, chuckle at, or examine our dreams with interest and fear. We almost never hear the suggestion that dreams can be *actively* used; we do not deliberately engage ourselves in our dreams to help ourselves.

It is understandable—although a novel concept—that a child will shape his dreams in accordance with the wishes of authority figures in his environment. Learning theory confirms that the attitude of the culture can condition a child's response. People who are first hearing about the Senoi often object that perhaps Senoi only shape the *reports* of dreams, rather than the dreams themselves. All-night recordings of Senoi sleep talkers, however, have verified that original songs, reported in the morning to be part of a dream, were heard and recorded while the same individual was observed to be sleeping. Thus, there is no doubt that the dreams themselves are shaped.

By the time a Senoi child reaches adolescence, he no longer has nightmares; his dreams change over the years until they reach the basic pattern required by their society. He is not considered to be a man until his dream characters cooperate with him and serve him in socially acceptable ways.

In contrast to the Senoi, the dreams of Westerners remain virtually unchanged from year to year. Nathaniel Kleitman, the contemporary American sleep researcher who codiscovered rapid eye movements, describes adult American dreams "as a manifestation of low-grade thinking." [12] He likens dream thinking to the thinking of the very old, the very young, the very drunk, or dreams of those with disorders of the central nervous system. Hall, in his extensive analysis of the manifest content of dreams, reports no change in dream style despite dramatic shifts in life style over the years. He finds threat and attempts to cope with it similar in both children and adults (italics mine):

> Children experience only slightly more anxiety in their dreams than adults do, and the kinds of situations that cause the dreamer to feel anxious are the same for children and adults. There are some differences in the frequency with which the various types of anxiety dreams occur. Anxiety in the child's dream is more frequently caused by being chased or attacked by animals and monsters. In adult dreams, the dreamer himself often produces the anxiety by committing some crime or socially disapproved act. The adult dreamer may use a more indirect approach to produce anxiety. He imagines some adversity that causes illness or harm to him or one of his possessions.
>
> It is interesting that there was *no difference between children and adults in their attempts to cope with the threatening situation.* Children tried as often as adults did, which was not very often, and they were equally successful when they did try to overcome the threat. *Success at any age is quite uncommon, however.*[13]

In most cultures, dream life is static; in the Senoi, it grows more positive with each year.

Let us assume that dream images represent internalized ideas the dreamer has about himself and others; assume furthermore that dream action represents the dreamer's way of interacting with himself and his environment. If these assumptions are true, then, *change in dream events can change the dreamer's ideas about himself and the world.*

This concept is central to dream control. If you change your behavior in your dream life; if this change "carries over" to produce a change in your waking life attitudes, then your *waking life behavior will change, too.* Changes in waking life behavior will result in further changes in dream life representation, and so forth, in a positive "growth circle." [14]

I have frequently observed this phenomenon of carry-over effect from dream life behaviors to waking life behaviors. It is similar to the effect of modern behavior therapy applied in a waking state. For example, if an impotent man is treated by an analyst who only helps him to uncover (over many years) his attitudes of resentment and fear toward women, he may or may not be able to change his impotence. If, however, the same man has his impotence directly treated by a behaviorist so that it is cured in a few weeks, he will definitely find that his changed behavior changes his attitude about himself.

In a similar way, if we simply "understand" our attitudes as expressed in our dreams, we may or may not be able to change our waking behavior. If we change our dream behavior, our waking behavior will change, too. There is considerable evidence to substantiate that this happens, as I will present shortly.

By deliberately changing elements in your dream life, you can learn to confront many of your problems at their origin—in your own mind, rather than years later in the therapist's office. Gestaltists regard each image in the dream as representing an aspect of the dreamer. Even if the dream image symbolizes another person, it is *your idea* of that person (not the person himself), thus, still you. When one dream image attacks another, you, the dreamer, are literally attacking part of yourself. These conflicting elements within your mind can be reorganized and unified in a positive way during the one and a half hours or more that you spend dreaming each night, by applying the Senoi concept of dream control. The dreamer who uses his dreams properly can become integrated; in Stewart's terms, he can "work for peace on earth by first establishing peace inside the earth that is his body." [15]

Once this peaceful unification of the dreamer's dream life is accomplished, it is not too far-fetched to speculate that, armed with these skills, he may well be able to relate to his society in a similarly peaceful, cooperative, creative fashion.

The dramatic change in dream life from fearful to creative comes about gradually. Even among the Senoi, the high level of dream control eventually achieved takes time to develop. Children do not immediately begin to dream in the elaborate pattern suggested to them by their elders. Day after day the dreams are reported, discussed, and criticized or approved. Night after night the child practices attempting to change his dreams in accordance with the belief system of his society. Year after year this process continues. Gradually, in bits and pieces, not all at once, the child begins to do in his dreams what he's been directed to do, until by adolescence he has attained a powerful control of his dreams.

The Senoi achieve dream control over certain images before they achieve it over other ones. According to Stewart,[16] the Senoi first gain control over things and animals in dreams, then over dream images of associates and peers, and finally over dream images of authority figures and of gods. At first these images die in dreams. Or, alternatively, they cooperate with the dreamer. They help him to conquer other images, which later he will be able to do by himself. Eventually important dream images from the dreamer's social and natural world (for example, father, mother, brother, friend, sun, wind, lightning) go beyond dying or cooperating, and give the dreamer something of value for his daytime use.

In this manner, control proceeds from year to year until finally the Senoi dreamer *always* arrives somewhere and finds a treasure in his good dreams or, in his bad dreams, confronts and conquers a dream enemy from whom he obtains a gift.

Despite the lack of cultural support for dream control in our society, the concepts of Senoi dream control can be taught and successfully incorporated into the dream life of the ordinary Western dreamer. The effect is almost surely as beneficial as it is for the Senoi, judging from the experiences of numerous students, family, and friends, as well as my own.

I have observed in myself, and students in my dream seminars have reported, great alteration in dream life as a result of exposure to these concepts. I suspect that the time required to develop the Senoi pattern fully is much longer for the Westerner than for the Senoi, who have complete societal support. The Western dreamer is not encouraged by his culture to change his dreams. In fact, current psychological thinking discourages, for the most part, "tampering" with one's own dreams. The student of dream control must unlearn many of his previous patterns as well as learn the new patterns.

Nevertheless, some of the Senoi dream concepts are incorporated fairly rapidly. The Senoi style of dreaming seems easier to establish, at least in its initial aspects, than any other type. This is probably because of its general, rather than specific, instructions.

If you are interested in experimenting with high levels of

dream control, you will do well to begin with the Senoi system. It is comparatively easy to program yourself with the general instruction: "If I am attacked [a very common dream occurrence], I will not run away; I will confront the attacker." The type of attack can vary widely; methods of confrontation can (and do) vary widely, as will be seen. You need only hold in mind the general rule, *confront and conquer danger* in a dream, which is much easier than requiring yourself to perform a specific dream action.

Many Senoi concepts immediately began to appear in my dream life after initial reading about them. I have often observed in myself a "first-night effect": I read about an idea related to dreams and directly incorporate it (or sometimes its opposite!) into my dreams of that very night. It does not necessarily follow that this element will remain a permanent part of my dream repertoire. Senoi concepts, however, seem easy to permanently incorporate.

Despite the fact that Senoi dream concepts are easily incorporated into dream life (sometimes even *despite* deliberate attempts), there seems to exist at the same time a fear response to control of dreams. People who no longer resist dream control on theoretical grounds (see Chapter 1) still seem to show resistance to it in their dream content.

For me, these resistances occurring within dreams lasted for several months, despite dramatic successes in Senoi-style dreaming. For instance, about three months after my first exposure to Senoi dream concepts, I decided in a dream to temporarily abandon attempts at dream control:

> *I am in a house and hear a noise outside. I go out the back door and see a guy on a motorcycle drive up, throw a thick Sunday newspaper, and drive away. I pick it up,*

*realizing it is tomorrow's newspaper. It is strange that I can
learn what will happen tomorrow. Then I am inside sitting in
a rocker. I am saying to myself that I can't control my dreams
too much because I am afraid I will lose control completely.
I don't want to do that. I'd better cool it for a while. If I do,
I'll probably find control increasing on its own.* ("Tomorrow's Newspaper," excerpted with story preceding and following, 1/22/73.)

Since I first read about and clearly understood Senoi dream
concepts about four months prior to this dream (on September
27, 1972), it is obvious that resistance lasted some time.

The "Tomorrow's Newspaper" dream was followed a
few nights later by a dream that seemed to urge me to continue
dream introspection, to not be afraid, as there were many
beautiful things growing inside:

*I see a dolphin drawn in cartoon style standing on his
tail with his mouth opened very wide. He holds his tongue
around the bottom of a girl so she can look inside his mouth.
She sees that all the flowers he has swallowed are growing. It
interests me.* ("Dolphin with Flowers," 1/25/73, with story
preceding.)

A few weeks after that, I seemed to be resisting the Senoi
dream control requirements I had imposed on myself:

*I am going to the opera with my husband. It used to be
that anyone, black or white, could attend, and there were no
clothing regulations. Now the rules have changed. People
inside the opera house come up to me constantly and say,
"Madam, no ladies in slacks allowed anymore," or, "No
sleeveless blouses." Apparently it is a period of warnings. I
can still do it, but not continue to do it. Rigid rules are being*

set up which puzzle me. ("Rigid Rules," 3/3/73, with story following.)

During the same time span, other more accepting themes appeared. I would comment to myself in dreams how helpful the Senoi system was:

> *As part of a story, I am flying through the air at great speed with some friends. We land safely in a kind of marsh. I think to myself, "This Senoi stuff has really helped, I'd usually be more frightened." I look around and see many interesting things: braided reeds that look Balinese, and build-ings reminiscent of Jerusalem. There is a sign posted, "Little Israel."* ("Little Israel," 3/10/73, with story preceding and following.)

And so I progressed, gaining some control, stopping ef-forts, starting again, resisting efforts, controlling more, resist-ing, controlling even more, and so on, in a similar pattern. The overall movement is toward dream control, but with care.

A student in one of my dream seminars showed far greater internal resistance. As part of a dream story, this student was trying to get out through a certain gate at college. A student guard let other students through but insisted that the dreamer go around the long way to another gate. When he was shoved around, the dreamer remembered to fight back and punched the guard. The guard proceeded to bodily pick up the dreamer and repeatedly pound him into the ground: "When I fought back, I got the shit beat out of me." In the Senoi system, he should continue to try, calling on dream friends to help him.

It seems to me that the Senoi dream concepts will not be incorporated by the dreamer, however receptive he is to the ideas, until he is at a state of development where he is ready for them. Thus, it cannot hurt you to make attempts at dream control. If you are not ready to utilize the concepts, you will reject them in your dreams. Dreamers have a kind of built-in safety mechanism.

Aside from the resistance noted above, the first change in dream life as a result of applying Senoi concepts was in the area of aggressive interaction. My husband and I discussed Senoi dream concepts with much interest in Malaysia as I visited the Senoi and in Singapore as I interviewed researchers and first read about the Senoi. He seldom recalls his dreams—an average of one or two dreams a month, unless prodded by me after a REM period. So it was unusual for him to report a dream altogether, yet he had incorporated the Senoi concept of *confront and conquer danger* three days after my first mention of it, and the very night after a long dinner conversation about it:

> *I was in a subway like the London tube system. I came to an escalator. The first three or four steps weren't going. I figured I had to walk up. After I got up the first few steps, I found that it was working. I looked up toward the top and saw all this yellow machinery above the escalator. I realized if I kept on going, I would be smashed by the machinery. I became frightened, and started to wake up. Then I said to myself, "No, I have to keep on going. I have to face it. Patty says I can't wake up." My heart began pounding and my palms sweating as I was carried nearer and nearer. I said, "This is bad for my heart," but I kept on going. Nothing happened. Somehow I passed it and everything was all right. Later I was going back down.* ("Yellow Machinery," 9/30/72.)

Although it was not a direct attack, the yellow machinery

in this dream obviously constitutes a threat. In Hall's categories of aggression this would be classified as an aggressive act that involves an attempt to physically harm a dream character, the only more intense aggression being that of the death of a dream character. By deciding to remain asleep and confront the machinery, my husband succeeded in the Senoi system. He would be advised, however, in future dreams, to explore the machinery, to learn something, to find something of value, and to bring it back to share with his family and friends. His observation that there is greatly increased heart rate in response to the feared stimulus may contraindicate this system for heart patients because of increased danger of nocturnal angina.

My own dream experiences with aggressive interaction show a similar incorporation of Senoi dream concepts. Before exposure to them, I frequently (although not always) played the role of victim; attack was common. Attack dreams with the dreamer as victim are typical, as already mentioned.

After exposure to Senoi dream concepts, my role often became different. I grew more capable of dealing with dream threats. This was literally a "growth." Occasionally, I would directly attack. Usually, I used techniques that were easier for me—I implored, I seduced, I appealed to pity. Later, however, I more frequently used another dream character to do the attacking for me or directly attacked myself.

For example, as part of a long dream story, my youngest daughter and I are being chased by a gang of guys who intend to rape us. This is a recurrent dream image for me, resulting from an actual experience at about age thirteen when I was chased through the woods by a gang of boys who said, "Get her!" and from whom I barely escaped by running to my grandmother's backyard where she happily was within sight and earshot. In the dream:

... we round a corner and see that the guys have blocked off the hallway and about six of them wait with their arms apart to grab us. I say, "Oh, no," and we turn and run. As I am desperately running, I suddenly realize I'm not supposed to do that. I stop myself and, with a feeling of great effort, yet certain I must do it, say, "Come on!" and force myself to turn around to face them. Then we are fighting them. We pinch and pull and bit. Suddenly I have something I am spraying in their eyes. In a few minutes we have successfully fought them off. Then the scene changes and I am with a man and woman, telling them about our experience. The woman is English-looking; she wears an attractive coat and matching hat of nubbly cream, green, and brown wool. They are both congratulating us on our escape. I wake. ("Spraying the Rapists," 2/19/73.)

I not only confront and conquer the dream attackers but provide my own dream reinforcement in the form of the congratulating couple. I should, however, go further in future dreams and require a gift from the conquered dream images.

I have not yet entirely eliminated from my repertoire chase and attack-type dreams in which I am victimized, but I have greatly shifted the balance: I *often*, instead of seldom, confront and conquer the dream enemies.

Students in my dream seminars report similar dramatic shifts in dream content shortly after exposure to the Senoi system. Within a two-week seminar, for example, a wide range of confrontation was reported. Some students confronted more successfully than others. For example, one student simply locked a dream aggressor out of a car, then drove away. Another student who dreamed she was being attacked by a dog she had previously restrained, was surprised and frightened yet stood still and faced it, confident that some nearby girls would help her. Another student made light remarks to a potential dream mugger while "physically holding him off gently but firmly." Still another student reported a more direct confrontation with a dream rapist who had been seducing girls by posing as a car salesman:

> *The man is driving by in a car with someone else. He stops, comes to the door, speaks, and comes in.*
>
> *He is attacking me! I am yelling for help from my friends. The three other people come and are pounding on him and I am out of his grasp. They are beating him. He is escaping, running out the front door and into a side room, glassed-in, in front of the store. I am rushing after him, alone. He is sitting in a chair. I am beating him over the head with a picture. His head is rolling back and forth, his chin on his chest. His eyes are almost closed and they, too, are rolling back and forth sideways. He is almost unconscious.*
>
> *I feel sorry for him, for the pain I am causing him. I lean down and am stroking his head—communicating my sorrow. I am aware I have to continue beating him, until it is done, even though I now do not want to. (It is as though I have to complete a task or role I have previously been assigned, and I am being watched or filmed.) I know I have to beat him to unconsciousness or death, and I am continuing to beat him.*

This student successfully confronted her aggressor but did not extract from him a gift. She did, however, continue the dream in a museum setting where all sorts of beautiful modern paintings and art pieces had been sent as gifts for a new police station (perhaps the police station is her version of my "Rigid Rules"). She even works in a hand (à la don Juan's system —see p. 174) holding a bouquet of flowers with the flower tops surrounded by aquariums. She observes many marvelous and unusual tropical fish that are also gifts. Note her "resistance" to the system: Pity for the rapist. Also note her feeling of having "to complete a task," that is, her awareness of the Senoi rule.

Although it is comparatively easy to advance against attack in a dream, it is more difficult to obtain a gift from the conquered aggressor. In fact, most dreamers incorporate gifts into their dreams in a direct, literal fashion. The first night after exposure to Senoi concepts, my dreams contained a gift—a package wrapped for a wedding. Students report such gifts as receiving ribbon-wrapped packages in their dreams, or opening a cabinet to find shelves of crystal glassware left as a present. Dreamers need to exert effort to shape these "gifts" into the creative pattern required by the Senoi. My own dream-written poems, songs, and paintings are more often just discovered or observed, rather than received from a dream character.

Sexual interaction is a category that can be easily and precisely measured in the Senoi system: Did the dreamer experience orgasm or not? No problem with sexual symbolism—trees in flame, houses burning, snuggling pussy cats, tall buildings being erected, exploring a cave. The dreamer either has an orgasm or doesn't.

Orgasm during dreaming is common for men. Kinsey [17] reported that 83 percent of the large sample of males he studied experienced "nocturnal emissions" (orgasm, presumably accompanied by dreams) by age forty-five. As mentioned in Chapter 1, the common "wet dream" has not (to my knowledge) been measured during all-night EEG recordings in dream laboratories. This itself suggests a measure of dream control. When researchers compare dreams in the lab to dreams at home, they confirm this difference in degree of sexuality (with home dreams being more sex-loaded). The dreamer apparently does not wish to be observed in this activity.

Female orgasm in dreams is rare, compared to males, just as it is in waking life. Kinsey reported that only 37 percent of females experience orgasm in dreams by age 45.[18] Researchers disagree about whether it is desirable for females to experience orgasm in their dreams or not. One research team [19] even relates frequency of orgasms in female dreams to degree of disturbance. (I leave it to women's liberation to determine why dream orgasm should be considered disturbed in women and normal in men.) At the other extreme, Abraham Maslow,[20] the American humanistic psychologist who originated the theory of self-actualization, stated that female sexual dreams are characteristic of women who are self-assured, poised, independent, and generally capable. Women with low self-esteem (who are more inhibited) usually have romantic, symbolic, anxious, or distorted sexual dreams, he found, compared to open dreams of the sexual act by women with high self-esteem. If this is so, then increasing orgasms in dreams could be another valuable behavior that might well carry over positive attitudes to waking life.

A recent researcher [21] found a striking difference in sexuality in the dreams of creative girls as compared with noncreative girls. From a class he taught on creative writing, an instructor selected a group of the most and a group of the least imaginative students, based on their originality in choice and treatment of their themes. Dreams collected from these girls were carefully examined. Among the many differences observed between the two groups was the form of sexuality in their dreams. The noncreative girls had dreams in which sexuality was only alluded to or represented symbolically—for example, a friend throws a black and red snake into the dreamer's room. The noncreative girls were sexually passive and felt vulnerable to aggressive sexuality of men in their dreams. The creative girls, like Maslow's women with high self-esteem, dreamed openly of sexual encounter. The creative girls often dreamed of active sexual intercourse in a variety of nonconventional settings. The researcher comments that the creative girls' open sexual dreams may correspond to greater actual sexual freedom, but he believes it goes beyond this: The noncreative girls have conventional interests and goals; their stereotyped thinking is "dream deep." By allowing open sexual expression in dreams, it seems to me, we may actually be freeing creative thinking on all levels of consciousness.

Now, recalling the Senoi principle of *advance toward pleasure in dreams* and their claim that one cannot have too many dream lovers, let us see the impact of this principle on dream life.

Prior to exposure to Senoi concepts, orgasm was rare in my dreams, usually occurring during time of deprivation or else, conversely, during periods of particularly heightened sexual activity. After efforts to advance toward sexual pleasure in dreams, not only did the orgasms increase (despite constant external sex life), but also directly experienced passionate dream feelings at all levels of sexuality increased. Students report similar increased sexuality and orgasms in dream life after exposure to Senoi concepts.

I must say that, subjectively, this change in increased direct dream sexuality is experienced as a very pleasant feature of dream life. In addition, it may be that by increasing sexual expression in female dreams, we are increasing attitudes of self-esteem that may carry over into waking life, in the same way that the aggressive dream behaviors can produce an attitude of confidence in waking life. If this is so, increasing sexuality in the dreams of a female may have particular value in developing feelings of self-esteem, capability, and other traits of independence. By freeing up our sexuality in dreams, as I mentioned above, we may be freeing creative thinking at all levels of consciousness.

The experience of flying in dreams is almost as subjectively exciting as orgasm. Prior to exposure to Senoi concepts, I often dreamed of flying; it seemed an interesting phenomenon. Following exposure to Senoi concepts, I experienced flying in a new dimension: I *felt* myself flying with what I imagine to be all the physical sensations of the act (the closest waking life experience was a parachute jump at Coney Island when I was fourteen). In addition to being a convenient method to get someplace quickly, to escape from pursuers, or to get an overview, dream flying also became a great pleasure:

> *I am with my youngest daughter in a large room that is mostly white. We have come here to see a special television show. The set is warming up. I go to get seated. I want a comfortable spot, as we plan to watch until very late. I pick out a seat on a green velvet couch, but it is too far from the set—the screen is out of sight. I see another green velvet couch nearer and decide on that, planning to curl up under the fuzzy green blanket to watch. The shades are drawn, but it is still bright and beautiful outside. I peep out at the colorful wooded countryside. I get my seat, then decide I should turn on one light—a floor lamp—across the large room to have when it gets completely dark late at night. I head over toward the lamp and decide to fly. I push off with my feet from the floor, like from the bottom of a swimming pool, and float up into the air. It is the most marvelous sensation. I go higher and higher. I am a little frightened and very excited. All the kinesthetic body responses of flying are felt very clearly, as*

*though it is really happening. I sail up and up. I extend my
hands above my head and gently bounce off the ceiling by
pressing on my fingertips. I see the white ceiling and ceiling
lamp fixture clearly. I float back down. I repeat this, up and
down, several times. It's a staggering sensation. I am amazed
I can truly do it. I know I'm showing off a lot for my little
girl. I want her to see, but wonder if I should. As I get more
self-conscious, I stop, drift down, and head back to turn up
the TV show. I think, "How can I explain that behavior?" I
reply to myself, "Probably self-induced trance and hallucination," but the sensation of real experience is startling. I settle
from the air to turn up the TV to watch the show. As I
settle, I see a large cloth of gold brocade with a Chinese
landscape embroidered on it, spread on something to the left.
It is glowing, exquisite. I realize my daughter has gone into
the other room to do something. I needn't have been self-
conscious at all. As the TV pictures come in, I see a woman
on the right with a man on the left, both with long curly
hair and dressed in Louis XIV costumes. The girl is very
pretty and smiling. She has a heart shape drawn to the right
of her mouth. She wears a low-cut blue dress. She reaches
over to the man and lowers a clear plastic, rose-tinted mask
from his face. I wake with the excited feeling of flying in my
face and body.* ("Late TV Show," 3/23/73.)

The dreams of flying increased as I applied the Senoi system, but it was the change in subjective quality that was most
striking. Dream flying became an adventure. Again, students
report similar dream flying experiences with great enthusiasm.
(The exciting quality of dream flying and its many possible
values are discussed in Chapter 6.)

The incidence of friendly or helpful images also greatly
increased for me with the Senoi system. Prior to exposure, I
was mostly reliant on myself in dreams, and if I failed, I failed

and that was the end of it. After exposure, I actively called on dream characters to help me when I could not manage myself. Helpful characters began to appear more frequently in my dreams, even without a particular need.

As you apply the Senoi rules of dream control to your own dream life, you, too, will experience many pleasurable changes. It is pleasant to experience orgasms in dreams, and it may contribute to feelings of self-confidence and freer thinking that carry over to waking life. Flying dreams can be an exciting physical experience, too. It may enable you to sense a freedom within yourself, to feel capable of novel adventures and able to cope with unfamiliarity in your environment. As you find your dreams filling with helpful figures that were not there before, you may experience a sense of confidence that also carries over to your waking life. As you wake from your dream with an original song or poem in your mind, you will enjoy the excitement of your creation, as well as obtaining a tangible product.

All of these dream changes are exciting personal experiences. There is, however, a more profound result of applying the Senoi system: The Senoi system clearly promotes emotional health.

One of the major goals of all therapy is to overcome fear that is unrealistic and inhibits the patient from enjoying a full life. Therapists have long advised patients to confront their fears. It is not so easy to do. Analysts spend years getting the patient to discover the source of his fears and giving him catharsis, so that he may eventually deal with his fears in his present-day life. Although the procedure is far shorter than analysis, behaviorists spend many sessions exposing the patient in graduated amounts to the fear-producing stimulus to "desensitize" him so he will no longer be afraid of it. The fear-producing stimulus is usually presented in imagined scenes, but sometimes it is actually present. It is rarely, if ever, suggested that a patient confront his fears in his dreams.

It seems that the Senoi system may provide us with the means to deal with a person's fears where they originate, in his own mind, instead of years later with a therapist. If you apply the Senoi rule of *confront and conquer danger* in your dreams, you will find that it is not only your dreams that change. There is a powerful carry-over effect. After you have successfully dealt with your enemies in your dream world, it suddenly becomes easier to deal with threat in the waking world.

I first noticed this carry-over effect in myself after several months of Senoi-type dreams. It occurred shortly after I dreamed of a chase and battle, with my husband and other men in the role of the attackers. At one point we all decided to be friends and celebrated by having a banquet together. This success involved the Senoi-type sharing of food, as well as making friends with the attackers. A couple of days later, I got into an argument with my husband. He was offended and angry, I became angry, too, but instead of dissolving into tears, my more typical response to anger, I suddenly realized I didn't have to be upset just because he was. Although I had been intellectually aware of this fact for a long time, I never *felt* it before. I stayed calm and was able to resolve the situation without stress. It amazed me because I had a strong internal feeling of control under attack, just as I did in the dreams.

Subsequently, students began spontaneously reporting similar effects. A painfully shy, quiet girl in one of the dream seminars came into class to report the following dream with great excitement:

> *I walked into an old-fashioned drugstore. I was waiting behind the counter for my turn to be served. The man asked who was next, and started helping a lady who came in after me. It was quite clear I was next. I told him so, and he told me to wait. I said, "No, you help me now." I rattled off three items I wanted and he just stood there. He wasn't about to get them. I said, "Look, you fucker, get them." I started to really carry on. I was swearing at the man and everyone in the store. "M" came in. I told her what happened. She tried to calm me down, and said, "Let's get out of here." I told her, "No, I've got to stick to my grounds." The man finally got me what I wanted. "M" and I walked out. Before I closed the door, I poked my head back around the corner and I yelled at the man, "You motherfucker!" "M" was really shocked at my language.*

This dream represents dramatically different behavior from the student's usual style, waking or dreaming. She said that the dream enabled her to subsequently speak up to her boyfriend in waking life about a behavior of his that troubled her, an unthinkable action before.

Another retiring student found herself able to insist on a right in waking life that she would have previously abdicated. She was sitting in a nonsmoking section of a plane and was bothered by a man smoking in front of her. She asked the stewardess to ask him to stop, but the stewardess said she couldn't do that because it hadn't been announced as a nonsmoking section (despite posted signs):

> *I was going to drop it at that, as I usually do, feeling there was nothing I could do. However, I continued to discuss it with her and asked her to please just ask him. She said OK. She asked him, and he stopped, and I was no longer feeling angry and victimized about having smoke surrounding me.*

It is a small beginning, but she was able in waking life to take herself out of the role of victim, after having done so in dreams.

We may be observing here a "behavioral rehearsal" that enables people who have previously dealt with problems by withdrawal to confront them in waking life. They seem to find waking problems less distressing and find themselves more able to cope with them.

As you control your dreams, you will discover that you have a powerful tool within yourself. You can practice overcoming your own fears, inhibitions, and phobias within your dreams. You can carry around within yourself your own self-therapy available to you several times each night.

We need follow-up studies and controlled studies, but the possibility is momentous: People can deliberately work on their problems in their dreams and make progress; they can both prevent fears from developing and treat fears that exist; they can carry over increased emotional maturity to waking life. Perhaps the Senoi peacefulness, cooperation, and creativity will become more of a reality, too!

By applying Senoi concepts of dream control, we can produce beautiful creations and solve problems at the same time as integrating our personalities. If we don't run in our dream life, we won't be afraid in waking life. If we are not afraid, we are free to create.

SUMMARY OF WHAT WE CAN LEARN
FROM SENOI DREAMERS

1. You can build an extraordinarily cooperative dream life within yourself by:
   a. Paying attention to your dream life.

b. Working on shaping your dream images every day.

c. Discussing your dream experiences with other interested people.

2. You can eliminate nightmares, produce creative products, and integrate your personality by applying the Senoi rules of dream control: *confront and conquer dream danger, advance toward dream pleasure,* and *achieve positive outcomes* in your dreams. These rules are summarized in detail below.

SUGGESTIONS FOR APPLYING THE SENOI SYSTEM OF DREAM CONTROL

1. Read through the summary of the Senoi system of dream control below.

2. Determine that you will shape your dreams in accordance with the Senoi rules, beginning with confrontation of danger in your dreams.

3. Each morning, review your dreams of the night before, using the Guide for Applying the Senoi System (below). See how far you are able to progress in "yes" responses to the guide.

4. Always consider Category VII on the guide carefully: What mistakes and successes occurred in your dreams, and what are your plans for future dreams?

5. Preserve an expression of all beautiful or useful gifts and treasures obtained in your dreams. Paint them, write them, sing them, dance them, or give them appropriate form in waking life.

6. Share your dreams and progress in the Senoi system, if possible, with a group of interested friends.

7. Don't get discouraged as mistakes occur. Successes will be even greater with persistent effort.

SUMMARY OF THE SENOI SYSTEM OF DREAM CONTROL

I. General rules in the Senoi system of dream control.

A. Always *confront and conquer danger* in dreams.

B. Always *move toward pleasurable experience* in dreams.

C. Always *make your dream have a positive outcome and extract a creative product* from it.

II. Applying the general rules to specific dream situations: Aggressive interaction.

A. If you are the victim (the recipient of any aggressive action), you should become reciprocally aggressive.

    1. Attack your dream enemy.

    2. Fight to the death, if necessary.

        a. The death of a dream enemy releases a positive force from the part of you that has formed the antagonistic dream image.

        b. The essence of the dream enemy you kill will emerge as a helpful, positive figure for you.

    3. Call on other dream figures to help you, if needed. Fight by yourself until they arrive.

    4. Any dream character that either is aggressive to you or simply refuses to help you is to be considered an enemy.

        a. Figures that appear to be friends but attack or refuse to help are disguised as friends.

        b. Dream characters are enemies only so long as you are afraid of them.

B. If the dream enemy is amorphous, rather than a specific image, you should also move toward it.

C. After you have confronted and subdued an aggressive dream image, force it to give you a gift.

1. The gift can be something beautiful, such as a poem, a story, a song, a dance, a design, or a painting.

2. The gift can be something useful, such as an invention or a solution to a problem.

3. Bargain only if necessary to get this gift.

4. The value of this gift should be such that you obtain social consensus of its worth while awake.

D. Certain actions should be carried out in a waking state, following aggression in dreams.

1. If the image of a friend has been aggressive or uncooperative in a dream (if you did not fight back in the dream, determine to do so in the future), advise him when you awake so he can repair his damaged image.

2. If you have been aggressive or refused to cooperate with a friend in a dream, you should make friendly gestures to him while awake.

3. If you have observed another dream character being attacked and this is a person known to you, you should advise him of this while awake, to warn him (in future dreams, kill the aggressive object before it has a chance to attack).

III. Applying the general rules to specific situations: Sexual interaction.

A. If you are experiencing pleasurable sexual contact in a dream, allow it to continue and intensify.

B. If you are having intercourse in a dream, allow it to proceed through orgasm.

1. Do not be fearful of what may seem to be incestuous or improper love, as these are parts of yourself that need to be integrated.

2. You cannot have too much love in your dreams.

C. Ask your dream lover for a gift, of the type described in II C.

IV. Applying the general rules to specific dream situations: Falling and flying dreams.

A. If you fall in your dream, allow yourself to remain asleep, relax, and land.

B. In future dreams, try to fly rather than just fall.

C. If you are flying in a dream, allow yourself to continue to do it, experiencing fully the pleasant sensations.

D. Whether you fall or you fly, let yourself arrive at some interesting place.

E. Observe something beautiful or useful in this place, as described in II C.

V. Applying the general rules to specific dream situations: Friendly interaction.

A. If dream images are friendly to you, accept their help.

B. Show appreciation to them for their friendliness.

C. Ask them to give you a gift as described in II C.

D. Share and use the things given to you.

E. Ask friendly figures to be your guides.

VI. Miscellaneous rules.

A. If you dream of food, share it with other dream characters.

GUIDE FOR APPLYING SENOI SYSTEM OF DREAM CONTROL

I. Aggressive Interaction in Dreams

1. Did you have an enemy in this dream?   1. yes____ no____

2. What type of enemy was it?   2. a.___ b.___ c.___

       a. Aggressive image

       b. Uncooperative image

       c. Amorphous threat

3. Label the enemy.   3. _____

4. Identify the category of aggression.   4. _____

5. Did you advance toward the enemy?   5. yes___ no___

6. Did you attack the enemy?   6. yes___ no___

7. Did you ask for help in attacking, if necessary?   7. yes___ no___

8. Did you receive help if asked for?   8. yes___ no___

9. If you were injured or killed, were you reborn?   9. yes___ no___

10. Did you injure your enemy?   10. yes___ no___

11. Did you successfully fight off your enemy?   11. yes___ no___

12. Did you kill your enemy?   12. yes___ no___

13. Did you ask your enemy for a gift?   13. yes___ no___

II. Sexual Interaction in Dreams

14. Did you have sexual contact in this dream?   14. yes___ no___

15. Identify partner or stimulus.   15. _____

16. Identify category of sexual interaction.   16. _____

17. Did you allow contact to proceed through intercourse?   17. yes___ no___

18. Did you allow inter-   18. yes___ no___

course to proceed through orgasm?

19. Did you ask your dream lover for a gift?   19. yes____ no____

III. Falling or Flying in Dreams

20. Did you fall in this dream?   20. yes____ no____

21. Did you allow yourself to remain asleep?   21. yes____ no____

22. Did you allow yourself to relax?   22. yes____ no____

23. Did you allow yourself to land?   23. yes____ no____

24. Did you fly in this dream?   24. yes____ no____

25. Did you enjoy flying?   25. yes____ no____

26. Did you find an interesting place?   26. yes____ no____

27. Did you observe a gift or treasure?   27. yes____ no____

IV. Friendly Interaction in Dreams

28. Did you encounter friendly figures in this dream?   28. yes____ no____

29. Label the friendly figure(s).   29. _____

30. Identify the category of friendliness.   30. _____

31. Did you accept the figure's friendly gesture(s)?   31. yes____ no____

32. Did you express appreciation for friendliness?   32. yes____ no____

33. Did you ask friendly images to be your guide?   33. yes____ no____

34. Did you share and use anything given to you?

34. yes___ no___

35. Did you ask friendly images for a gift?

35. yes___ no___

V. Miscellaneous Interaction in Dreams

36. Did you share any food in the dream with other characters?

36. yes___ no___

37. If there was food in your dream, what was it?

37. _____

VI. Gifts or Treasures

38. Did you extract, receive, find, or observe a gift or treasure in this dream?

38. yes___ no___

39. What type of gift or treasure was it?

39. _____

40. Describe it briefly.

40. _____

41. Did you bargain for this, if necessary?

41. yes___ no___

42. Did you get social consensus on gift when awake?

42. yes___ no___

VII. Summary

A. What *mistakes* did you make in the dream (count "noes")

_____

B. What do you determine to do in future dreams?

_____

C. What *successes* did you achieve in this dream (count "yeses")

_____

D. Congratulate yourself on your successes.

CHAPTER SIX

Learn From Lucid Dreamers

You will have an unusual, exciting experience when you have a "lucid dream." Very simply, a lucid dream is a dream in which the dreamer is aware he is dreaming. Awareness can range from the mere thought, "This is only a dream," to an unbelievable freedom from all restrictions of body, time, and space. When you become lucid you can do *anything* in your dream. You can fly anywhere you wish, experience love-making with the partner of your choice, converse with friends long dead or people unknown to you; you can see any place in the world you choose, experience all levels of positive emotions, receive answers to questions that plague you, observe creative products, and, in general, use the full resource of the material stored in your mind. *You can learn to become conscious during your dreams.*

Dreams are, according to Ernest Rossi,[1] a contemporary theorist, a composite of (1) forces and figures expressing the autonomous process [2] that are not under the dreamer's control, and (2) the dreamer himself interacting with these forces and figures. When dreams are dull and routine, the autonomous process is blocked out; when dreams are too bizarre, the autonomous process is overwhelming the dreamer's identity and cannot be assimilated. The ideal balance is a dream life in which you interact with your dream figures in stimulating adventures. From encountering your dream figures, Rossi believes you can develop new awareness, which becomes integrated with former awareness, leading eventually to a new identity.

When you have a lucid dream you are in a favorable position to maximize your interaction with dream figures. Your dreams are not dull because you are invested in them with a feeling like waking consciousness, you experience them as yourself, and you have the freedom to create almost any event you desire. At the same time, your dreams are not too bizarre, for you have the power to either turn them off or to alter the negative aspects of them. Your dreams became, indeed, a "stimulating adventure." You do not know in advance what the autonomous process will present to you in dream figures, so you are sure to be surprised, if not delighted. Nevertheless, you know you can control, stop, or change negative events and evoke positive ones. Like the feeling of competence that you may sometimes have in waking life—unexpected events and frustrations appear, but you know that you can deal with them, do so, and proceed to go about achieving your own desired goals. *As you practice competence in lucid dreams, you will increase its probable occurrence in waking life.*

The seekers of lucid dreams have been many. As you will see, the Yogis of the dream state have as their primary purpose to *enter* the dream state in full consciousness, just as the lucid dreamer's intention is to *attain* consciousness during the dream state. The two approaches differ in timing: The Yogis of the dream state strive to never let go of consciousness; the lucid dreamers usually struggle to *become* conscious during the dream. There are, of course, other differences—in purpose, in experiments performed, and so on, as will be described.

In my opinion, lucid dream control is more difficult to achieve than any other type of dream control we have discussed. (Yoga dream control is probably even more difficult to attain.) In the first place, few people are aware of the possibility of becoming conscious while dreaming. Dreamers rarely develop lucid dreaming without hearing about it (although it can happen). Even when presented with the possibility of lucid dreaming, many people do not believe it. Or they say that if the experience occurred it was not a dream. Or they regard it as a "miracle." My experience with my own dreams and reported dreams of students suggests that, to the contrary, lucid dreaming is a skill that can be acquired. It is difficult to attain, but once experienced it is so exciting that the effort is nothing and the sense of joy and adventure immeasurable.

Why it is so difficult to attain consciousness in a dream state is unclear. For some reason it is easier to attain a semiconscious awareness—for example, to remember that one must fight off dream attackers (Senoi). In this case, the dreamer knows in a vague way that he is dreaming, but the awareness is not central. He is focused on the action required. In lucid dreaming, as in Yoga of the dream state, awareness of dreaming is central. It must be held on to above all else. Action is secondary and can take unlimited forms.

Once you attain awareness of the dream state, it is not ensured. You must be constantly alert in a lucid dream. You will find yourself going in and out of awareness, having to remind yourself, "Don't forget, you're dreaming, you can do anything." If you relax your awareness, you lose it and fall into ordinary, uncontrolled dreaming. On the other hand, if you have strong awareness, there is a danger that excitement over the joy of your freedom and power will wake you. You must exercise your will not to become overexcited and wake, yet at the same time not become distracted and slip into ordinary dreaming. Like crossing a narrow board, you must keep your balance to avoid falling one way or the other. Your reward is exquisite pleasure. You will see how to find and develop this special state.

Lucid dreamers of the West were recently reviewed by Celia Green,[3] currently director of the Institute of Psychophysical Research in Oxford. Green examined published accounts of lucid dreaming by Arnold-Forster, Delage, van Eeden, Fox, Hervey de Saint-Denys, Ouspensky, and Whiteman, as well as unpublished material from four subjects who reported to the society. Much material in this chapter is drawn from her work, as well as the original publications whenever possible.

Combining the reported experiences of other people and my own experiences with lucid dreams, I have extracted a set of suggestions that I believe will help you discover the remarkable state of dream consciousness. If you already possess the skill of becoming aware during a dream that you are, in fact, dreaming, you can learn to extend and intensify the experience with remarkable results.

Please assume, for the moment at least, that it is possible for you to become conscious during a dream. The next step is to recognize when you are in a *prelucid state*. If a lucid dream is a dream in which you are aware that you are dreaming, a prelucid dream is one in which you *suspect* that you are dreaming without fully realizing that you are doing so. You adopt a critical attitude toward your dream experience. You may even specifically ask yourself, "Am I dreaming?" and proceed to test whether your experience is real or dreamlike.

Prelucid dreams, according to Green and my own experience, can defy all detailed inspection to test their reality. In one such prelucid dream, I believed myself to have awakened. I dreamed that I turned on the light by my bed. I looked at the night table beside me, observing the red of the lampshade, the glow of the light on the leather-top table—all was as in a waking state. Yet I suspected something. I reached out my hand and rapped vigorously on the table top. Quite solid. I decided that the experience was real because I could feel it. So concluding, I continued to dream in the usual manner. Upon actual wakening, the symbolism was obvious to me—I had been considering whether the professed affection of a particular friend was genuine; "It *must* be real because I can *feel* it." (This prelucid dream would also be classified as a "false awakening," to be described below.)

Thus, you may conclude, on the basis of examining your dream, that it is reality. If you do so, the dream continues in an ordinary manner. If, on the other hand, you determine that your experience is indeed a dream, you can proceed into a lucid dream experience. *Try to test the reality of your experience during a dream.*

My prelucid dreams usually involve comments on the dream, within the dream:

> As part of a story I see the face of a decorative clock on an upright piano that has just been opened. It is literally a face, with a lovely expression on it. I see closer and closer views of it. It rather resembles a Buddha's face, white, constructed of seamed metal. Then I see it drawn on my notepad, and I say, "I'd usually wake up at that part." The dream continues. ("Buddha Clock," 11/5/72.)

Obviously, I had some awareness I was dreaming in order to make the statement, "I'd usually wake up . . ." Yet the awareness was not clearly focused enough, so the dream went on in an ordinary manner. *As you become more aware of such prelucid moments, it becomes easier to push the dream into a lucid state.*

On one attempt to induce a lucid dream, the result was a dream *about* lucid dreams. In the second dream I recorded that night, I saw myself reading a book that described a series of dreams in which thirteen out of fourteen dreams were lucid. There were numerous facts and illustrations related to them. In another dream there was a story about a girl named *Lucy*. At the end of the fifth and final dream that night, I saw my notepad with a recording about a lucid dream I'd had. I looked at it and thought, "I didn't think I'd had a lucid dream." This critical, analytical thought woke me rather than precipitating the lucid dream I desired. *You can induce a lucid dream but it takes time.*

You can successfully initiate a lucid dream from several types of dream events. Brief lucid dreams commonly arise from an emotionally stressful situation. A nightmare in which you are terrified becomes lucid at the point you say to yourself, "This is only a dream; I don't need to be afraid. I can wake up." This realization usually terminates the dream. Dreamers commonly experience this rudimentary level of lucid dreaming, usually without recognizing it as such. The level of awareness is enough to reduce fear in the dream situation and allow the dreamer to escape by waking. It is an improvement over the usual nightmare, from which the dreamer wakes out of sheer terror. He has a few seconds of lucidity and uses it to wake.

However, some dreamers who have developed this skill of waking themselves from nightmares go further. They decide that since they are dreaming, they can't really be hurt, so it is all right to continue the dream. In these cases, the dream goes on, but with the frightening element either altered in form or in the same form but no longer capable of producing fear. *As you hold on to your awareness of your dream state, your lucid dream continues, instead of being just a momentary flash.*

Mary Arnold-Forster, a nonprofessional but highly perceptive English observer of dreams who described her adventures in dream control, developed this skill to a high degree. She devised a formula: "Remember this is a dream. You are to dream no longer," or "You know this is a dream; you shall dream no longer—you are to wake." [4] She repeated this silently to herself from time to time during the day and before going to sleep, sometimes even aloud, to imprint it powerfully on the "dream mind," always using the same words. *Keep reminding yourself that dreams are only dreams, not real, until you can remember that fact during a dream.*

At first she found the formula waked her at once, but later, having once said the formula in her dream, she found, "I do not have to wake, though I may do so, but the original fear element always ceases. It is simply 'switched off' and a continuation of the dream, but without the disturbing element, takes its place and goes forward without a break." [5] Arnold-Forster was haunted by dreams that she would receive news of the death of her husband or four sons at the warfront (World War I). This was a realistic fear during the war years, yet by using the formula, she was happily able to free herself from anguish about it in dreams. She relates:

> In most cases the disordered dream is stopped by a simple word of command, which either ends it abruptly as the falling of the stage curtain brings the play to a close, or which ends it by changing the dream scene, as one magic lantern picture fades out and gives place to another. [6]

As you become lucid in a frightening dream, don't use your awareness to wake up. *You can benefit yourself further by using lucidity to continue the dream in a changed form.*

When a lucid dreamer decides not to allow dream images

to frighten him he is practicing a form of the Senoi concept of *confront and conquer* and the Yoga concept of *fearlessness of dream images*. (In this case, however, there are no clear-cut instructions as to how to proceed after the negative image is turned off. You choose what happens next.) Thus, *one way to become lucid is to be frightened in a dream and then realize it is a dream*. There are other ways.

A lucid dream may begin as a result of recognizing the strange dreamlike quality of the experience. The dreamer examines his dream experience and realizes he is dreaming. For example, in one dream that became lucid I recognized the strange dreamlike quality of my experience:

> *In the midst of a long, unpleasant dream in which my youngest daughter has been raped and stuffed into a closet, and I am caring for her, I walk by a bowl on the shelf with a plant growing in it. I see with horror some small moldy snake-lizardlike animals crawling in the earth. "I'll have to discard the whole thing later," I think. I feel a wave of disappointment at the vague thought. "I haven't dreamed anything like that in a long time." Then I look out a nearby window and see my daughter, who has sneaked outside, running over to a boy. Now she begins to change form, bubbling and turning into a large, similar snakelike object herself— like a huge ball formed of, or covered with, snakes, but with her own head. This is even worse (to dream about). Suddenly, I am struck with the full realization that I AM DREAMING altogether. I become very excited . . .* ("Looking at Myself," 6/6/73, with following story.)

My recognition of the dreamlike quality of this experience in my prelucid state was also combined with some emotional stress and thoughts about the incongruity of the present images compared to usual dreams. *Alert yourself to strange happenings in your dreams; they are a handle on the door to lucid dreaming.* When you recognize it in the dream, you can open it.

In another case, I probably recognized the dreamlike quality without emotional stress:

> *I am in a place, perhaps dreaming, waiting for my husband. I go down to a wooden door which is an entrance to or exit from a men's room. I begin to carve upon the door: "A strange happening." As I continue to carve, I realize it is a dream . . .* ("Carving My Name," 7/29/73, with story following.)

Here I am alerting myself to "a strange happening" by spelling it out for myself. This is surely a cooperative dream state.

Another route to lucid dreaming is to begin to analyze your thought processes in a dream. Any dream situation that would initiate critical thought in waking life can precipitate a lucid dream. For instance, in a prelucid state that became lucid, I dreamed:

> *In the course of a story I find myself in a kind of garage on a huge bedlike arrangement, with several people. There is a huge, fat, black woman whom I hug and hug, and she, me. She says, "I love you," and I reply, "I love you, too." Then I wonder. "Whatever would give me such an image? Oh, yes, it is probably from R—the woman who took care of me while Mother was in the hospital having my brother— that's why I have an image like that in a dream—and it is a dream! IT'S A DREAM AND I'M DREAMING!" I am joyous with the realization and happily hug the spread, with the woman in it . . .* ("Big, Black Woman," 7/20/73, with story following.)

There is nothing in my current life to explain such an image.

Its incongruity struck me in the dream. Yogis, as you will see, achieve remarkable dream consciousness by analyzing ongoing dreams. *Alert yourself to incongruities in your dreams. Attempt to analyze them critically during the dream.*

A critical attitude is essential in order to tip the scale from prelucid dreams to lucid dreams, according to Oliver Fox. Fox maintains that there are four levels of this crucial critical attitude:

> 1. The dreamer recognizes an incongruity in his dream only after he is awake. For example, in one of the above dreams I might have puzzled about the image of my daughter turning into a ball of snakes *after* I woke.
> 2. The dreamer notices an incongruity during his dream, is somewhat curious about it, but accepts it—for example, I might have observed the image of my daughter with some mild curiosity during the dream.
> 3. The dreamer notices an incongruity in his dream and is surprised by it at that time—for example, I might have seen the image of my daughter and said, "That's peculiar," in the dream.
> 4. The dreamer notices an incongruity in his dream, says in effect, "But that's *impossible*; I must be dreaming," and thus becomes lucid. This is essentially what I did when confronted with the image of my daughter turning into a ball of snakes.[7]

Develop a critical attitude during your dreams and you will be able to move into lucid dream adventures.

It is also possible to enter a lucid dream from a waking state. In this case the dreamer observes his own mental processes as he falls asleep, entering a lucid dream. Green claims this happens only to dreamers who *deliberately* attempt this experience. The Yogis of the dream state have developed this to a high degree. Few Westerners claim this ability.

Ouspensky,[8] the Russian philosopher, reported making a practice of voluntarily entering a lucid dream from a waking state. He wrote that his attempts to preserve consciousness in sleep created for him "a particular half-dream state." He found that if he had a lucid dream early in his sleep period, he thought about it, and could not go back to sleep afterward. He found it easier to experience lucid dreams in the morning when already awake but still in bed:

> Wishing to create these states, after waking I again closed my eyes and began to doze, at the same time keeping my mind on some definite image, or some thought. And sometimes in such cases there began those strange states which I call "half-dream states." Without definite effort, such states would not come . . .[9]

Notice Ouspensky's practice of holding a definite image in mind. This would tend to induce a dream on that subject. You may wish to try entering a lucid dream state from a waking state. *All lucid dreams*, whether consciousness is attained during the dream or never let go of, *are obtained more easily after several hours of sleep.*

The Dutch psychotherapist Frederik van Eeden [10] claimed to be a habitual lucid dreamer. Van Eeden, who had written his most interesting dreams in a general diary for two years, then began a separate account of his lucid dreams for the next fourteen years (January 20, 1898, to December 26, 1912). Altogether he recorded 500 dreams, of which 352 were lucid. This is an amazingly high percentage of lucid dreams. Modern research suggests that the number of dreams he *experienced* was greater than he reported, probably between 1,000 and 1,500 per year, at an average of three or four REM periods a night. (My own dream record contains about 900 dreams a year since employing the technique described in Chapter 8.) Nonetheless, van Eeden reported a lot of lucid dreams. He stated that his frequent lucid dreams were highly pleasant, often involving floating or flying. He said that he had almost complete recall of his waking life during them and he could perform acts of will in them. His memory of them was clear (lucid dreams are easily recalled). He further stated that he was in excellent health when he experienced them, and their effect was very beneficial and refreshing. Van Eeden went on to say (italics mine) "that without exception *all my lucid dreams occurred in the hours between five and eight in the morning.*" My own experience confirms van Eeden's finding: All my lucid dreams occurred between 5:00 A.M. and 8:30 A.M.[11] Perhaps it is easier to assert consciousness when more rested. *Our efforts to become lucid will be more successful in the late morning.*

What is this elusive creature, the lucid dream, like once you catch hold of it? You will find your lucid dreams differ from your ordinary dreams in several ways, beyond the obvious striking difference that you are aware of your dream state. Lucid dreams appear more realistic than ordinary dreams. Animals or objects rarely start talking or acting like people, as they often do in ordinary dreams. Your body will rarely change form in a lucid dream. Other dream figures act in psychologically realistic ways. There are some common exceptions to this observation of physical realism, including flying, miraculously manipulating the environment, and falling or traveling through a tunnel to represent displacements of time or space. Generally, however, lucid dreams are realistic.

Perceptions in lucid dreams seem particularly vivid. Colors are lifelike. Sounds, noises, tastes, odors, the feel of textures, temperatures, pain, kinesthetic sensations—all seem quite real. In fact, lucid dreamers appear to delight in experimenting to see how realistic they can make their dream sensations. Van Eeden, for example, reported:

> On Sept. 9, 1904, I dreamt that I stood at a table before a window. On the table were different objects. I was perfectly well aware that I was dreaming and I considered what sorts of experiments I could make. I began by trying to break glass, by beating it with a stone. I put a small tablet of glass on two stones and struck it with another stone. Yet it would not break. Then I took a fine claret-glass from the table and struck it with my fist, with all my might, at the same time reflecting how dangerous it would be to do this in waking life; yet the glass remained whole. But lo! when I looked at it again after some time, it was broken.
>
> It broke all right, but a little too late, like an actor who misses his cue. This gave me a very curious impression of being in a *fake-world*, cleverly imitated, but with small failures.
>
> I took the broken glass and threw it out of the window, in order to observe whether I could hear the *tinkling*. I heard the noise all right and I even saw two dogs run away from it quite naturally. I thought what a good imitation this comedy-world was. Then I saw a decanter with claret and tasted it, and noted with perfect clearness of mind: "Well, we can also have voluntary impressions of taste in this dream-world; this has quite the taste of wine." [12]

Thus, the physical world appears real, psychological behavior seems real, and the dreamer's perceptions seem like waking life. Thought processes, however, are less realistic than

waking life in lucid dreams (although still more so than in ordinary dreams). Memory and analytic thought serve the lucid
dreamer best for general psychological reflections and intentions. For example, you will be able to remember and think
about theories of dreams during a lucid dream. Next the lucid
dreamer recalls general information about the physical world,
his specific intentions about what to do in his lucid dream, and
personal information of long standing. You will remember, for
instance, who you are and that you planned to fly in a lucid
dream. The lucid dreamer's memory is least accurate regarding
immediate and specific details of his current life, which may
appear in a distorted form. You may find yourself living again,
in a lucid dream, in a house you recently left. Recent concrete
details may be inaccurate in lucid dreams. Green notes, however, that memory "varies from subject to subject, and increases as a given subject develops lucid dreaming." [13]

It is interesting to note that waking memory *about* a
lucid dream is extraordinarily clear. The lucid dream usually
generates great excitement and is more easily recalled than an
ordinary event in waking life. When you experience a lucid
dream you will know it and remember it.

Emotions in lucid dreams cover the range of waking
experience, extending from a neutral acceptance of the lucid
dream to heights of liberation and excitement. I mentioned
earlier the need to remain calm during a lucid dream. "Habitual lucid dreamers almost unanimously stress the importance
of emotional detachment in prolonging the experience and
retaining a high degree of lucidity." [14] In one lucid dream I
became so excited at the prospect of flying that I almost woke.
I shifted my decision to a less exciting activity and the dream
continued. Emotional conflict, too, appears to terminate lucidity. If you do things in a lucid dream that seem too

physically dangerous to you or you lose yourself in the emotion, lucidity will be lost. *Enjoy the lucid dream without allowing yourself to become too emotionally involved.*

There are two dream events that often occur close to a lucid dream: false awakenings and flying dreams. A false awakening is a state in which the dreamer seems to look back on his previous dream experience and believes himself to be awake when he is actually still dreaming. This state may follow a lucid dream, a nonlucid dream, or sometimes no remembered dream at all. There may even be a series of false awakenings. Dreamers may apply extreme measures to prove to themselves whether or not they are dreaming, misjudge the experience as reality, then believe themselves to waken, later finding that this apparent waking state was still another dream. A cycle of dreams within a dream can continue through three or four dreams. Philosophers who have experienced a series of false awakenings have speculated that what we believe to be life may be only another layer of dream.[15]

There are two types of false awakenings, according to Green. The first is fairly common. The dreamer has a dream in which he seems to be talking or thinking about some previous dream experience. This may or may not start with a fairly realistic representation of the dreamer waking up in his own bed. It sometimes occurs to the more sophisticated dreamer to examine his environment for clues to test its reality.

My own dream record has many examples of this type of false awakening, one of which is described above. My false awakenings often revolve around my method of dream recording on a notepad during the night (see Chapter 8). For example, in one dream I had mixed up the direction of turning the pages of the notepad as I picked it up. I dreamed I opened my eyes in order to see if the pad was clear of writing. To my surprise, I saw pages and pages of dream notes with marvelous drawings in black felt-tip pen. In this case the dream continued in an ordinary manner. Other times I will dream I am writing my dream, have a flash of lucidity in which I realize I'm not actually doing so, and wake myself up in order to record.

Other false awakenings of this type involve different topics. In one dream I heard noises and tried to look to see what time it was. In the dream, I couldn't manage to get my eyes open. Then, the clock seemed to be blocked. The dream continued as though it were real. An unusual aspect of this dream is that before going to sleep, I had placed a pillow in front of the clock-radio to smother an annoying vibration it had developed. Was I simply aware that I'd done this, or was it a case of "seeing with eyelids closed" that others report? [16] *Always try to test the reality of apparent awakenings from a dream.*

The second classification of false awakenings is one in which the dreamer seems to awaken in a realistic manner, in his own bedroom setting, but in addition, there is a strange atmosphere of suspense. The dreamer usually remains in his own bed. The length of time varies before he realizes something is unusual. Suspense, excitement, or apprehension come immediately or in a few minutes. This type of false awakening differs from the first type in that it *always* (rather than sometimes) begins with the dreamer in bed and there is an extraordinary atmosphere of suspense.

This type of false awakening is rare, not all lucid dreamers report it, and few unsophisticated subjects experience it. The dreamer at first becomes aware it is not a normal waking state. He then actually awakens or remains in it and sees apparitions. Fox claims that he could easily enter an out-of-the-body state from this dream state.

My lengthy dream record contains only one example of this type of false awakening:

> *I was in my bed sleeping when I heard a running noise and breathing like that of a "presence." I roused and called, "Who's there?" I finally caught hold of something in the dark—it was my youngest daughter. Her hands were icy cold. "What's wrong?" I asked. "I've come to tell you I'm leaving," she replied. "I have a ride tonight and I'm going."* ("Presence," 6/14/73.)

At this point in the dream I got up and struggled with her, and the dream continued in an ordinary manner. The strange part was the atmosphere when I "woke" in the dream. It had a spooky feel—hearing the breathing in the dark but seeing no one. I had read Green's description of this type of false awakening prior to this dream, so perhaps it was simply an incorporation of the experience of others into my own situation. It was a fact that I was afraid that my daughter would leave at the time this dream occurred. *Always try to determine whether an awakening from a dream is actual or false. If you discover it is false, you can precipitate a lucid dream.*

Flying dreams often precede lucid dreams. In fact, lucid dreamers have many more flying dreams than the ordinary dreamer.

Flying dreams are fairly common for the ordinary dreamer. One research team [17] studied dream events reported by students in Kentucky and by students in Tokyo. Approximately 39 percent of both groups of students said they had experienced dreams of flying or soaring through the air.

Psychiatric patients report a lower percentage of flying dreams.[18] When asked if they could remember dreams of "yourself flying through the air, being able to fly; not in an airplane, but with your own body" only 19 percent of 748 psychiatric patients said yes. Were these patients being careful not to sound too crazy? Or are there actual differences in amount of flying dreams between these two populations?

Whatever the explanation, lucid dreamers, in contrast, report an extraordinary amount of flying dreams (italics mine): "Virtually *all* habitual lucid dreamers refer to flying dreams." [19] Flying dreams seem to indicate to van Eeden that lucid dreams are coming:

> When I have been flying in my dreams for two or three nights, then I know that a lucid dream is at hand. And the lucid dream itself is often initiated and accompanied all the time by the sensation of flying.[20]

Whiteman and Fox also speak of attaining lucidity while floating or flying in a dream. Arnold-Forster describes increased ability to fly in dreams as she gained lucidity and control of her dreams. Sure enough, checking my own record shows that two out of four recent lucid dreams of mine were preceded by nonlucid flying dreams that occurred *during the same night. Induce dreams of flying and you are on your way to lucid dreaming.*

Strange as it may seem, you can *learn* to fly in your dreams. See how it happened with Mary Arnold-Forster. She related in 1921 how her ability to fly in dreams developed over the years. She first recalled flying dreams when she was a very little child living in London. At night, on the staircase, she was afraid to pass the landing that opened onto a dark conservatory. She dreamed of being alone and frightened on the staircase:

> It was then that the blessed discovery was made, and that I found that it was just as easy to fly downstairs as to

walk; that directly my feet left the ground the fear ceased—
I was quite safe; and this discovery has altered the nature of
my dreams ever since. At first I only flew down one particular
flight of steps, and always downwards; but very soon I began
to fly more actively. If anything began to alarm me in my
dreams, I used to try to rise in the air, but for some years I
was unable to rise to any great height, or to fly with real
ease. It was only gradually that the flying dream ceased to
be connected with the sensation of fear and escape. For a
long time it was often an effort to fly; every year, however,
made it easier and more sure. By degrees "bad dreams" left
me. When once I realized that I could always escape by
flight, the sense of the something unknown, to be escaped
from, became a thing of the past; but the power of flying
grew and has steadily improved all my life.[21]

Modern-day psychologists would describe Arnold-Forster's
application of her flying skill to situations other than need for
escape as generalization.[22] Her statement, "Each dream of
flying makes the next flight easier," [23] is pure learning. *You can
learn to fly in your dreams*, too, if you do not already.

Arnold-Forster described her two methods of dream
flying. In one case, she pushed or sprung with her feet from
the ground and flew without further effort. "A slight paddling
motion by my hands" [24] enabled her to go faster, rise higher, or
steer, especially through a doorway or window. It also gave
her confidence and power in long flights. In the other case, she
simply glided a few inches above the ground not moving her
feet, as though she were walking effortlessly. Her commonest
flying dreams were in "lofty rooms and the great staircases of
palatial buildings which I do not know," although they sometimes occurred in the British Museum or other public galleries.
She would fly "as a bird does," along the ceiling, coming down

to pass through doors and windows. She states she always wore her 'flying dress'—it is a dress of straight close folds which fall three or four inches below my feet." She explained that this dress appeared in her dreams following a dream in which she was gliding along a busy sidewalk and became fearful that people might notice that her feet never moved as theirs did and so attract undesirable attention. Her flying dress avoided this possibility. She seemed to learn something new from each dream experience of flying.

Arnold-Forster, like van Eeden, found both flying and gliding dreams extremely pleasurable and easy to recall. She attributed her steady increase in flying dreams to the following system: After having discovered how to get rid of her bad dreams, she tried to find out how far she could go in inducing pleasant dreams. By concentrating her thinking on a particular dream such as flying, it would come to her *in two or three nights* or sometimes longer, depending, she felt, on the degree of concentration she was able to achieve with the waking mind. She noted, "Especially after talking about flying I find that I am certain very soon to dream of it." [25] We have observed that timing before: two or three nights. You remember how Stevenson's production of *Dr. Jekyll and Mr. Hyde* came after "racking his brains" for two days for a plot. *Concentrate on flying or lucid dreams intensely for two or three days, and talk about it. They may come to you.*

In addition to concentration, Arnold-Forster planned some definite accomplishment for a dream—for instance, a new and different act of flight.

> It was a long time before I could fly higher than five or six feet from the ground, and it was only after watching and thinking about the flight of birds, the soaring of the larks above the Wiltshire Downs, the hovering of a kestrel, the

action of the rooks' strong wings, and the glancing flights of swallows, that I began to achieve in my dreams some of the same bird-like flights.[26]

Thus, she was able to produce a new type of flight by waking life observation. Similarly, she thought a great deal about flying over trees, high buildings, and the sea before she was able to achieve these flights in her dreams. She found herself dreaming she was steering a small airplane with the confidence that if mechanical difficulties occurred, she could take refuge in her natural form of flight.

This observation of birds and so on that Arnold-Forster engaged in is similar to the experience of Guareschi in which he taught Margherita how to ride a bike, change tires, and mountain-climb in waking life in order to use these skills to solve a problem in dream life (see Chapter 1). *Concentrate on the objects you wish to produce in your dreams while you are awake.*

In addition to concentrating waking thought on the desired dream, talking about it, and observing elements she wished to incorporate in her dreams, Arnold-Forster went further—she developed a "second formula" to induce the desired dream (her first formula turned off or altered the undesirable dream). She came upon this in the course of a dream in which she was a guest at a party. In the dream, her brother-in-law explained to several men present her method of flying and asked her to demonstrate it, which she did. They discussed it critically. However, one gentleman stepped forward and offered an explanation to the puzzle. Then she took the hand of someone and was able to persuade him to fly a few inches.

Arnold-Forster used the gentleman's explanation given in her dream as the basis of her formula: "You know that the law of gravitation has no power over you here. If the law is suspended, you can fly at will. Have confidence in yourself, and you need not fear." [27] *You can also try these techniques or hit upon others of your own to sustain flying power.*

Although Arnold-Forster was not focusing directly on consciousness in these flying dreams, it is clear that they were lucid.[28] In applying her formulas, Arnold-Forster must have discerned that she was in a dream state where the law of gravitation was suspended. She used this awareness to alter unpleasant dreams and to increase pleasurable elements of dreaming. We can change our unpleasant dreams and increase our pleasant dreams, too.

I am not a habitual lucid dreamer, at least at the moment. My dream record, however, shows, in addition to several characteristics of lucid dreams described above, many flying dreams. During the last year, I had an average of three flying dreams a month—flying dreams ranged from zero (only once) to as high as five a month. Subsequently, I have been experiencing about six flying dreams a month. My experience with flying dreams confirms many of Arnold-Forster's findings.

Dreamers evolve individual "flying styles." Arnold-Forster's method of flying by pushing or springing with her feet, then using a paddling motion of the hands to steer, or simply gliding along a few inches above the ground, has already been described. Some dreamers "fly" in a series of earth-terminated bounds over houses and trees, their leaps decreasing in magnitude.[29] Other dreamers lean backward as though floating on water,[30] fly in an armchair or small plane, or use a combination of flying techniques. Some dreamers report that great physical effort is required to fly, while others feel propelled by a force.

My own flying style shows a wide variety. In flying, I usually push off from the ground as though from the bottom

of a swimming pool, hold my arms in front of me, and sometimes move them as in a breast stroke. Lately, after reading
Arnold-Forster, I tried some paddling motions with the hands.
In other instances I have flown in dreams (1) by leaning
backward and being propelled upward at an angle, (2) by
catapulting myself from a swing and then being blown by the
wind, (3) by throwing myself down from a high place, (4)
by sliding downhill and lifting my feet to sail, gliding, (5) by
hovering in a curled up position, (6) by bouncing at great
heights while waiting, and (7) by flying in a plane or
spacecraft.

I am usually the dream character doing the flying (it was
I who flew in thirty-six of the forty-two flying dreams of the
past year). Other flying dreams included such images as
watching a flying horse act, seeing a flying coffee pot, watching a marvelous dancing "snowbird," looking at a drawing
of a flying bridal couple, and seeing two images of flying
butterflies.

A few of these flying dreams are extraordinarily vivid
and full of the physical sensation of flying (see "Late TV
Show" dream in Chapter 5). These dreams are probably prelucid, as they involve analytic comments on the flying activity.
In addition to flying sensations, I sometimes experience other
sensations—of the five *vividly* sensed flying dreams of the past
year, two were clearly accompanied by sexual sensations as
well as sensations of flying. Another type of sensation emerged
from a false awakening after which I flew. I felt certain I could
fly in reality until I actually woke. Even after really waking,
the strange sensation lingered. In other dreams, the activity of
flying may suddenly appear without dreaming of starting to
fly, and it is more like watching a picture of flying than fully
experiencing it.

The various styles of flying I use are employed for a

variety of purposes. The most common reasons for flying in my dreams include escape from a threat, a quicker means to accomplish something, a more convenient way to do something, a means to check on or direct things better, and a way to get an overview of a situation so I can plan what to do next. Occasionally I've used bouncing as an activity while waiting for something else, flying as a symbolic representation of where I might wander, or flying to see and do fantastic things.

My flying dreams show, as Arnold-Forster's did, a learning effect. When sailing downhill in a standing position, I discovered I could control the direction of movement by aiming my leg. I used this discovery in a dream eight months later when I was taking care of my plants by flying in an upright position. Water flowed from my toes and by directing my legs I could regulate the amount of water for each plant. In another dream, I found that after escaping threat by flying, I could use my aerial position as a new and superior position of attack. In these and many other ways, flying has increased in value as a dream activity.

Surprisingly often, my flying dreams are the final dreams of the night (twenty-one out of forty-two flying dreams of the last year).[31] This observation that flying dreams are usually the last dreams of the night fits well with both the finding that dreams become more bizarre as the night progresses and the claim that lucid dreams usually occur after a reasonable amount of rest (between 5:00 A.M. and 8:00 A.M.). *You will more probably have success in inducing flying dreams if you direct your efforts at your morning dreams.*

Lucid dreamers not only have more flying dreams than ordinary dreamers, as we have seen, but deliberately increase the frequency of their existing flying dreams and learn movements over a series of dreams to make flying easier and even more pleasurable than its usual pleasant state.

Why should lucid dreamers experience flying more often than nonlucid dreamers? Explanations of flying dreams [32] cannot account for the fact that lucid dreamers experience flying dreams more frequently. Nor do they explain the puzzling observation made by Ellis that flying dreams are among the earliest dreams to appear in childhood and become less frequent after middle age. He says an acquaintance found his flying dreams ceased at the age of fifty, while his own disappeared, or became rare, at an earlier age. Freud, as usual, believed that the wish to fly "signifies in dreaming nothing else but the desire to be capable of sexual activities." He observed that patients usually found them pleasant and he thought they reproduced genital stimulation from such activities as swinging. Be it noted that Freud admitted to being mystified by flying dreams and *he himself never experienced one*.[33]

All of my flying dreams, in whatever style and for whatever purpose, are pleasant—particularly those with accompanying physical sensation. If I can moderate my delight at the prospect of flying enough to continue an ongoing lucid dream, I will most certainly choose to fly in future lucid dreams. (Since originally writing this chapter, I have flown in lucid dreams.)

I wonder if we have here the explanation of the frequency of flying dreams in lucid dreamers: Flying dreams are extraordinarily pleasurable. The lucid dreamer can perform the activity of his choice. He chooses to fly.

Another possible explanation is that there is something about the unique state of feeling conscious while dreaming that precipitates a sensation of flying. Saints in religious ecstasy and persons on the borderline of death commonly report a flying sensation.[34] The sensation of flying may accompany an altered state of consciousness.

The value of flying dreams is not clear at this time, but we can speculate. Perhaps flying dreams have a psychological impact of feeling free, feeling capable of adventurous experience, and feeling able to deal with novelty and change. Maybe if we fly in our dreams we will feel freer in waking life. It is certain that people who regularly fly in their dreams almost without exception find the activity delightful. And such dreams provide an easy "flight" to lucid dreaming.

When you have a lucid dream you will find that you have an extraordinary amount of control in it compared to your usual dreams. We have already seen how lucid dreamers use their control to turn off or alter unpleasant dreams and to increase the number of pleasant dreams like flying, as well as introducing specific skills (such as new types of dream flying). In addition, many lucid dreamers delight in experimenting with their dream environment to test their power of control. For example, one subject reported:

> *Dreaming that I was walking along a road—straight and I think walled on one side—and realized I was dreaming. I knew this was a thing I had been trying to do and thought, "Now I can make something happen." I thought I would like to have an apple. I saw a patch on the road ahead and thought, "By the time I reach that it will be an apple." Before reaching it, I found I had another apple in my hand. I examined it, thinking, "Quite a creditable imitation of an apple."* [35]

Later, this same subject was working in a dream with a model of an atom:

> *I came to an atom which had a small bead stuck into the hole in it where I wanted to insert a connection, so I said to the little bead, "I command you to get out"—which it did.*[36]

The sensation of directing action in a dream is quite remarkable.

P. D. Ouspensky, the Russian philosopher, tried similar experiments with mixed results:

> *. . . Let this black kitten be transformed into a large white dog. In a waking state it is impossible and if it comes off it will mean that I am asleep." I say this to myself and immediately the black kitten becomes transformed into a large white dog. At the same time the opposite wall disappears, disclosing a mountain landscape with a river like a ribbon receding into the distance.*
>
> *"This is curious," I say to myself; "I did not order this landscape. Where did it come from?" Some faint recollection begins to stir in me, a recollection of having seen this landscape somewhere and of its being somehow connected with the white dog. But I feel that if I let myself go into it I shall forget the most important thing that I have to remember, namely,* that I am asleep and am conscious of myself, *i.e. that I am in the state for which I have long wished and which I have been trying to attain. I make an effort not to think about the landscape, but at that moment some power seems to drag me* backwards. *I fly swiftly through the back wall of the room and go on flying in a straight line, all the time backwards and with a terrible noise in my ears, suddenly come to a stop and awake.*[37]

You can choose to have almost anything you wish happen in lucid dreams. It is interesting to observe in yourself what choice you make.

In examining my own long dream record, I find many prelucid dreams and many false awakenings. Lucid dreams, however, are few. For example, in a recent eight-month period, I recorded only three unquestionably lucid dreams, all clustered rather closely around the time I was reading and thinking a great deal about lucid dreams. My dream life apparently was responding to my intense occupation of the moment. All the associated characteristics of lucid dreams—including prelucid dreams, false awakenings, and flying dreams—have increased with my efforts to induce lucid dreams. And I learned how to become lucid. The different methods I used, discussed above, successfully initiated lucidity in these three recent dreams. After becoming lucid, my first thought was to wonder what to do. In "Looking at Myself," I initially wanted to fly, but the thought was so exciting I started to awaken. By remembering not to get too emotional, I was able to continue the dream, deciding instead to see myself. This proceeded to happen in a pleasant and interesting manner, quite different from the preceding, frightening, nonlucid dream.

In the other two lucid dreams, I decided to have an orgasm. Although passionate feelings followed, they were not complete, since I had to exercise care not to wake myself. (However, in an even more recent lucid dream, "Naked Babies," 9/15/73, I succeeded in experiencing an orgasm, suggesting that it *is* possible to learn to have strong emotional experiences in a lucid dream if one is accustomed to the state of dream consciousness.) In addition, in "Carving My Name," I proceeded to do just that on the door where I was already carving. I read it and realized why Ouspensky [38] believed it is impossible to say one's name in a lucid dream: The whole atmosphere vibrated and thundered, and I woke. It's not impossible to say one's own name in a lucid dream, but it *is* disruptive.

In all of these lucid dreams I continue to see the operation of symbolism—my reaction to the possible sexual activity of my child, a wish to know how I see myself, the closer, more comfortable relationship to my "big, black" unconscious, a wish to "carve my name"—to make a mark. Symbols still occur, but the dream adventure becomes even more alive.

My dream record contains an unusual category of very brief lucid dreams combined with a false awakening: I often dream I am recording my dream on a notepad (or other surface) in my special technique (see Chapter 8), only to realize that I am not actually doing so. For example:

> *At the end of a dream I am writing my dream with a pencil across the pillow. It is something about Western philosophy. I force myself to sit up and see whether the writing is clear. I find it is only a series of dots and dashes. I then force myself actually awake to write.* ("Dots and Dashes," 1/7/72.)

The moment I realize that I am not awake and writing, there is the implication that I realize that I am dreaming, so there is a brief flash of lucidity which I use to actually wake in order to write. There is, then, a frequent occurrence of false awakening followed by brief lucidity that leads to actual awakening. Thus, I am using the dream control lucidity brings in a variety of ways: to awaken in order to write my dream, to "see myself," and to experience orgasms. These were choices made *during* the dream, not preplanned. You can do either: *Decide what you will do when you become lucid, or wait and see what you choose to do while in a lucid dream state.*

Many lucid dreamers preplan paranormal experiments to perform while in a lucid state. They have, for example, attempted to travel in their dreams to gather information of the type that would be labeled clairvoyant or telepathic or have made attempts at extrasensory perception. Dream travel is, according to Green, "a somewhat unreliable process, with a high probability that the subject will lose his state of lucidity or wake up before the termination of the journey is reached." [39] Nevertheless, Oliver Fox relates a striking success of this type, in which he had been spending the evening with two friends, Slade and Elkington, when their conversation had turned to the subject of dreams. Before parting, they agreed to meet, if possible, on Southampton Common in their dreams. The same night, both Fox and Elkington had dreams in which they were aware that they were dreaming, traveled to Southampton Common, greeted each other, remarked on Slade's absence, and ended their dreams. The next day on the street, Fox met Elkington, who immediately reported to him the same dream he had experienced. Along came Slade, who stated that the experiment was a failure because he hadn't dreamed at all. Fox and Elkington were astounded at this explanation for Slade's inability to keep his dream appointment with them. They were unable to repeat this success. However, other people have reported amazing successes along this same line.

If you want to try ESP in a lucid dream you need to remember your intention to do so while in a dream state. You must also recognize that spatial location is no longer relevant. This is no easy matter. If I am on the East Coast, where I frequently visit, and I want to "travel" in my dream to the West Coast, where my permanent home is, I am troubled by the thought "But it is so *far*" or even "It will be too cold to go there at night." Green suggests impressing on the waking mind that dream events are independent and prearranging with yourself techniques to attempt ESP, such as summoning the person you wish to visit or commanding the appearance of a door on the other side of which will be the person or place you desire. Some lucid dreamers attempt to relay messages to other people. *Lucid dreaming offers you unlimited opportunity for experimentation.*

The degree to which it is possible to push dream control is unknown at present. Lucid dreamers vary among themselves in the extent of success at dream control. Arnold-Forster was perhaps able to go further in dream control than many of her fellow lucid dreamers because both of her parents were involved with their dream lives. This may have provided her with a more congenial setting to develop her skill, in much the same way as the Senoi parents provide to their children. A less advanced lucid dreamer, Jean-Paul Richter, reportedly admitted "that it was impossible forcibly to obtain or prevent the appearance of certain images and that it was impossible to know whether even induced images were friendly or terrifying." [40] Clearly, his skill at dream control was not so developed, since we know that it is possible to transform frightening dream images.

Yet, even the most successful lucid dreamer asserts there is a limit to dream control.[41] All agree that "the will" can only be asserted so far and no more. They may be wrong. Consider the fact that their remarkable successes have been achieved in the face of general public opinion that their experiences are impossible. Perhaps in a setting where lucid dreaming is accepted we can go even further. The Yogis of the dream state maintain that dream control can be total.

Despite the fact that lucid dreamers disagree on the extent to which dream control is possible, *all* of them are able to control their dreams far beyond what we have been led to believe is possible. We can remarkably influence the "involuntary" process of dreaming.

Lucid dreaming is available to you now. With it, you can experience unusual, exciting personal adventures.

I have already described how, when in a lucid dream, you can choose to do anything you wish—fly anywhere, engage in love-making with anyone, and enjoy all sorts of positive experiences. You may wish to draw directly on the vast resources of your mind by posing personal questions or by asking for creative products to appear while you are in a lucid dream. If you wish to test ESP, lucid dreams provide an unparalleled opportunity. All this might be value enough. But there is more.

You might wish to use a lucid dream state to induce crystal clear images in your dreams and hold them still for careful examination. Dreamers often see magnificent paintings or read marvelous books in their dreams, yet their waking recollection of them is blurred, vague, and fuzzy; they cannot reproduce them while awake. Lucid dreamers can learn to catch hold of fleeting dream images, turn them over and over, and study them in such vivid detail that producing their likeness in waking life is almost as simple a task as copying.

The process of using a lucid dream to hold images in clear focus is similar to the method described by the anthropologist Carlos Castaneda [42] in one of his books about his adventures with the elderly Yaqui Indian don Juan Matus, who is said to be a sorcerer. Castaneda relates don Juan's instructions on learning to sustain dream images almost indefinitely by formulating an intention to see your hands (or any other object) in your dream, remembering this intention during your dream, and carrying out the act of gazing steadily at your hands during a dream. The image is held only so long as it is clear and unshifting, gradually building up the repertoire of clear dream images. Castaneda's purpose was to use his dreams to gain access to power to become a "warrior." I was able to induce the elaborate pattern of dream images that Castaneda describes. However, I prefer to use skill in sustaining dream images to examine idiosyncratic dream images. As you gain skill in lucid dreaming, you may wish to examine dream paintings, to read the text of dream books, or observe any interesting dream image with remarkable clarity.

Lucid dreamers have the potential to accomplish even more, however. In a lucid dream it becomes possible for you to use your special state of awareness as a kind of personal laboratory in which you can deliberately engage in a "behavioral rehearsal" of skills you wish to increase in waking life —anything from perfecting tennis strokes to assertive behavior can profitably be practiced during a lucid dream. Choose your topic and perfect it.

The notion of a personal laboratory can be extended further to a therapeutic level. For example, a lucid dreamer with a phobia of any sort could present himself with the feared object (during a dream in which he knows he is dreaming and therefore cannot be harmed) and thus "desensitize" himself just as a therapist might help him to do in waking life using imagination to visualize the feared object. Recovered alcoholics sometimes experience "drunk dreams" in which they believe themselves to have slipped into drinking behavior again. If such a person were also to become a lucid dreamer, he could dispel the fear in his dream and deliberately engage in dream behavior he finds acceptable, smashing the bottle or walking out of the bar, thus strengthening it for waking life. The possible therapeutic application of lucid dreaming is considerable.

Furthermore, lucid dreams offer a great value in the possibility they provide for communication between the waking world and the dream world. Consider this unique situation: You are asleep, but you feel conscious and can perform acts of will in your lucid dream. Now, even ordinary dreamers have been trained to perform simple motor responses during sleep. Charles Tart,[43] the editor of *Altered States of Consciousness*, has suggested the possibility of a "two-way communication system" between a dreamer and a waking subject. Would it not be possible to train lucid dreamers to respond even more easily?

If subjects were able to indicate to experimenters the exact moment when lucid dreams were occurring, researchers could accurately observe if differences between lucid dreams and nonlucid dreams are measurable on the EEG. We could, perhaps, for the first time learn about the dream from the subject while it is ongoing rather than by later report.

The possibilities of communicating with a lucid dreamer *during* his dream, combined with their therapeutic potential and the marvelous personal adventure the lucid dream offers, give lucid dreams a special position in both the waking and the dream world.

Summary of What We Can Learn From Lucid Dreamers

1. You can learn to become conscious during your dreams. It is more difficult than other types of dream control but it is possible.

2. As you practice skills in lucid dreams you increase the probability of their occurrence in waking life.

3. Once lucidity is attained, you must be constantly alert to avoid falling back into ordinary dreaming on the one hand or, on the other, becoming so excited with the power of lucidity that you awaken.

4. Learn to recognize when you are in a prelucid state (become aware of the possibility you may be dream-

ing). Suspect it. Try to test the reality of your experience during a dream.

5. As you become aware of prelucid moments, it becomes easier to push the dream into a lucid state. Inducing lucid dreams takes time but can be done.

6. Brief flashes of lucidity can be extended into prolonged states.

7. Keep reminding yourself that dream events are not real events until you can remember it during your dream. Devise your own formula, such as: "You know this is a dream, it can't hurt you. See what will happen next."

8. You can learn to "turn off" unpleasant dreams. You can awaken from them. It is better for you, however, to allow them to continue in an altered form.

9. One way to become lucid is to become so frightened you realize you are dreaming.

10. Another way to become lucid is to recognize the dreamlike quality of strange happenings in your dreams.

11. You can also become lucid by recognizing incongruities in your dreams.

12. You can become lucid as you develop a critical attitude during your dreams.

13. All lucid dreams are obtained more easily after several hours of sleep—between 5:00 A.M. and 8:00 A.M., for most people. Exert your efforts during this time span.

14. Lucid dreams are generally realistic (with some notable exceptions, such as flying). Dream images look and act as they do in waking life, emotions and sensations are vividly experienced by the lucid dreamer. Memory and analytic thought are better in lucid dreams than in ordinary dreams, but specific recent details may be distorted. Lucid dreams are vividly recalled.

15. Don't allow yourself to become too emotional in a lucid dream or you will awaken.

16. If you appear to awaken from a dream, test the reality of your experience. If you discover you have had a false awakening, you can precipitate a lucid dream.

17. Lucid dreamers have frequent flying dreams, much more so than ordinary dreamers. Induce dreams of flying and you will increase your probability of a lucid dream.

18. You can learn to fly in your dreams. Concentrate on it. Talk about it. Repeat an induction formula during the day, such as "Gravitation has no power in dreams. You can fly." Observe things relevant to your desired dream. Plan a new flying accomplishment. Direct your efforts to induce flying dreams to a time when you are well rested. Flying dreams may have psychological value in that they give the dreamer a feeling of freedom and power that carries over to waking life.

19. You can choose to have almost anything you wish occur in a lucid dream. You can plan what you will do in a lucid dream ahead of having it, or you can wait and see what you will choose during the lucid dream itself.

20. Lucid dreams offer unlimited opportunities for experimentation: You can try ESP; you can rehearse skills you wish to increase in your waking life; and you can help yourself to overcome irrational fears in lucid dreams. Remember, anything is possible in a lucid dream.

CHAPTER SEVEN

Learn From Yogi Dreamers

> O nobly-born, whatever fearful and terrifying visions thou mayst see, recognize them to be thine own thought-forms.
>
> —*The Tibetan Book of the Dead* [1]

You can become totally fearless of your most frightening dream images. You can learn to recognize them as no more than your thoughts shaped into a form, dressed in clothes, living and acting only by the breath you put into them. You are the god who creates your dream creatures; you give them life. You are the author of the plot they act out, the director, and the producer. You can allow them to improvise a show to entertain or inform you, but always, always, you can intervene. Your dream characters work for you. They can become a Frankenstein, destroying their creator only if you forget that they are of your making and you have both the power to change them and to put new thoughts into new forms to interact with them. The Tibetan Yogis of the dream state say that the awareness of your role as creator of your dream images can become total.

Yogis [2] claim to have evolved control to a point that their bodies can enter a physical state of sleep while their minds remain fully conscious. They proceed to consciously experience the dream state, in which they carry out various acts of will. These Yogis assert that ". . . the character of any dream can be changed or transformed by willing that it shall be." [3] Then they return to the waking state with complete memory of all that has passed. This is an astonishing and almost incredible claim to Western ears. Westerners find it difficult enough to believe that a dreamer can *become* conscious in a dream, as the lucid dreamers do, to say nothing of *maintaining* unbroken consciousness between sleeping and waking. Yet, it may well be fact. Yogic skills in body and thought control clearly surpass those of Western culture. Why not in dream control as well? What we know of these "ear-whispered" [4] teachings on dream control is chiefly from the writings of W. Y. Evans-Wentz, an Oxford scholar who lived in India and Sikkim for several years, studying occult doctrines; material in this chapter draws heavily on his works. Let's see how an imaginary young monk, Ram, [5] is taught to achieve this remarkable goal and what we can extract from these ancient secret techniques for our own lives.

Young Ram gathers his saffron robe and sits cross-legged on the stony ground before his guru. They are alone at the edge of the monastery, high upon a cliff. Through the cool mist, he can see the tiny stone houses of the villagers in the distant valley and the hairy yaks wandering the hillside, but they are as remote to him as another world. Nearby, the wind carries to him the tinkling bells of the temple, the soft murmur of the monks at prayer, and wafts of pungent incense. However, it is time for his private lesson and he shuts off all awareness except that of his guru. These moments of special instruction from the master who guides him on the path from ignorance to right knowledge are the most important in his life. The paths to knowledge are many, true, but it is impossible to find one's way alone. He must discipline his unenlightened human mind before he can unite it with enlightened divinity.[6] Ram nods his shaven head to indicate his readiness. The meditation begins.

Deeper and deeper into himself, Ram withdraws. All sense of the external world vanishes. Far within himself he holds one pinpoint of concentration. Ram spent many years learning to achieve this "one-pointedness" [7] of mind. First he had to conquer his body, to attain total command of his lower self, before he could learn to direct his mental processes by will. An ancient lama (monk) [8] wrote down, more than 300 years ago, the secret methods taught to disciples for centuries prior to that time. Ram has faithfully followed these doctrines under the tutelage of his guru. First, he learned how to generate his own body heat. By meditations and exercises he acquired the power to endure the most extreme cold with comfort. His skill at generating "psychic heat" was tested one bitter winter [9] evening: Naked, he and his fellow disciples sat cross-legged in the cutting wind at the frozen lake shore. With their bodies, they dried sheets that had been dipped into the icy water. Those who could not dry at least three sheets failed and those triumphant could wear the insignia of a single cotton shirt or robe and be reverently addressed as "repa" (cotton-clad one).

Most men in Tibet must protect themselves from the bitter winter winds and freezing temperatures by wearing fur hats, cloaks lined with wool, and boots and by drinking *thirty to fifty* cups of hot buttered tea each day. In such a country the man who can endure, clad only in cotton, is respected indeed.

Now Ram is immune to all extremes of heat or cold by the power of his concentrated and disciplined thoughts. By these and many other exercises and trials Ram became convinced that his body is only an illusion created by his mind. He is ready to proceed.

Westerners find this kind of thinking baffling. Yet it is not so far as you might think from conceptions that we can accept. You know how your internal attitude can greatly influence your perception and ability. A woman who suffered a severe car accident was able to lift the car from the body of her injured child and drive to a hospital without feeling pain. Once the child was in safe hands, she collapsed and was found to have a broken back. Impossible? Perhaps. But intense occupation with a crucial matter—an injured child—could block out all awareness of pain for a period of time. We often "forget" a mild headache or toothache or stomachache when something exciting happens. Maybe people can learn to direct their attention in this total manner without an emergency or exciting distraction.

In many ways we construct or "create" our experience. We select that part of the multitudinous events happening in and around us that we will attend to at the moment. When we feel sexually aroused, *everything* seems stimulating; when we are satiated, we see the same stimuli differently. There are endless numbers of ways to experience the same event. The same movie will be perceived very differently by each person in the same audience. No one way is "right." Perhaps saying the world is an illusion is another way of saying, "There are thousands of ways to see things. All are a product of the viewer." Perhaps we can learn to produce the internal state that determines our perceptions. Let us see how Ram proceeds on his path.

Ram has six doctrines to master on his path to "right knowledge." He has acquired the skill of generating body heat (Doctrine 1: psychic heat). Now that he has also mastered his body (Doctrine 2: the illusory body), he is ready to master his dreams (Doctrine 3: the dream state). If he realizes that both waking perceptions and sleeping dreams are products of his mind, "illusions," he may experience ecstatic clearness of perception (Doctrine 4: the clear light) in which he understands that everything in the universe is but a part of the content of the "Supreme Dream," the dream of Buddha. When Buddha awakes, his dream (creation) ends. The Yogi is a tiny particle of this great dream. When he becomes fully awakened to this fact (enlightenment), he experiences at-one-ness (Nirvana) with all the world.

Ram will eventually die and experience an after-death state called the *Bardo* (which lasts symbolically 49 days but may go on for 500–1,000 years or more, depending upon Ram's stage of spiritual development). The *Bardo* is believed to be a kind of prolonged dream state.[10] Here the deceased experience terrifying visions, which depend upon the beliefs they held while living. Ram's guru will prepare him for this experience by "setting him face to face," describing to him what to expect in the after-death state (Doctrine 5: the after-death state).

Ram must know how to deal with these horrific visions of the after-death state in order to gain freedom from the endless rounds of deaths and rebirths. Otherwise, he will endure great sufferings in the *Bardo* and feel forced to escape by seeking rebirth. Thus, learning to control dreams has a quite different goal for the Yogi: freedom from rebirth. Finally, Ram's guru will be sure to teach him how to transfer his consciousness (Doctrine 6: consciousness transference) from the after-death state into a new body. In this way, he will be prepared to cope with whatever happens. We will concentrate here on two of these doctrines: the dream state and the after-death state.

Esoteric as they seem, they both give helpful additional skills in dream control.

In the doctrine of the dream state [11] Ram has four steps to master. He must "Comprehend the nature of the dream state, transmute the dream content, realize the dream state is an illusion, and meditate upon the dream state."

In order to comprehend the dream state, Ram begins by resolving to maintain unbroken continuity of consciousness throughout waking and dreaming. His guru advises him to hold in mind, under every condition during the day, that all things are of the substance of dreams, that this is their true nature. At night, when he lies down to sleep on the thin pad in his tiny cubicle, Ram prays to his guru that he will be able to comprehend the nature of the dream state and resolves that he will do so.

Now Ram begins to practice special breathing methods and visualization powers. All is dark and quiet. It is especially easy to paint vivid mental pictures. Thus, Ram goes to sleep. We can liken this practice to *immersing oneself in the subject one wishes to dream about up until the last few minutes before sleep.* We have seen how effectively this can induce a desired dream. It may well induce dream consciousness, too.

The next morning Ram practices his "pot-shaped" breathing [12] seven times. Eleven times he strives to comprehend the nature of the dream state. Then he concentrates his mind upon a dot "like unto a bony substance, white of colour, situated between the eyebrows." [13] Again at nightfall, he meditates upon the dot. The following morning, once more, he makes twenty-one efforts to comprehend the nature of the dream state, and now he concentrates his mind on a black dot, the size of a pill, situated at the base of his genital organ. By now he should be comprehending that the dream state is an illusion.

Notice that the efforts to induce the desired point of view are focused in time (two or three days again) and that they are intensified. How often do we concentrate even five minutes upon *one* thought? Try it. It's much longer than you would think. Our minds flit from thought to thought almost as fast as a hummingbird beats its wings on each pass at a flower. It may be that *steady concentration on a single thought* can have a profound effect upon producing that thought again in an altered state of consciousness. And twenty-one efforts! *Intensifying concentration may in some way increase probability of the thought's recurrence in the dream state.*

Ram must guard against the "spreading-out" of his dream content, which seems to mean losing hold of consciousness during the dream. Ram is warned that he may wake up when he is just about to comprehend the nature of the dream state. This sounds suspiciously like a brief flash of lucidity that the dreamer uses to escape from his dream by awakening. His guru advises nutritious food and physical work to fatigue him and evoke deep sleep, curing the tendency to awaken when about to become conscious.

If Ram is troubled with a recurrent dream that does not change in content, he is told to meditate often upon that dream, with pot-shaped breathing and dot visualization, and firmly resolve to understand the nature of that dream.

Ram may also be aware that he has dreamed but be unable to remember his dreams. In this case his guru cautions him to "avoid pollutions and impurities." *You, too, will be able to concentrate on inducing and controlling your dreams more easily when life is peaceful.*

Perhaps Ram will not be aware of dreaming at all. This is referred to as "the spreading-out into negativeness." Students in my dream seminars often report this experience the first few nights of class, calling it "stage fright." The antidote the guru suggests to Ram in this case is particularly interesting. As usual, he is told to meditate on pot-shaped breathing and to visualize the dot at the root of his sexual organ. In addition, Ram is told to offer propitiatory offerings to the *Viras* (the "heroes") and the *Dakinis* ("fairies"). According to Evans-Wentz,[14] the gurus believe that certain nonhuman entities try to prevent the disciple from acquiring supernatural powers at this stage of his development. Therefore, before Ram can establish himself securely on this plane and be free of interference, he must make friends with its inhabitants, the *Viras* and *Dakinis*.

This belief that the disciple must make friends with the inhabitants of the strange realm he wishes to enter is rather like the practice of the Senoi making friends with all of their dream images. The form differs. Ram will make offerings while awake; the Senoi struggle with their enemies, while dreaming, to convert them into friends. The effect may be similar: more cooperative dream figures. *You need to build your own dream friends to help you to progress.*

Ram is concentrating daily upon recognizing that his dream images come from his own thoughts and remaining conscious during his dreams. His guru now tells him to begin changing the form of his dream images:

> If, for example, the dream be about fire, think, "What fear can there be of fire which occurreth in a dream!" Holding to this thought, trample upon the fire. In like manner, tread under foot whatever be dreamt.[15]

Clearly, this advice is similar to the Senoi concept of confrontation of danger in dreams. I experienced the yogic form of this principle during a period of intense concentration on their ideas while writing this chapter. In the course of a dream I am climbing over a small hill:

> *Going down the hill there are branches in my way and suddenly many large yellow buzzing bees appear. I am fearful that they will sting me. Then I say to myself, "They can't hurt me.* Bees in a dream are not real bees, so they can't hurt me." *I swing my arm back and forth as I descend. The bees are still there but I am not troubled by them and they move out of my path as I move my arm.* ("Yellow Bees," 10/7/73.)

Both Senoi and Yogis confront the fearful dream image.

Unlike the Senoi, however, the Yogis are urged to transform dream content to test the dreamer's ability to impose change, regardless of whether the images are threatening or not. If a dream is of fire, Ram should sometimes transform it into water, the antidote of fire. If the dream is of minute objects, he should transform them into large objects; or if it is of large objects, transform them into small, in order to comprehend "the nature of dimensions." If the dream is of a single thing, he should transform it into many things; or if it is of many things, he should transform it into one thing, in order to comprehend "the nature of plurality and unity." This practice is more like that of lucid dreamers who change their dreams around just to see what will happen—making an apple appear, breaking a wine glass, and so on. *As you develop consciousness in your dreams you can produce any change you wish.* The potential value of this skill, discussed below, is almost limitless.

After Ram becomes proficient at changing his dream content by his will, his guru tells him to think about the various paradises (Buddha realms) [16] and how they are attainable.

Now, when he lies down to sleep, Ram visualizes a red dot within his throat psychic center and firmly believes that he shall thereby obtain a vivid dream of whatever Buddha realm he wishes to see, complete with all its characteristics. He proceeds to dream of the chosen realm. Obviously, Ram is inducing a dream in a similar manner to the practice of the ancient Greeks, Egyptians, and Chinese in their dream incubation ceremonies. The dreamer expects he will see a god (or a Buddha realm) in his dream and he does so. As you gain skill in dream control you can more easily induce desired images.

Ram continues to practice changing the content of his dreams and inducing specific dream images until he becomes thoroughly proficient in it. His guru asks him to visualize his own body and all other bodies seen in the dream state as being illusions of deities. Ram is further told to abandon all fear or dread of any dream images. This is difficult advice to follow on the face of it. However, *when you are aware that you are dreaming and that the fearful dream image cannot hurt you unless you let it, it becomes much easier to be unafraid.*

Notice the similarity to Senoi concepts again at this point. The guru's advice to the disciple to abandon all fear of dream images is similar to the Senoi's belief that dream images can only hurt the dreamer as long as he runs from them; he must not be afraid of them, but turn and fight. The advice is essentially the same; the reasoning behind it is somewhat different. The Yogi should not be afraid of dream images because they are merely illusions of his mind and can be dismissed; the Senoi should not be afraid of dream images because they are illusions (the tiger in his dream is not the same as the tiger in the jungle in the day), and they can be conquered and made to serve him. The common denominator of *abandoning fear of dream images* seems to be an important aspect of developing control. Confronting and conquering may not even be necessary, if you can become conscious that you are dreaming and that dream images cannot hurt you. *Become aware of your dream state and you can abandon fear of any dream image.*

In addition to comprehending the nature of the dream state, transmuting the content of dreams, and fully realizing that dreams are illusion, Ram meditates on the forms of the deities he sees in his dreams and keeps his mind quiet and free of thoughts so that these images become attuned to the "non-thought condition of mind." This sounds almost as though the disciple is inducing his dream images to meditate. If the disciple masters this process, he realizes that the content of both the waking state and the dream state are illusions. All subjective experience will be known to be born of the clear light (that is, to be a product of the mind of Buddha), and the illusions and the mind will blend. According to Evans-Wentz, once he has realized that the content of both waking state and dream state are illusion, ". . . the disciple is ready for further advance on the Path, the Goal of which is the Dreamless State (free from the illusoriness of both the waking and sleeping condition) . . ." [17] Thus, the doctrine of the dream state ends. It is followed by the doctrine of the clear light, the doctrine of the after-death state, and the doctrine of consciousness transference.

The ordinary Western dreamer might well wonder how this esoteric material can apply to him. Yet we have seen that the practices the Yogi engages in are variations of concepts we are already familiar with: peacefulness to concentrate on dreams, building of dream friends, inducing specific desired dreams, developing consciousness in dreams so as to change dream images and become fearless of them.

The Yogis differ in their maintenance of consciousness

while falling asleep and the completeness to which they push dream control. Perhaps their strict discipline of mind and body in meditations and exercises enable the Yogis to accomplish these behaviors unknown to Westerners. We will probably not know for certain until we undergo their rigorous training. Yogis extend their concept of fearlessness of dream images beyond the living state: A Yogi is to be fearless of his dreams even when dead.

The *Bardo* is a term for the after-death state, the state between one death and the next rebirth. It is believed to be a kind of dream state. Yet, the after-death state is not an ordinary dream state since the "dreamer" is dead. The *Bardo Thödol (The Tibetan Book of the Dead)* gives instructions, a guide, for the deceased to follow during his after-death experience. Although these instructions are not for ordinary dreaming (as the dreamer is dead) you will see that they can be helpful to the Western dreamer wishing to deal with his own dream images while in a living state. In fact, Carl Jung, in his psychological commentary to a later edition of *The Tibetan Book of the Dead*, remarked on the extraordinary value this text had for him (perhaps for different reasons):

> For years, ever since it was first published [in 1927], the *Bardo Thödol* has been my constant companion, and to it I owe not only many stimulating ideas and discoveries, but also many fundamental insights.[18]

We, too, will find it useful.

The guide for the deceased, the *Bardo Thödol*,[19] consists of three *Bardo* parts: (1) the *Chikhai Bardo*, which describes the psychic happenings (the subjective experiences) of the moments of death and how a Yogi is to die; (2) the *Chönyid Bardo*, which deals with the dreamlike apparitions that arise during

the *Bardo;* and (3) the *Sidpa Bardo,* which deals with the rebirth instinct and how a womb is to be chosen. When any Tibetan person is dying (Yogi or not), the *Bardo Thödol* is read
to him at his deathbed (unless it is certain he will directly attain Buddhahood). Yogis have been instructed in the *Bardo
Thödol* while living. Since the Yogis already know the *Bardo
Thödol* well, the reading at their deathbed simply serves as a
reminder for their imminent after-death experiences. However,
the reading of the *Bardo* for the common people is considered
indispensable. They may be helped to attain Buddhahood without meditation. The mere hearing of it alone gives them a
chance in the after-death state. For this reason, the *Bardo Thödol* is referred to as "the doctrine of liberation by hearing."

There is similarity to certain Senoi concepts in the second
part of the *Bardo Thödol.* The first part of the *Bardo,* the *Chikhai Bardo,* which gives instructions on how to deal with the
symptoms of death, does not help us with our dream states.
However, in the second part of the *Bardo,* the *Chönyid Bardo,*
there is much similarity to certain Senoi concepts—the main
theme, like the instructions on the dream state, is to abandon
fear, to face the images no matter how terrifying, and to go
forward. The Senoi are advised to advance toward frightening
dream images and conquer them (although it is not clear
whether the Senoi regard dream images as actual external
spirits, rather than parts of themselves). The Yogi is advised to
advance, but without the additional Senoi advice of counter-
attack. Just as in the doctrine of the dream state, *the important
thing is fearlessness of your dream image.*

In the *Chönyid Bardo,* the deceased is daily exposed to
images of terrifying "Peaceful Deities" and horrendous
"Wrathful Deities." For example, at one point the deceased
is faced with all fifty-eight "blood-drinking deities":

> They will come having their upper teeth biting the
> nether lip; their eyes glassy; their hairs tied up on the top of
> the head; big-bellied, narrow-waisted; holding a [*karmic*]
> record-board in the hand; giving utterance from their mouth
> to sounds of "Strike! Slay!", licking [human] brain, drinking
> blood, tearing heads from corpses, tearing out [the] hearts:
> thus will [they] come, filling the worlds.[20]

This is surely as terrifying as any nightmare experience in the
dream state of life. If one can cope with it, nightmares should
be easy to deal with.

The Yogis refer to dream images as "thought-forms."
(This concept is similar to the concept of the Gestaltists that
all dream images are parts of the dreamer.) I am not sure that a
Westerner is particularly comfortable with the idea that terrifying dream images are his "own thought-forms." However, it
is undoubtedly a more comfortable position to take than the
belief that the terrifying images are gods or devils who have
come to punish the deceased "dreamer." *Recognize that your
own frightening dream images originate from your thoughts.
Ability to recognize dream images (while living or while dead)
as being one's "own thought-forms" is the secret to Yoga
dream control.*

The third state of the *Bardo*, the *Sidpa Bardo*, is referred
to as the "transitional state of rebirth." Here the deceased is
exposed to further illusions:

> Apparitional illusions, too, of being pursued by various
> terrible beasts of prey will dawn. Snow, rain, darkness, fierce
> blasts [of wind], and hallucinations of being pursued by
> many people likewise will come; [and] sounds as of moun-
> tains crumbling down, and of angry overflowing seas, and of
> the roaring of fire, and of fierce winds springing up.[21]

He is urged to realize that all he suffers is a result of his behavior and a product of his mind.

Whatever the experiences, the deceased should set them aside and meditate. He will begin to yearn for another human body. He must resist this desire.

If recognition of the illusions has not yet come, the deceased will next experience a judgment of his good and evil deeds, followed by horrendous suffering imposed on him by "The Lord of Death." His salvation here is, as always, to recognize the illusion as coming from himself. He should meditate. "If it be an illiterate boor who knoweth not how to meditate . . ." [22] he is advised to "merely analyse with care the real nature of that which is frightening thee" [23] (that is, in reality it is not formed of anything). Notice the similarity of this advice to the lucid dreamer's process in which analytic thought is used in a prelucid dream in order to produce lucidity. *Try to analyze your dream images during your dreams.*

The deceased will see different lights issuing from the six different worlds.[24] His own body will take on the color of the world to which he is to be reborn. He should meditate upon the "clear light" and try to obstruct his rebirth. If all this fails to bring recognition, the deceased will be greatly tempted to be reborn. The womb will seem to him to be a place of refuge wherein he can escape the snow, rain, darkness, fierce wind, and hallucinations. He must resist allowing himself to be reborn. He can prevent rebirth by not allowing himself to enter the womb, or by "closing the womb-door." [25] If he cannot resist being reborn, he should try to choose rebirth in a country where religion prevails, a difficult task. He will then enter a womb.

When the reader has completed reading the *Bardo Thödol* three times, he recites various rituals and prayers. It is suggested that the *Bardo Thödol* be read for forty-nine days, giving the deceased every chance to become liberated at one stage or another.

From *The Tibetan Book of the Dead* we can draw helpful concepts that we can put to use in our dreams this very night. The first of these useful principles is that of *concentration on the dream state*.

We have observed rudimentary forms of concentration on the dream state with ancient dreamers and past creative dreamers who induced specific dreams. We saw it again in American Indian dreamers, the Senoi, don Juan, and lucid dreamers. Mary Arnold-Forster, especially, planned during the day how she would deal with frightening dream images she might encounter and she thought extensively about pleasant dream images and producing informative and creative dreams. Contration on the dream state developed "one-pointedly," as the Yogis do.

There is no doubt that most Westerners fall into the category of "an illiterate boor who knoweth not how to meditate." Ability to concentrate attention apparently confers tremendous power to the thought processes of an individual. It may be that the disciple who follows the *Bardo Thödol* and meditation instructions is learning to produce a special dream state unknown to most Westerners.

The special dream state of which the Yogis speak sounds remarkably like the "half-dream state" that the Russian philosopher Ouspensky describes. There is a tenth-century Tantric text (the *Spandakârikâ* of Vasagupta) that alludes to an "intermediate state" between waking and sleeping in which alone it is possible to induce and master dreams.[26] The disciple must learn to hold himself at this junction of sleeping and waking. I have had some small experience in entering a dream state while *remaining* conscious (rather than becoming conscious), but not enough to merit discussion.

I speculate that the Western dreamer who develops skill in concentration would be able to proceed both more swiftly and more efficiently in such goals as increasing helpful dream images and producing informative and creative dreams. Concentration could be used to increase and sustain all sorts of positive creative dreaming goals. *Increase your skills in concentration and meditation and you will probably increase your control in dreams.*

Another important concept *The Tibetan Book of the Dead* underlines for us is that of *fearlessness of dream images.* This principle, like concentration, is not unique to Yoga of the dream state. Yet, the extent to which this concept is carried is special. For example, the images that the deceased is said to suffer unless he recognizes them as his own thought-forms are indeed horrendous. To liken them to a nightmare in the living state may be too mild. They are perhaps more like the hallucinations of the psychotic or the agonized visions of drug-induced "bad trips." If the Westerner could learn to avoid terror responses and learn coping responses to hallucinations from drugs or psychotic states, as well as to nightmares, what a benefit that would be! If Yoga of the dream state can indeed accomplish this, as it is claimed, it would be of great value to teach these methods to Westerners.

We would need to study all available materials, consult with masters of this system, and adapt it to our way of life. As Ralph Metzner puts it in his recent book, *Maps of Consciousness*:

... we cannot simply use the Indian ways, or the Japanese ways of Zen. Our culture is different, our children are programmed differently, our body constitution is different, and the evolution of consciousness has not stood still since the Middle Ages. We need to extract the viable essence from the *tantras* and other ancient ways and convert it to our needs, using what we can, experimentally, in a context of testing and verification.[27]

Fearlessness of dream images is surely an "extraction" we can use. It is important, I think, to notice the form in which this is taught. In a way these horrendous visions are induced, just as we have seen pleasant ones induced. The Yogi who reads and hears and commits this material to memory during his life will surely experience some of it during his dream life while alive. The "nightmare" is stereotyped, just as the American Indians and others stereotype the appearance of their gods. However, it is crucial, I believe, that the instructions contain *at the same time* the method to deal with these images, how to prevent fear from accompanying them.

While working on this chapter I experienced a weird hallucination-type dream:

> *In the dream I am part of an audience. I see men high in a balcony of the huge auditorium throwing small pellets into balloons, which burst and release a drug into the atmosphere. The lights go out. I close my eyes and can feel the effect already. "Oh, yes," I say knowingly. I float up in the air into the balcony level and, hovering in the air, observe myself in a mirror. I know the image will be distorted because of the drug (I've never experienced drug hallucinations but have read descriptions of them and heard experiences related). Sure enough, my face appears in a series of bizarre forms. In one of the reflections, my face is covered with a network of scars. In another, I appear wild, with long flowing hair, a*

bikini top, and a native skirt. Waves of passion flow through my lower body as I move and my eyes are wild and staring. Such views of myself would ordinarily be very disturbing in a dream. In this case I am not afraid, in part because I expect the distorted images. I think how afraid I'd usually be. I say to myself, "Remember, all this comes from your mind! It's a good thing I was prepared by the Yoga stuff." I have moments of almost slipping into the feeling and becoming frightened but manage to stay on top of it. The story continues. ("Balloon Drug," 2/3/74.)

Awake, it is easy to see the symbolism—a concern over my aging reflection, the wrinkles-scar network, a view of the sexually wild part of myself. These are truly pictures of my thoughts; they are my "thought-forms." I do not find them frightening when I "recognize" them. In my dream I saw them vividly at the same time as experiencing them (a mirror provides the opportunity to simultaneously see the image and experience being it). Yet, I was able to "recognize" them. Ability to feel fearless in the face of frightening images is indeed a worthwhile skill. *As you recognize your own frightening images as your thought-forms you will free yourself from fear of them.*

Our ability to deal with everyday life (as well as horrendous visions) can also benefit from an extension of the concept of fearlessness. For example, it is possible to extend to everyday life the idea that the deceased should not fear the wrathful deities because they are merely different aspects of the peaceful deities. If my husband is "wrathful" and I react to him only as he is at the moment, I have a negative response. If, however, I hold in my mind the idea that my angry husband is the same as my peaceful, beloved husband, merely a different aspect—if I "recognize" him to be the same—then it is much easier to respond in a positive, constructive way to the situation.

Notice the parallel between recognizing the frightening images of the after-death state to be illusions of one's own mind and the urging of lucid dreamers to recognize dream images to be dreams. In the case of the Yogis, recognition leads to liberation from the after-death state and the attainment of Buddhahood. In the case of the lucid dreamers, recognition leads to the experiencing of a lucid dream in which one is free to perform whatever he wishes. In both cases *recognition leads to fearlessness, which leads to freedom.*

We should not entirely dispense with the possibility that there is an after-death state in which visions appear. If so, knowledge of how to deal with frightening dreams becomes not only therapeutic in life but also possibly soul saving, a crucial element to survival after death.

The essential element in dispelling fear of dream images is to recognize that one is dreaming. Again, this concept is not unique to the Yogis (lucid dreamers hold it as well), yet it is carried to a far greater extent. The fact that dreams are not real is impressed over and over on the mind of the disciple throughout his lifetime both by his guru and by himself in his own meditation. *The Tibetan Book of the Dead* explains how fearlessness emerges from the recognition that dream images seen in the after-death plane are illusions:

> Through the *guru's* select teaching, one cometh to recognize them to be the thought-forms issuing from one's own intellectual faculties. For instance, a person, upon recognizing a lion-skin [to be a lion-skin], is freed [from fear]; for though it be only a stuffed lion-skin, if one do not know it to be so actually, fear ariseth, but, upon being told by some person that it is a lion-skin only, one is freed from fear. Simi-

larly here, too, when the bands of blood-drinking deities, huge of proportions, with very thick-set limbs, dawn as big as the skies, awe and terror are naturally produced in one. [But] as soon as the setting-face-to-face is heard [one] recognizeth them to be one's own tutelary deities and one's own thought-forms.[28]

Once we recognize a dream image to be a "lion-skin only," we need no longer fear it. Our dreams, known to be dreams, can become completely fear-free. The Yogi uses this fear-free state to dispense with dreams altogether and to proceed to merge himself with the great dream of Buddha.

Both the Yogis and the Senoi obtain dramatic changes in the content of their dreams, but they differ markedly in the form of the changed dream and the long-term result of these changes. The Yogis eventually detach themselves from the world, their bodies, and their dreams, regarding all as illusions. The Senoi seem to relate more and more successfully to their internal structure and the external world. Thus, control of dreams can lead in different directions, depending on one's philosophy.

We may wish to use a fear-free dream state differently from the Yogis. We may wish to use a fear-free dream state as a realm of consciousness in which we can engage in all manner of self-knowledge. We may choose to allow what will happen in our dreams to happen, knowing that whatever images arise they cannot hurt us. We may choose to induce a particular pleasurable dream experience and, as it occurs, observe its manner and meaning to us. We may choose to produce creations from this state. We may choose to use our fear-free dream state to practice skills and attitudes we wish to emit in the waking state. We may choose to pose questions to ourselves and observe the responses that arise. In these and many other ways, a fear-free dream state known to be a dream offers great value to us. We may wish to think of the dream state not as another illusion but as another form of marvelous human reality.

SUMMARY OF WHAT WE CAN LEARN FROM YOGI DREAMERS

1. You can learn to maintain consciousness throughout your dream state.

2. Determine to remain conscious during your dreams. Induce dream consciousness. Immerse yourself in the idea of dream consciousness during the day and immediately prior to sleep. Intensify your concentration on the idea of dream consciousness for two or three days.

3. Provide yourself with a peaceful setting to help you concentrate on inducing and controlling your dreams.

4. Increase your skills in concentration and meditation and you will increase your skill in dream control.

5. Build up your dream friends.

6. As you become conscious during your dream, you can induce any change in it you wish.

7. As you develop dream consciousness, you can become totally fearless of any dream image.

8. Recognize that your frightening dream images originate from your thoughts.

9. Recognize that your dreams are dreams while you are in a dream state.

10. As you recognize that your dream images are your own thought-forms and become aware that you are dreaming, you will become fearless. As you are fearless of your dream images you become free to use your dreams for creative and therapeutic purposes.

part three

How to Develop Dream Control

CHAPTER EIGHT

How to Keep Your Dream Diary

Your dream life can provide you with many marvelous gifts: creative products, delightful adventures, increased skill in coping with waking life, and a personal laboratory to develop any project of your choice. The party is held several times each night. You are the guest of honor. All you need to do is attend, enjoy, pick up your presents, and return to waking life. Of course, you need to be aware. Otherwise, unconscious and tipsy, you'll forget who was there, what they said, what you did, and lose your gifts before you reach home. *You can develop almost total recall for your nightly dream parties and become able to record and use your gifts in waking life.*

Skill in remembering your dreams begins with your attitude. Value your dreams. Don't reject any one of them. The dream you dismiss as ridiculous or trivial, like an orphan child, may be the very one with great potential to blossom beautifully when it's more developed. Accept each dream you remember. Treat it with respect. Write it down. Give it permanent form. You will be amazed to find, after you keep a dream diary for a few months, that seemingly unimportant symbols appear again and again. They change in shape and size but are clearly recognizable when written down. They literally grow. You can trace their development over time. Each dream you have is a child of your own. *Attend patiently to all your dreams and they will provide you with remarkable insights about yourself.*

Let's assume that you already value your dreams and are willing to accept them as they come, silly or fragmentary. How can you get in touch with them close enough to recall and record them in order to relate to them in the exciting ways that are possible?

Your attitude immediately prior to sleep is important: Plan to remember your dreams. Suggest it to yourself. One student found it helpful to drink half a glass of water before sleeping, determining while drinking that she would recall her dreams. In the morning she drank the remainder of the water while trying to recall. The same effect can be achieved by self-suggestion: "Tonight I will remember my dreams." *Remind yourself before going to sleep that you will remember your dreams.*

If you are not already a vivid dream recaller, the best time to begin developing skill in dream recall is *in the morning from a natural awakening.* When you awaken spontaneously in the morning (not by an alarm clock, not by phone ringing, not by children's calls), you are awakening directly from a REM period. Any time that you awaken by yourself you awaken from a dream. The morning dream, however, is the longest of the night's series, sometimes lasting a half to three-quarters of an hour. You have much more to catch hold of. If you ordinarily must wake up by alarm clock and you begin thinking about the day's activities even before opening your eyes, you are likely to lose all trace of the night's dreams. You will find it helpful to begin catching hold of your dreams by arranging a time to sleep in and awaken naturally. A weekend or peaceful vacation time can give you an opportunity to start. I personally prefer this method to artificial awakenings designed to catch a dream [1] because it is possible to develop it into the special system described below. It also allows your dream to come to a natural conclusion rather than intruding into the theme with bells or buzzers. (These methods may be necessary however, with chronic nonrecallers of dreams.) *Arrange a time when you can spontaneously awaken.*

Knowing that you have just completed a dream, the next step is crucial: Don't open your eyes! *Lie still with closed eyes and let images flow into your mind.* Don't begin thinking about what you must do for the day. You've chosen a peaceful unpressured time. Just let yourself feel. Very often this is enough to allow the images of your just-ended dream to return. The tiniest fragment of the last dream can serve as a hook for the whole night's series. I often recall the last dream scene first. I wake up hearing the words that I or some other dream figure is speaking, dancing the dance, laughing at the joke. It is the closing scene of the play. By reviewing it in my mind, the scene before that flows back, then the preceding one, and the one that preceded that. In reverse order the scenes of the last dream appear. It is not like a film run backward; the whole scenes, in complete sections, line up in reverse order. "Oh, before that so and so happened. And before that . . ." Occasionally the dream will return *in toto,* but it more commonly comes with the last scene first. Some small scrap that seems inconsequential, when considered, is found to be attached to a richly woven intricate garment. In a similar way, remembrance of the last entire dream will stimulate association to previous dreams of the night. *When you awaken naturally from a dream, close your eyes (preferably don't open them at all), lie still, and let the dream images flow back.*

Suppose there is not even the slightest fragment of a dream to let your mind wander on. You may sense that you dreamed or have a vague feeling without an image or there may be nothing at all. Don't give up. If a couple of minutes produces no dream recall, try this: Let your mind wander over images of the people close to you, your family, your intimate friends. Like riffling the pages of a book you may hit upon the image you seek in passing. You will *know*. There is a feeling of certain recognition that you dreamed something about that person that is inescapable. It's like trying to recall a forgotten name. The shape and rhythm and even initial sound may be there, but the whole name is elusive. When you hit upon the correct name yourself or someone supplies it, you recognize its accuracy. *Run through the important people in your life in your mind; it may trigger associations to your recent dream.*

Strange as it may seem, the position of your body in the morning is important in recalling your dreams of the preceding night. Hermann Rorschach,[2] who invented the famous "ink-blot" test, observed that it was necessary to lie still when awakening because any quick motor movement like jumping out of bed disrupts memory of the dream. This is true, but you can go beyond it. Allow yourself to recall whatever dreams come to you in the position in which you awake. Lie still and let the images flow. *Then roll over.* If you find yourself lying on the left side, roll over to the right; if you are on your stomach, roll over slowly onto a side or onto your back. For some as yet unknown reason, additional dream recall often comes when you move gently from one position and settle into another. One contemporary theorist[3] speculates that dreams may be stored in codes that are more readable when we are in the original posture in which the dream occurred: "Trying to recall a dream while in an inappropriate posture feels something like trying to write left-handed."[4] When we recreate the original sleeping posture in which the dream occurred, memory of it often flows back. *When you feel as though your dream recall is complete in the position in which you awoke, move gently*

*into other sleeping positions you use, with eyes still closed, and
you will often find additional dream recall.*

You may find yourself recalling scraps of dreams during
the day. Some incident, some tone of voice, something someone
says to you, something you hear yourself say, or something you
see may trigger the response, "Oh, I dreamed about that last
night!" Just as with morning dream recall it is important to
capture these birdlike wisps of dreams, to put them into cages
of writing or tapes or drawings before letting them go. No
matter how vivid and accessible they seem at the moment, you
will find they have vanished completely in a day or two and
your memory of them, if you have any at all, will be a pale,
distorted reflection. Recorded, even in fragmentary form, they
can become extraordinarily useful to you later. Dream recall
triggered by some stimulus in the environment may even occur
several days after the dream in question. However, the sooner
you can catch hold of it after the dream, the more complete
and accurate your recall will be. Timing is crucial.

One research team [5] clearly established that *dream recall
is richest and most detailed immediately after a REM period
ends.* Researchers awakened sleepers at four different times:
(1) when the EEG machine showed they were experiencing
REM: sleepers reported, as expected, an ongoing dream story;
(2) during a body movement immediately after REM stopped:
sleepers awakened at this point described complete, vivid, specific dream stories; (3) sleepers were awakened five minutes
after REM stopped: they reported vague snatches of dream
stories; and (4) sleepers were awakened ten minutes after REM
stopped: most of these sleepers had no dream recall or only a
blurry impression of a dream. Thus, only *five minutes* after a
dream finishes, recall of it breaks up into fragments, and ten
minutes after a dream, recall is almost, if not completely, gone.

If you are going to catch an ordinary dream in its full expression, you must get hold of it quickly. Lucid dreams, in contrast, are vivid enough to stay in memory because you were there—conscious—just like an exciting event in waking life. Nightmares, too, are often vividly recalled. The ordinary dream, however, needs immediate attention to capture it.

Now, you may believe it is impossible to capture a dream within five minutes of its completion. It can be done. I am not speaking of artificial awakenings. Of course, if you sleep in a dream laboratory and an experimenter watches the unfolding record of your brain waves, he can see when the pattern of dreaming occurs and can wake you. Although an interesting experience, it is hardly convenient and not one you would wish to employ every night. You could also arrange with a good friend to stay up all night and watch you sleep. An alert observer can see the rapid eye movements indicating a dream state without an EEG machine. In one of my dream seminars, a student with poor dream recall made such an arrangement with his girlfriend. She passed the long hours of the night by reading at her friend's bedside and apparently missed some of his REM periods, much to their mutual frustration. Those she caught were interrupted too near the beginning of the dream story so there was not much to recall. Having a friend watch you sleep and wake you at appropriate times can be done but is tedious and uncertain. Another artificial awakening method involves setting your alarm clock at approximately the time you would expect a dream to occur—about ninety minutes after falling asleep and every ninety minutes thereafter. Again, this method interrupts an ongoing dream story, if it catches a dream at all. Otherwise, sleep is disrupted. Another student of mine, who underwent surgery, was subsequently waked by a nurse for shots throughout the night while she was in the hospital. She was delighted to find herself in the midst of dreams and busily recorded them while getting her shot. Generally, however, I do not recommend artificial awakenings of any sort unless other methods of capturing dreams do not produce results.

You can actually train yourself to awaken after a dream story is completed naturally. As you develop the habit of valuing your dreams, taking time to recall them in the morning, and recording them regularly each day, you will find that your memory for dreams increases dramatically. This is how it happened for me.

I became interested in recording my dreams when I was about fourteen. People in my family were discussing Freud's views on dreams, then much in vogue. I wanted to check for myself. I had been a heavy dream recaller all my life (and still recollect some unrecorded childhood dreams). At fourteen, I began to write down my dreams that seemed striking. I recorded the date, a description of the dreams I recalled in the morning, often adding events of the preceding day, feelings and associations, and sometimes drawings and attempts at analysis. I was mainly curious about the symbolism. The records I made were sporadic. As I grew older and went through typical teen-age trauma, I found that dream recording was cathartic; it helped me understand my shifting feelings and cope more effectively. My descriptions were more complete and I kept steadier records. As a clinical psychology doctoral student I became aware of the considerable possibilities of a scientific examination of the record spanning several years. Dreams, unless examined by EEG, were in some disrepute at my university, however, so I did my dissertation [6] in an area more concrete and measurable. Records from this time forward were comprehensive, with additional data and rare gaps. As I made daily records, I found I had developed extraordinary dream recall. There was rarely a morning wakening without a vivid dream in mind.

Suddenly, during this time of regular recording, I found myself awake in the middle of the night. This was a rare event and I puzzled, "What am I doing awake?" Nothing had happened to arouse me. Then I realized I had just been dreaming. I was waking from a dream in the same way as I did in the morning. How to remember it? At first, I tried reviewing it in my mind with the intention of recording it in the morning with the most recent dream. Anyone who has attempted this knows how futile it can be. Two or even three "replays" of the dream seem to have it firmly set and you return to sleep, only to discover in the morning that a ghostly trace of the once vivid dream is all that remains. This method was useless and time wasting for me. Yet, I continued to wake during the night following a dream. How to record it? Too lazy to get up, unwilling to turn on the light and disturb my husband by writing in bed, I scribbled a few short phrases on my ever-present bedside pad and returned to sleep. Again I woke. Another dream. Another scribble. In the morning the scrawls done in the dark were hard to decipher because they often overlapped. And so I hit upon a special way to capture these fleeting dreams so they would survive until morning.[7]

When I self-awaken from a dream, during the night or in the morning, I remain still with my eyes closed. I pick up the 5″ x 8″ pad on my night table with the pen that lies on top of it and record the dream *with eyes still closed* in the following special way: I grasp the note pad with the 8″ side held horizontally with my left fingertips. I brace the pad on the bed or night table beside me (lying on my left side) or upon my chest (while lying on my back). I hold the right hand in normal writing position except that the little finger is extended upward in order to feel the top edge of the pad. I write a complete description of the dream (not just phrases) across the pad making the line straight by feeling the top edge of the pad as a guide. When I reach the end of a line, I lower my left hand fingertips to indicate the starting position of the next line and return the pen in my right hand to the spot marked by my left fingertips by tactual contact. It's rather like a typewriter carriage returning to the next line. Keeping the little finger extended while writing corrects for the tendency to write in a downward curve in the dark. This method virtually eliminates superimposition of lines. After one page is filled with writing I turn the page, press it flat, and continue the same process, using both sides of the paper until recall is complete.

Each new entry is marked with a paragraph symbol to indicate clearly that it follows a period of sleep. I have already noted when I retired the approximate time of falling asleep and I note the time of awakening. In the morning I have several pages of wobbly notes which usually describe three or four dreams, but may range from one to seven dreams.

This method may sound very complex, but it quickly becomes easy and automatic with practice. At first it requires tremendous effort to pick up the pad and pen, but this, too, soon becomes simple. The method provides a record of dreams immediately following REM periods. I checked this point by spending several nights in a dream laboratory attached to an EEG machine and verified that I do, indeed, awaken following each REM period (and occasionally outside of REM). Once the written record is made I can easily dismiss thinking about the dream and return quickly to sleep. There is no need to "rehearse" the dream or exert effort to remember. I believe recall is more complete with this method. Opening your eyes and sitting up in bed, however gently, and turning on a light, however dim, break into visual imagery of the dream. As the dream is recorded with eyes shut, previous dream scenes flow back into mind. Experimenters who use tape recorders to describe the dream also disrupt total recall, in my opinion. The drowsy dreamer must rouse considerably to speak clearly and loudly enough to record immediately after a dream. Such arousal is very likely to disturb dream recall as well as a bed partner. My personal preference is for the writing technique described above. It gives, for me, the most complete recall with the least effort. You may wish to experiment with it. Each dreamer, however, should use the method that is most comfortable and appealing to him or her. *Whatever method you use, record your dreams, preferably with eyes closed, in the order that you recall them.* This practice will enable you to maximize your dream recall.

If you want to try my dream recording technique, the equipment you choose is important. Select unlined 5″ x 8″ note pads that are sealed with string embedded in the plastic binding. Pages on pads with only a plastic edge break off as the page is turned, rather than remaining firmly attached. It's impossible to write legibly on loose, moving paper. Pads with spiral bindings or thick tops with perforations are bulky and hard to handle. It's better to choose a standard size pad and stick with it, because each change requires accommodation and is confusing. Pencil is too light for sleepy note taking; use a high-quality inexpensive ballpoint pen such as an accountant fine point. Become aware of the feel of writing with the pen with ink flowing. Alert yourself to the draggy, scratchy feel of writing with a pen out of ink. Many pages of notes can be lost in the dark if this escapes you. Keep a second pen within easy reach in case you run out of ink during the night.

If you happen to know shorthand, as I do, you will have to guard against lapsing into it. For several weeks I found my midnight dream entries partially or entirely in shorthand when I awoke, even though I had determined not to use it. Transcribing is too difficult a task to add to deciphering the shaky notes. On a few occasions I found the first entry in longhand and later entries on the same night in greater amounts of shorthand until the last entry was *entirely* in shorthand, although I had no awareness of writing in that form. Extra effort has eliminated the appearance of shorthand.

Another aspect of this technique that requires attention is to be certain you are actually recording on the pad with the pen. When I first evolved this technique I often dreamed I was recording the dream (so there was no necessity to wake to do so). Occasionally, however, I felt certain I was actually recording because I could feel myself writing with what I believed to be the pen on what I believed to be the pad. On rousing further, I discovered I was actually tracing the words with my fingers on my skin. In one case, the thigh of my right leg served as a pad and in another my right cheek. Now, after long use of the method, this does not happen. In fact, my dream state cooperates with the intent to record. For example, at the end of one dream segment, I saw a dark-haired, moustached reporter holding a pen and note pad. He was looking at me and pointing to the right. Turning my head to see what he was pointing at, I opened my eyes and saw my own pad and pen. It was as though the dream image were saying, "It's time to write now." In another dream, a character said, "Now it's time to pause for a commercial." I found myself awake obviously for the purpose of writing. *As you establish a habit for dream recording and work on building dream friends, you will develop a more cooperative dream state.*

I mentioned above the importance of writing down your dreams in the order that you recall them. There is one exception to this rule: Always record a unique verbal expression immediately. If I awaken with a dream poem in mind and I also recall the entire preceding scene, I dare not describe the scene first and then the poem in the order that the images appeared and were recalled. I write the poem itself immediately, then describe the story that led up to it. When I come to the place where the poem originally appeared I often write it again, if possible. Later when I have my eyes open and am fully functional, it is interesting to compare the first recording to the second. Within the few minutes it took to describe the dream scene, several words of the poem may have changed. *When you record a unique verbal expression immediately you have a better chance of preserving it in its original form.* You will find it helpful to follow this practice with unusual phrases, names, or impressive quotations, too. Such dream-concocted expressions as "Scandia Rose," "Engrabble," "Emmanual Styles," and "Wemberly" would have escaped me long before their proper place in the story had I not recorded them first. *Note your unique productions first.* The story will come back with association to other elements in it, the strange dream creations may not. You will see how, in Chapter 9, these unique productions can have special value for you.

As I record my dreams during the night and in the morning, I also make note of any unusual occurrences. For example, on rare occasions I may be so tired that I start to fall asleep for a few instants while writing. When I rouse, I note "F.A." (falling asleep) or even "fell asleep," if that's the case. On other rare occasions I may begin to dream again—probably hypnogogic experiences—while recording the just finished dream. When I become aware of this fact, I record "O.D."

(overlaid dream) and a description of it in parentheses. Again, the telephone may ring and disrupt recording and recall of the dream. (With four children this can happen even in the middle of the night.) Such a fact is also noted. *Note any unusual happening that may affect your record.*

There is one *common* happening that I often note: The dream imagery that occurs as one drifts off to sleep is technically called hypnogogic visions or hypnogogic experiences. You have perhaps experienced these with a startle response that sometimes occurs at the onset of sleep. Hypnogogic experiences are not usually dream stories but more images or scenes that one is aware of while still semiconscious. One researcher [8] studied this type of imagery extensively. He observed the moment of transition from abstract thought to concrete imagery. The more you become aware of this type of visual thinking, the more you notice its occurrence as you drift off to sleep. In fact, Hervey de Saint-Denys found that it was so frequent he asserted, "There is no sleep without dreams, just as there is no waking state without thought" [9] (my translation). He woke himself completely each time he had a hypnogogic vision in order to capture and record it. I choose to note only one or two of these hypnogogic experiences with "D.O." (drifting off) if the images seem particularly interesting but do not count them as dreams or attempt to keep track of them. They are endlessly available and I prefer to concentrate on the dream state *per se.* *You may wish to make note of interesting hypnogogic experiences. They, like your dreams, will help you understand your own symbol system.*

There are some aspects of dreams that seem impossible to describe. Most dreamers have experienced changing from one form into another—you turn into a bird and escape, or the cat becomes a pig. Sometimes the setting shifts while you and the action continue—you are inside a house doing something and the area around you becomes a marketplace while you continue just as before. However, other shifts are subtler. Sometimes the texture of a dream is complex beyond ability to express. Everything seems to be happening simultaneously; or there are several levels of dream action, intricate beyond Lawrence Durrell's *Alexandria Quartet,* and all occurring at once; or a story repeats two or three times in different versions. When a dream is impossible to describe, I state what I can of it and add "complex" or "many-layered," as the case may be. *Try to at least identify the elusive elements of your dreams.*

Many people find that telling a dream to a friend helps them to recall it. The very act of putting the dream into words and trying to explain or express it seems to stimulate both recall of the dream and insight into aspects of it. Sometimes, if you "forget" (suppress or repress) the dream, your friend can recall it readily. However, it's tempting not to record a dream once it has been told, so be sure to write it down, too. *Share your dream experiences with a friend, if possible, as well as record them.*

Let us assume that you have collected your dreams in some way in the morning and during the night (or just in the morning). You have written them complete, or in phrases, or taped them. Now you need to give them permanent form to get the most benefit from them.

I take the several pages of wobbly notes that I have collected during the night and morning and copy them over sometime during the day into a standard form with date, location (I often travel), dream description, time of retiring and rising, waking state recall or lack of it, associations to the dreams, and facts of the day preceding the dream. Sometimes I add sketches of unusual images and analyses. These dream record forms, on one side of plastic-reinforced loose leaf notebook paper, are kept in chronological order, with monthly dividers, in yearbooks. The current collection covering twenty-five years is contained in twelve volumes filling a three-foot bookshelf. There are over 10,000 dreams recorded. The latest are most complete, with approximately 1,000 entries each year. (With the method described above, for example, the 1971 record has 900 entries from 362 nights of dreaming—no sleep on three nights—with a typical month of about 75 dreams and an average of 3.12 dreams each night.) You may not wish to bother with so complete a record. There is much to learn from it if you do. However, if you merely record those dreams you recall in a systematic method where you can examine them, in chronological order, you can gain a great deal of insight. Here is another way written records are, I believe, superior to tapes (unless the tapes are transcribed). You can *see* the changes. You may wish to keep an extensive record for a limited period of time. *Keep a written record of your dreams and you can learn a great deal about yourself.*

In examining my own record and making comparisons I find it helpful to use the suggestion of one of my students to give titles to the individual dreams as though they were stories. Thus, it is much easier to recall a specific dream by the title "Dancing Vegetables" than by date. I choose distinctive elements of the dream for its title. Idiosyncratic elements of a dream are believed to be emerging parts of the dreamer's personality. (This concept is discussed in Chapter 9.) By selecting one of the unique aspects of a dream for its title, you will not only be increasing your ability to recall it but also will be identifying elements in it which deserve special attention. *Select titles for your dreams from their unique characteristics.*

When you have your dream record in a permanent written form, you can examine it from many points of view. I cannot, in this book, discuss the numerous approaches to working with your dream record. I will discuss, however (in the last chapter), an unusual and, I believe, especially valuable approach. Here, I want to mention briefly a method I've devised that I find particularly helpful. In my permanent record, I have written a description of the dream in the main section of the form. In the right-hand column, I have noted associations to the dream imagery. In this approach to working with dreams, I now make a "translation." I take the dream plot as it appears and substitute my associations to the symbols. For example, my dream as originally recorded may read: "I am with my husband outside at the foot of some hills when an attractive woman with her hair in a long brown braid appears. I see that she is blind. She has come to consult with him, so I leave them alone." Assuming for the moment that all parts of the dream are parts of myself, my "translation," incorporating the associations, would read: "The wise part of me is near some rough terrain (difficulties). The old-fashioned part of me cannot see something. It needs help." Or suppose my record reads: "I am with —— (my daughter) in a living room. I want her to help me put out a small fire that has started. I yell at her to get some water. She is unbelievably stubborn and annoying." The "translation," again using my associations, might read: "There is a small problem that needs attention. The childish part of me resists cooperating. I feel angry at myself." I proceed through a dream record sentence by sentence "translating" in this fashion. The resulting document can lead to amazing insights. It is important to incorporate associations of current feelings. My daughter, for example, can represent childishness, vulnerability, betrayal, potential talent, or emerging strength, depending on the relationship of the moment or her current condition. Of course, she may also represent herself. In one dream I was holding on to her at the edge of a ledge. She was about to fall over and I yelled at her to do something. I couldn't support her weight if she didn't help. In this case, the dream image of my daughter represented my conception of *her* and her need to perform in a specific situation rather than a part of me. However, it is always informative to first try a "translation" from the point of view that all dream images are parts of yourself.

Dreams are perhaps the most highly personal expressions you have. No one else can tell you what your dreams mean. A therapist, if sensitive and intimately knowledgeable about you, can make some good guesses. But only you can supply the pertinent associations. *Try translating some of your dreams in their entirety with your current associations to the symbols in them. You can learn much about yourself.*

Some people are able to recall their dreams easily and often (high dream recallers) while other people remember their dreams only rarely and with difficulty (low dream recallers). Researchers have tried to discover why. Are there personality differences between high dream recallers and low dream recallers? Results of current studies are inconclusive. However, researchers seem to agree that, in general, low dream recallers are more likely to repress (keep from conscious awareness) or deny important psychological experiences.[10] Low dream recallers seem to be conformist, self-controlled, and defensive; they are likely to be more confident and less self-aware than habitual high dream recallers. Conversely, high dream recallers tend to be more anxious, less self-confident, yet have more self-understanding. Researchers [11] more tentatively conclude that high dream recallers have greater capacity for visual imagery outside of dreams; they use visual imagery more often and more effectively, which may make their dreams more recallable. Other researchers [12] have noted other differences.

I have observed, in my many conversations with dreamers

around the world, a difference between high and low dream re-callers that is striking enough to mention: Females seem to re-call dreams more often and more completely than males. Let me emphasize that I did not make a careful study of this; it is purely an impression. There is, however, one study that may support my observation. Researchers [13] collected written dreams from a large sample of schoolchildren. Records of dreams from female students were clearly longer and more complete than those of male students. It may be that this find-ing is a variation of the usual finding of female superiority on verbal tests. Another possible explanation is that greater fe-male dream recall, if it is found to exist, could be a result of attitudes taught by our culture. It is considered all right for females to be interested in dreams, but men are more practical and work-oriented. The man who must get up and go to work often begins planning his projects for the day while still in bed. Plans calling for assertiveness, competition, and problem solving may be well under way before eyes are open. We noted earlier that distraction immediately following a REM period disrupts recall of the prior dream.[14] The man who is involved in rational thinking from the moment he wakes up is very likely to disrupt dream recall. A less pressured woman with less immediate distractions may have greater recall simply because of leisure to contemplate the night's dreaming. Male-female roles are taught; they are in the process of change. Perhaps life style plays a more important role in dream recall than sex *per se*.[15] *If you regard your dreams as important and take time to recall them, they will come to you more easily and more often.*

Regardless of your current level of dream recall, you can learn to increase its quantity and enhance its quality. Ordinary dreamers can learn to establish extraordinary dream recall. In one study,[16] researchers found that dreamers who have trained themselves to self-awaken from REM periods can do so with remarkable accuracy. In another study,[17] students learned to substantially increase their dream recall during the first two weeks of keeping a regular dream journal and meeting with a group three hours a week to discuss dreams. When they were given a special task one night to use their dreams to creatively solve a problem there was *four times* as much dream recall as on other nights. Dreamers who were usually low in dream recall showed the most improvement in amount of dream recall. Dreamers who were usually high in dream recall showed more qualitative changes as they intensified efforts to recall and record their dreams: Their dreams became more detailed, more colored, and they remembered other sensations and emotions more clearly. Many dreamers in this study felt that as their acceptance of dreams increased they felt more accepting of themselves. This observation resembles the carry-over effect we noted as my students succeeded in the Senoi technique of confronting and conquering danger in their dreams and consequently felt more capable in waking life. We noted, too, that societies that give dreams an important role produce dreamers with frequent, vivid, detailed recall, and dreams that relate well to waking life.[18] *As you practice valuing, recalling, and recording your dreams, you will increase your recall. Your dreams will become more vivid, complete, and relevant to waking life.*

I believe that low dream recallers can benefit by increasing their dream recall. By using methods suggested above they can learn to recall and record their dreams on a regular basis. Motivation will increase dream recall. *If you are a low dream recaller, you can learn to increase your dream recall and, with it, reach a greater understanding of yourself.*

High dream recallers can increase color, vividness, and detail of their dreams. By employing creative dream techniques outlined in this book, high dream recallers can reduce anxiety and learn to become more self-confident in waking life. *If you are already a high dream recaller, you can get even more learning from your dreams and at the same time increase skills and confidence.*

Recalling your dreams and then recording them in a permanent form will give you an invaluable document from which you can both contribute to knowledge in general and learn, in depth, more and more about yourself. You can not only learn *about* yourself, but also *from* yourself.

Summary of Suggestions for Keeping Your Dream Diary

1. You can develop almost total recall for your dreams. Accept and value each dream, no matter how foolish or fragmentary it may seem at the time. A complete record of your dreams can provide remarkable insights.

2. Before retiring, plan to remember whatever dreams come to you. Place a pad and pen within easy reach of your sleeping spot.

3. The best time to begin developing skill in dream recall is during an unpressured time in the morning when you awaken naturally (it will be from a REM period). If you have trouble recalling your dreams, plan a time when you can spontaneously awaken and be unhurried.

4. When you awaken from a dream, lie still and allow the dream images to flow back into your mind. If no images come, let yourself run through the important people in your life; visualizing them may trigger association to your recent dream.

5. When dream recall is complete in one bodily position, move gently into other sleeping positions to see whether you have additional dream recall in these positions. Always move gently into any recording position.

6. Record your dreams whenever they come to you, immediately, later in the day, or several days later.

7. Dream recall is richest and most detailed immediately following a REM period. You can learn to self-awaken from your REM periods throughout the night and make accurate records without disturbing your sleep. Record your dreams regularly in the morning with closed eyes in the method described and you may find yourself waking spontaneously from earlier REM periods. Recording dreams after spontaneous awakening from a REM will give most complete and accurate dream recall.

8. If you prefer, or if self-awakening does not develop, you may wish to use an artificial awakening method such as having a friend stay with you while you sleep and wake you at approximate ninety-minute intervals, when you are likely to be experiencing REM. Or, your friend can watch directly for rapid eye movements. You can also use an alarm clock. Remember that REMs toward morning are longer and you have a better chance of catching dreams then.

9. Regardless of the method used to collect your dreams, by writing or by tape, make the first record with your eyes closed. Opening your eyes will disrupt dream recall.

10. As you value your dreams, accept them, record them regularly, and work on building dream friends, you will develop a more cooperative dream state.

11. Make your records in the order that you recall your dreams. Exception: Make note of unique verbal expressions first (poems, names, unusual phrases), regardless of the order, before they are forgotten. Note unusual happenings while making your record (falling asleep, inter-

ruptions). You may wish to note hypnogogic experiences. Try to identify elusive elements such as simultaneous layers of dreams.

12. Sharing your dream with a friend will help you to remember it, but you need written records as well to get the most benefit from your dream diary. Put your dreams into permanent written form (even if originally taped) and into chronological order.

13. Selecting titles for your dream stories from their unique aspects helps you recall your dreams and also identifies elements deserving special attention.

14. You may wish to try a "translation" of your dreams in the method described. You can learn much about yourself from this practice.

15. Regardless of your current level of dream recall, researchers find that you can increase the amount of your dream recall and enhance the quality of it. As you give dreams an important role in your life, and time to attend to them, they will come more easily, more often, and be of more value to you. Keeping a dream record can lead to greater self-understanding and help you increase your confidence and skills.

CHAPTER NINE

How to Develop Dream Control

You have within yourself a source of great knowledge. You can reach it by relating creatively to your dreams. I have presented several systems of dream control that other people use. We can learn from them and apply the principles to our own dream life. Ancient dreamers, past creative dreamers, American Indian dreamers, Senoi dreamers, a Yaqui Indian dreamer, lucid dreamers, and Yogi dreamers all can teach us ways that help us to relate to our own dreams. (I will summarize this body of information shortly.) However, in addition to learning from other dreamers, it is important to realize that you can also learn a great deal from yourself. As you keep your own dream diary over a period of time and examine its contents carefully, you will learn things about yourself that you cannot learn from books or therapists or in any other way.

What of the people who have kept careful dream diaries for many years? Who are they? What did they find? Many researchers [1] maintain records of other people, their patients or their subjects, but seldom share their own dreams. There are only a few researchers who have kept track of their own dreams and left them open for us. These deeply personal documents are often kept in code, abandoned, or destroyed.[2]

Sigmund Freud,[3] the father of psychoanalysis, for instance, is believed to have maintained an extensive dream diary, which he apparently destroyed in April 1885, at the age of twenty-eight, along with general diaries that he had kept for fourteen years. His reason: "The stuff simply enveloped me as the sand does the Sphinx." Freud drew heavily on forty-seven of his own dreams for the theories presented in *The Interpretation of Dreams*. Aside from the forty-seven dreams and other casual references, we know little about his dream record or how he kept it. We would perhaps be richer if he had preserved his dream diary.

Carl Jung, in contrast, persevered longer and drew more upon himself. Some of his original record remains. After his break with Freud, Jung [4] related, he experienced a period of inner uncertainty that led him to withdraw. He became absorbed with his fantasies and attempted to understand them. At first he recorded his fantasies (both waking and dreaming) in "The Black Book," which eventually consisted of six small black leather-bound notebooks. Later, he transferred them to "The Red Book," a folio volume bound in red in which he wrote the fantasies in elaborate literary form and language in calligraphic Gothic script, embellished with drawings, in the style of a medieval manuscript. As he recorded his fantasies and worked with them he was struck by their power and was unable to continue as a lecturer at the university when he felt he knew so little about himself. Therefore, he abandoned his academic career and devoted approximately four years to attempts to understand his fantasy life. Like Freud, he felt overwhelmed. He stated that the chaos of his fantasies would have "strangled me like jungle creepers," had he not been able to take a scientific view of them. He says that his family as well as his profession gave him strong support in the real world. Jung particularly valued making daily drawings of a mandala [5] that he felt was a cryptogram of his momentary state of self. With a series of his mandalas he could observe his psychic changes from day to day. The material that emerged during Jung's period of intensive self-study formed the basis of his life's work:

> Today I can say that I have never lost touch with my initial experiences. All my works, all my creative activity, has come from those initial fantasies and dreams which began in 1912, almost fifty years ago. Everything that I accomplished in later life was already contained in them, although at first only in the form of emotions and images.[6]

Jung felt that the years in which he pursued his inner images were the most important in his life. Although he felt swamped by them at first, his fantasies formed a base of learning from himself that lasted for his lifetime and influenced, in turn, many other lives.

You are not likely to be able to devote several years of your life to intensive examination of your dreams. But I hope you will not be like Freud and, feeling overwhelmed, discard what is probably the most precious material you possess. Neither extreme is essential. You can learn a great deal by keeping a moderate record over a long period of time. You might also choose to keep an intensive record for a shorter period of time.

Julius Nelson,[7] an American psychologist, kept careful track of his dreams for three years (from 1884–1887). His records contained over 1,000 dreams a year, suggesting that his recall for REM periods was fairly complete. Nelson noticed a curious fluctuation in the *amount* of his dream recall: He found that his regular rise and fall in dreaming varied with the lunar month, and he speculated that this would be true for women, too, since their menstrual cycle follows a lunar month.

This idea of Nelson's intrigued me, so I made a study of my own dream record from this point of view. I compared the amount of my dream recall to the stage of my menstrual cycle (a record I had kept independently for different reasons).[8] Sure enough, a basic pattern of dream recall emerged: Dream recall is lower during menses (the first five days of the menstrual cycle, for me, counting the first day of bleeding as day 1). There is a high peak of dream recall somewhere during the middle of the cycle (days 6–19), followed by another period of low dream recall just before the next menses (days 20–27, for me). *The highest point of dream recall is never during menses or immediately prior to the next menses.* Other factors such as illness or fatigue have an effect, but less than the stage of the menstrual cycle. I later found that a biologist [9] had been making similar measures in a sleep lab, measuring REM rather than amount of dream recall, with similar but not identical results. The value of this discovery, at least for women, is an awareness that low dream recall is common during and prior to a menstrual period and that dream recall will return to normal and reach a peak in midcycle. A woman who feels "flooded" with dreams can rest assured that dream recall will not continue to build but will soon abate for a period of time. As for men, we simply do not yet know whether others, like Nelson, have a rhythmic shift in dream recall. Neither do we know whether men have periodic shifts in measurable REM as women do. And we are uncertain of the cause for the monthly waves of dreaming and memory of dreams that occur in women. We have much to learn. Nevertheless, careful individual records of dreams kept for a long time have taught us something about all dreamers and pointed the way to new knowledge. Who knows what discovery you may make as you study your own dreams?

When you have collected a set of your own dreams, you are in a better position to examine them and learn from them than when you have only isolated dreams. Jung observed that when you examine a series of dreams, you can find certain themes recurring. An important personal point will be underlined by repetition; glaring omissions become apparent; later dreams comment on or interpret preceding ones. Calvin Hall, in his monumental study of the manifest content of dreams, also found it helpful to have a collection of dreams. Given a series of 100 dreams from the same person, Hall declares he can get an accurate and comprehensive picture of the dreamer. You will be able to learn more about yourself as your dream diary grows. Where should you begin?

You can learn amazing things about yourself as you attend to the unusual images in your dreams. Dreams often contain strange creatures or objects: a long furry white animal-bird with hundreds of legs that dances and glides over the snow (the marvelous snowbird); a creature as round as a ball, covered in feathers, with dark eyes, sitting on a stone wall (the puffball); a tiny green woman with a water lily on her bottom who dives and swims in a pond (the water-lily lady); an object the size and color of half an orange, covered with candylike shreds, that turns into a jewelry box . . .

Each idiosyncratic dream image offers us a chance to learn more about ourselves. When similar images recur over a series of dreams, they are shouting to their dream originator for attention. According to Ernest Rossi,[10] a contemporary American dream theorist, any dream image that is unique, odd, strange, or intensely idiosyncratic in a dream is an emerging part of the dreamer from which new patterns of awareness may develop. Unique dream images are the "growing edge" of your personality. If you reflect on an unusual dream image, Rossi says, it can lead you to a new awareness; if you integrate your new awareness with your present self, you will be forming a new identity; as you form a new identity, you will be able to behave in new ways in waking life that will lead to new sensations and emotions, and eventually to new and different dream images. And so the cycle of growth continues.

The process of integrating new awareness from images is called psychosynthesis. The emphasis is upon making dream images part of your conscious awareness, rather than simply breaking down the parts of a dream to analyze them (as in psychoanalysis). For example, I used the psychosynthesis process with the following surprising dream:

> *I am with a group of professionals at a conference. At first I sit on the floor or a bench close to my husband, touching him. My husband has some exchange with his brother while I look into a mirror. My hair is long and wavy, and I wear a long skirt. I experiment with different ways to wear my hair. I hold it up and decide it looks good that way. I let a piece fall down near each cheek and like it even better. I'll have to try it this way. I am surprised to realize that although I thought there was nothing from the freedom movement I wanted for myself, I'd actually enjoy changing some things like this. I'll let my hair grow even longer.*
>
> *The discussion in the conference is about various aspects of dreaming. Several people have spoken on the symbolism involved in "leaving," which refers to leaves falling down from trees. Now my husband and I are seated on chairs in the front row. Everyone is eating. I stand up and say, "We've talked about 'leaving,' I'd like to discuss the concept 'branching.' I've had several dreams in which there was a growth. There was a woman's head and from it grew branches, almost like antlers, but many of them, more and more, each subdividing until it grew thick and dense." I describe more, feeling invested and excited and finish with a flourish. All is quiet for a second. My husband leans over and kisses me on the*

cheek, saying, "You did that really well." The head person, to whom I'd directed most of my remarks, gets up and goes to get more food. No one responds. I feel frustrated but at the same time exhilarated from having expressed myself. As food is brought out I don't get the kind of cake I prefer, but a blonde girl and I eat what we want of a crushed pineapplelike cake. ("Branching Woman," 3/9/73.)

This dream expresses, in part, the frustration I felt just prior to the acceptance of my first professional paper on dreams: No one but my husband was listening and approving. There is much more symbolized here, but I turn to the unique dream image: the woman with branches growing from her head. What was that? I didn't remember ever having such dreams before. Was it a fact? Going into my massive volumes I checked back, searching for other branching women. Sketches of unusual images that I make in the left hand column were helpful in scanning the record.

Two years before the "Branching Woman" dream I located a strangely similar one.[11] On May 1, 1971, I had dreamed that I discovered a great power in myself: I found I could make the vines of a strange, blue-flowered, slightly frightening, plant come toward me by internally willing it to do so. Then I could say, "Up!" or "Down!" and the vine would obey. I could do the same thing with my hair (which produced an image like the branching lady), and then with my whole body, up or down in the air. I demonstrated all this for my husband, who was impressed. I was very excited with my great discovery that I could produce these changes by a certain state of mind, but also somewhat fearful that the power would get out of control.

Although the dream image of myself with my hair standing straight up by power of my will and the woman with antlerlike branches in a thick growth on her head were not identical, their similarity led to a realization that hair in my dreams symbolizes growth, too. This led to reflection on the image of seeing myself in a mirror (self-reflection) putting my hair up in the "Branching Woman" dream, finding my freedom, and deciding on more growth. Now the growth is welcomed without fear. I located among my dream records other antler-branch dreams. One was an incidental detail of a story in which the main female character had two small curly antlers. I came across a later dream in which a girl wore a cap from which many green leafy branches arose. This, too, was a trivial part of a dream focused on other action. In "Branching Woman" the image became central. I could no longer ignore it. By reflecting on it and tracing its development in dreams over the previous two years, I came to new awarenesses about my creative growth, my "branching." This helped give me a new sense of identity and made it easier to behave in openly creative ways. I formed the branching lady dream image out of clay in waking life, a deeply satisfying piece of work. You have growing images inside you, too. *Notice your unusual dream images, reflect upon them, trace their change throughout your dream diary, give them a waking life form. Make your dream images part of your conscious self: You will be shaping a new and better self from your dream state. You will learn from yourself.*

The way that you relate to your unique dream images will determine your future psychological development:

> If we ignore the new images we may miss an opportunity for growth; if we actively reject them they may take malignant and frightening forms that can eventually confuse us to the point of mental illness; if we engage them in an imagina-

tive drama and dialogue, they will evolve into new patterns of awareness, identity, and behavior.[12]

Dreamers must take an active role within their dreams to integrate the newly emerging elements.[13] As you actively cope with your dream images you will affect your waking behavior. The Senoi system is particularly helpful in becoming active. Dreams in which you are overwhelmed by your dream images, chased, abused, ignored, or frustrated can leave you with a "dream hangover," clouding your waking activities. Dreams in which you successfully confront danger, have fascinating experiences, and discover creative products can leave you feeling covered with "dream dust," confident, happy, and full of zest for waking life.

I have presented several approaches to consciously influencing the content of your dreams. Here I will summarize them. What do the systems of dream control have in common? What general rules can we extract? We can organize a general system for creative dreaming by planning our behaviors before, during, and after dreaming.

In every system we have reviewed, the dreamer's attitude is of prime importance. Creative dreaming is rather like believing in the possibility of love; if you have never experienced it, it is difficult to believe it can exist for you. Once love has become a reality for you, no cynic on earth can persuade you that it does not exist. So it is with creative dreaming. Once you have been fully conscious during a dream, you *know* it can be done. Once your dream state has provided you with your own poem, or painting, or solution to a problem, you *know*. Ever after you will be able to seek inspiration and help from your dream state. Sometimes it may fail you, sometimes even still alarm you, but you know its potential and you attend lovingly to the relationship. Those who do not "believe in" dreams or who believe them to be nonsense [14] do not remember their dreams or have only nonsensical ones.

Dreams are what you make of them. If you believe them to be meaningful, you will have and remember meaningful dreams; if you believe them to be creative, you will have and remember creative dreams. Dream states respond to waking attitudes. Perhaps, like the existentialist's view that the meaning of life is the meaning we give it, the meaning of dreams is the meaning we impose on them.

Thus, the first step in creative dreaming is to regard dreams as important and meaningful aspects of life. If you do not already have this attitude, you may wish to adopt it temporarily, as an experiment. You can proceed with the other steps, in any case, but you will be more likely to get good results if you value your dreams. We saw how dreams became relevant to waking life as societies used them. Since our society does not reward the dreamer for dreaming, you will need to provide yourself with satisfaction for dream accomplishments. Creative products shared with friends, insight, and personal growth are powerful rewards for dreaming.

The bulk of this book presents evidence that it is possible for the dreamer to induce both the general and elaborate content of his or her dreams and to become conscious during the dream state. We have seen it happen again and again in many cultures, including our own. Dream induction can also be accomplished by hypnotism and other powerful external suggestion, but self-suggestion is, I believe, far preferable. The dreamer is then in control; he can move at his own pace and relate to his dreams in the ways most beneficial to him. Self-suggestion may be more believable to the dreamer and more powerful than suggestion by others. [15] In addition to valuing your dreams, *it is important to realize that you can consciously influence the happenings in your dream state.*

We carry around in our minds our own Library of Congress. Vast volumes, endless collections of every experience our senses have ever been exposed to since our conception, are recorded in some unknown way in our own brains. The more we experience of life, of interesting and beautiful things, the more we have fascinating texts to take down from a shelf in our dream wanderings. It is all there, available to us, waiting to be read, browsed through, carefully examined, and recombined into our very own creative products and solutions. The greater your experience, the greater your chance of making a unique combination. *Give yourself wide and varied experience, while you also develop specific skills in your chosen field; you will be able to draw upon your experience and skills during your dreams.*

Assuming that you value your dreams, and you accept that you can consciously influence them, and you have accumulated much that is interesting to dream about, you can hasten creative dreaming by immersing yourself in the specific subject you wish to dream of. Every system employs this step. Ancient dreamers concentrated on thoughts of the god they expected to appear in a dream to heal them; past creative dreamers such as Stevenson exerted intense efforts to invent a story for a few days prior to his induced dream; American Indian youths on their vision quests endured hungry days and nights thinking about and waiting for their spirit guide's arrival; the Senoi are occupied almost constantly with the subjects of their dreams; don Juan urged Carlos to concentrate on his desired dream imagery; lucid dreamers such as Mary Arnold-Forster focused intensely on the flying dreams she wished to produce; and Yogi dreamers meditate upon the events of their dreams to come. Skills in meditation may increase dream control.[16] *Whatever subject you wish to dream about, immerse yourself fully in it. Concentrate on it. Many creative dreamers stay deep in their subject up until a few minutes before sleep.*

Some of the systems we have considered advise the dreamer to participate in activities relevant to the desired dream. Ancient dreamers worshiped the god they wished to dream of and past creative dreamers steeped themselves in poetry or tried to decipher inscriptions; Mary Arnold-Forster observed birds in flight; Guareschi taught Margherita to change bicycle tires—all activities intended to help induce the desired dream. This is a kind of immersion in the subject, to be sure, but the *waking action* may have an effect beyond thinking about the subject. Many studies [17] have demonstrated the value of personal action in changing subsequent behavior. For instance, one researcher [18] attempted to eliminate nightmares in a group of twenty-five normal children who were suffering terror dreams following a traumatic life experience. One child was frightfully awakened in the middle of the night by fire alarms and bells when the house across the street from his own caught on fire; he was troubled thereafter with terror dreams of fire engines. Some of these children were asked to choose something they would prefer to dream about, such as visiting children in different lands; others were told that their terror dream was foolish and to tell themselves they would sleep peacefully all night; still others were taken to do things relevant to their terror dreams. The child who dreamed of frightening fire engines, for example, was taken to visit a fire engine station, where he talked with the firemen about their job and the engine. All the children were eventually able to eliminate their terror dreams, but those who engaged in relevant activity in waking life were, as a group, quicker; their terror dreams disappeared, on the average, within two months. Those children who suggested pleasant substitute dreams to themselves averaged three months before the terror dream vanished, and those who were given suggestions to ignore the terror dream averaged five months before it disappeared. Waking activity can change your dreams. *Engage in activities relevant to the dream change you wish to produce; expose yourself to the positive thing you wish to dream of; experience the negative things that you dream of in a positive way.*

Concentration on the subject of a desired dream appears to be aided by a peaceful setting. Many, but not all, of the systems we have considered provide the would-be creative dreamer with a serene spot—ancient dreamers had their beautiful temples, American Indian dreamers withdrew to isolated spots, Yogi dreamers create their own peacefulness by internal set of mind. *Provide yourself with a peaceful place, if possible.*

As you concentrate on the subject you wish to dream about, *form a clear-cut intention to dream of that subject.* All systems employ this step, directly or indirectly. *Decide specifically what you want to dream about; intend to dream about it.* For example, if you choose to follow the Senoi system, you will be helped to induce it by rereading the chapter on the Senoi, reviewing their rules, thinking about them, talking about them, and intending to dream according to them. "To think a thing is to dream it." [19] *Pick the topic of your dreams.*

After a clear-cut dream topic is decided upon, many dreamers put their intention into a concise phrase, such as, "Tonight I fly in my dreams. Tonight I fly. Tonight I fly." Only a few systems of dream control employ this step, so it may be helpful rather than essential. Those who advocate it repeat their phrase at intervals throughout the day and, while the body is deeply relaxed, repeat it again just prior to sleep. *You may wish to put your dream intention into a phrase, relax, repeat it, and visualize its fulfillment.*

All this *prior* preparation discussed so far will help you to remember what to do *during* your dreams. The more you think about what you want to do in your dreams while awake, the easier the same thoughts will come to you in your dreams. Think about the fact that dreams are not waking life and the things in them cannot hurt you, until you can remember this in the midst of a dream. Think about the cues that you might have used to become aware that you were dreaming until you can recognize them during a dream. For this is the crucial transition: *Remember while dreaming what you previously intended to do in your dream.* Once you have remembered your intentions during a dream, it is fairly easy to execute them.

One important principle to remember during your dream state is to find friendly dream images. All systems achieve a more cooperative dream state in some way: Ancient dreamers and American Indian dreamers induced helpful spiritual figures; the creative Stevenson had his "Brownies"; Senoi dreamers transform dream enemies into dream friends, or call on dream friends and they appear; don Juan achieves the dream images he desires; lucid dreamers can make friendly figures appear (or any other type); and Yogi dreamers are urged to be fond of, and merge with, their dream figures.

Build friendly figures into your dreams. Value the ones that appear spontaneously; respond to them in friendly ways during your dreams. Call on dream friends when you need them, induce them, make them part of you.

The most important thing to remember during your dream is *fearlessness of dream images.* Successful creative dreamers accomplish this goal in a variety of ways. Some develop fearlessness of dreams as their dream characters work for them, as Stevenson did with his story-providing Brownies. The Senoi develop fearlessness of their dream enemies by confronting them, conquering them, and extracting a creative product from them. The Yogis focus upon "recognition" that the dream state is a dream, not waking life. As you gain control over various aspects of your dream life, you become aware that there is no need for fear because you can determine what will happen in your dreams. You can totally eliminate nightmares. You can both master and befriend your dreams. Fearlessness of dreams is easier if you are aware that you are dreaming.

Lucid dreaming, a feeling of consciousness during dreams, is one of the most exciting experiences a person can have. You can develop the skill of lucid dreaming from a brief flash of awareness to a prolonged dream adventure. As you learn to recognize prelucid moments you can test your dream experience and go into lucid dreaming. Frightening dream experiences, incongruities, or a strange dreamlike quality can alert your critical thought processes to the point that you realize you are in a dream state. You can learn to easily alter unpleasant dream experiences as they occur without having to escape them by awakening. To hold on to lucidity, you need to maintain a delicate balance between not becoming too emotional and not forgetting that you are dreaming. You may be able to maintain, as the Yogis do, consciousness throughout the transitions from waking to sleeping to dreaming to waking again.

Only two of the systems require high consciousness during the dream state: lucid dreamers and Yogi dreamers. You need *some* degree of dream consciousness to recognize that you are supposed to confront danger rather than run (in a dream) or to recall that you intended to look at your hands (in a dream). Lucidity is unimportant in the other systems and hence may limit their usefulness. You can shape your dreams without high consciousness, but the more aware you become of your dream state while you are in it, the more you will be able to actively relate to it and use it to your benefit. *Become conscious of your dream state.*

You may be able to develop lucid dreaming by increasing your number of flying dreams. My records confirm that both lucid dreams and flying dreams occur more often after several hours of rest and frequently occur in the same night. I made a special analysis of the appearance of color in my dreams and found that color, too, appears more frequently in my dreams after several hours of rest.[20] Perhaps there is an underlying common chemical base for these findings. Or perhaps the cortex is more aroused at this time since, according to my records, various types of dream control often occur during the same night.[21] In any case, consciousness in dreams is achieved more easily after several hours of sleep. Even before full consciousness occurs, you may become aware of directing aspects of the dream while it occurs, a phenomenon I call "dream composing."[22]

As you become conscious in your dreams, you can have limitless positive dream adventures, as well as turn off negative dream happenings. Delightful things can happen to you without dream consciousness—you can see a beautiful painting, get a brilliant idea for reorganizing the office, experience waves of passion, observe strange animals and people, or fly to a different land. However, when you become conscious in your dreams, your range of choice is multiplied a thousandfold. You can do all that can be done in other systems—and go beyond them. You are conscious. Your choice is unlimited. Would you feel all the joy of flying? Would you make love to orgasm with a particular person? Would you converse with a dead friend? Would you learn from a great sage? Would you travel to another place? Would you obtain answers to a question? Would you use the full creative resources of your mind? You can do any of this during your dreams because all the material exists within you. *Become conscious in your dreams and you can do all this—and more.*

Your behavior *after* your dreams is important, too. Visualize your dream, record it in the present tense, put it into a permanent form. Work with your dreams—question dream images; give particular attention to recurring dreams and idiosyncratic dream images. All systems use the valuable information they obtain from the dream state. Treasure your creative dream products. Produce them in waking life. Use them. Share them. Discuss your dreams with friends, as well as record them. Since this means listening to your friends' dreams, too, you may want to form a creative dreaming group.[23]

Developing creative dreaming takes time. It takes practice to develop the necessary attitudes and behaviors before and after dreaming, so that awareness of previous intentions comes back to you *during* dreaming. One researcher [24] found that children needed an average of *five weeks* before a self-suggested dream appeared. Some children were able to produce the desired dream in two weeks, several of them took less than four weeks, while one took as long as six months. It seems there are great individual differences in creative dreaming skills.

Hervey de Saint-Denys,[25] a French nobleman of the nineteenth century who was a specialist on the Orient, kept careful track of his dreams from the age of thirteen to forty-five (and probably longer). He described his experiences in a book published in 1867, *Dreams and Ways of Directing Them*

(*Les rêves et les moyens de les diriger*). His collection of dreams at that time consisted of 1,946 nights of dreaming recorded in 22 notebooks. He stated that he had numerous gaps during the first six weeks he kept his dream diary, but from the 179th night onward he never experienced sleeping without some dream recall. His first lucid dream took place on the 207th night of his dream diary, his second lucid dream on the 214th night; six months later he averaged lucid dreams on two out of every five nights, and *after fifteen months of record keeping he had lucid dreams almost every night.* This is a high dream consciousness, indeed. We can learn much from the Marquis d'Hervey de Saint-Denys. When I have completed the translation of his work I will be writing more about his ideas. Meanwhile, we can see that dream control takes time and practice. Don't be discouraged. It comes more easily to some people than to others. And it comes and goes in spurts. But it does come. *If you persist in your efforts, eventually you can achieve dream control.*

The fact that it is possible to become conscious during dreams and to control many events within them raises a question: Is there such a thing as "unconscious"? Perhaps dreams are simply part of the continuum of life. Perhaps there is no unconscious. *Perhaps there are only levels of awareness. Relate to your dreams creatively and you will become more aware at every level.*

Your dreams can become your own personal laboratory. All of the systems use dreams to make life better: Ancient dreamers got cured or received advice; past creative dreamers had products, such as a violin concerto or inspiration for a book; American Indian dreamers received permission for a life's career and assurance of support and help; Senoi dreamers receive daily creative products to share with their tribe; don

Juan and some lucid dreamers feel able to obtain useful paranormal information; Yogi dreamers believe they attain salvation from the endless cycle of death and rebirth. Confronting and conquering danger in dreams has helped people to develop self-confidence in waking life and to develop independence. Successful problem solving in dreams carries over into waking life. By relating to your dreams in creative ways you can help integrate your personality. Here, then, is the beauty of creative dreaming: *You can use creative dreaming for your own purposes.*

Whatever you wish to do in your dreams you can do, especially as you develop dream consciousness. You can experiment. You can practice whatever skills you wish while dreaming and they will carry over to your waking state. You can overcome your fears. You can pick whatever matters to you, plan ahead, or decide during the dream what *you* want. It is an open system. You decide. *Use your dreams to help you. Decide what is important to you and dream on it.*

In conclusion, you can develop your dream control by keeping a careful diary of your dreams, working with it before and after dreaming, and learn from yourself. The most important goals to achieve *during your dreams* are developing dream friends, becoming fearless of dream images, and becoming conscious of your dream state. As you become conscious during your dreams, you can create more dream friends and become totally fearless of dream enemies. Once you are fearless of your dreams, you become free to use them in any way you desire. Anything becomes possible. You can create a better self. You may not dream and grow rich (although even this is possible), but you can assuredly dream and grow happy, dream and develop yourself, dream and contribute to your society, dream . . . and discover the wonders within.

Reference Notes

CHAPTER ONE

1. This figure is approximate, of course, based in part on the belief that we spend a third of life in sleep, so that by age seventy we have spent twenty years or more sleeping. See Julius Segal and Gay Gaer Luce, *Sleep* (New York: Arena Books, 1972), p. 11. Most people spend about 20 percent of their sleep time in a dream state. It is extremely unusual for a person to dream less than 15 percent or more than 30 percent of his sleep time as a young adult. See Ernest Hartmann, *The Biology of Dreaming* (Springfield, Ill: Charles C Thomas, 1967, p. 11). Newborns, however, spend as much as 45–65 percent of their sleep time in a dream state, while young adults (eighteen to thirty years old) spend 20–25 percent, adults (thirty to fifty years) spend 18–25 percent, and older adults spend 13–18 percent of sleep time in dreaming (Hartmann, *ibid.*, p. 19).

2. Although data are inconclusive at present, researchers suspect that the drugs that *decrease* dream time in man include barbiturates, phenothiazines, alcohol, and amphetamines; caffeine, aspirin, and benzodiazepines seem to allow approximately normal dream time while reserpine and LSD seem to increase dream time in man. See "The Chemistry of the D-State," in Ernest Hartmann, *ibid.*, p. 51, for details.

3. Leonard Handler, "The Amelioration of Nightmares in Children," *Psychotherapy: Theory, Research, and Practice*, Vol. 9, No. 1 (Spring 1972).

4. Giovanni Guareschi, *My Home, Sweet Home* (New York: Farrar, Straus & Giroux, 1966).

5. As described in Hartmann, *op. cit.*, p. 5.

6. For example, monkeys were "conditioned" (trained) to press a bar to obtain food when they saw an image on a screen in a waking state. Later, while asleep, they performed the same action during a REM state, suggesting that they saw dream images. Described in Segal and Luce, *op. cit.*, p. 206.

7. The so-called "night terrors" have been observed, however. (For

example, see E. Kahn, *et al.*, "Mental Content of Stage 4 Night-Terrors," *Proceedings of American Psychological Association*, 8[Pt. 1] [1973], 499–500). "Night terrors" appear to be a panic reaction emerging from the deepest stages of sleep, without association (as far as researchers can tell) with a dream. The type of nightmare rarely, if ever, observed in a dream laboratory is the more common type of nightmare involving a frightening dream experience that occurs during a REM period.

8. Robert Ornstein, *The Psychology of Consciousness* (San Francisco: Freeman, 1972). Ornstein, research psychologist at Langley-Porter Neuropsychiatric Institute in San Francisco, writes about his idea that the left hemisphere of the brain is specialized to perform rational thinking functions, while the right hemisphere of the brain specializes in intuitive and creative functions. Our Western culture emphasizes rationality, while the Eastern culture emphasizes intuition, yet both functions are important in a "whole" human. We need both halves of our brains. Perhaps by rationally using our waking mind to shape our dream life and by accepting and using the creative products of our dream life in our waking state, we are literally integrating the powers of our minds.

9. As quoted in Segal and Luce, *op. cit.*, p. 262. Master bricklayers were able to recall thirty or forty features about one brick that they had laid ten years earlier—for example, in the seventh brick of a specific wall, in a specific row, in a specific year, in the lower left-hand corner is a purple pebble.

10. For example, see Montague Ullman and Stanley Krippner, "ESP in the Night," *Psychology Today*, Vol. 4, No. 1 (June 1970), p. 47.

CHAPTER TWO

1. Theodore Papadakis, *Epidauros, The Sanctuary of Asclepios* (Athens: Art Editions, Mcletzis-Papadakis, 1971), p. 5.
2. The number of reported Asclepieia varies from 300 to 420, depending upon the reference source.
3. As described in Norman MacKenzie, *Dreams and Dreaming* (London: Aldus Books, 1965), p. 43.
4. As described in Edwin Diamond, *The Science of Dreams* (New York: MacFadden Books, 1963). In fact, researchers of primitive tribes believe that the primitive people developed the idea of the soul's existence after death on the evidence of their dreams.

5. Stelae were found at Epidaurus that relate histories of forty-three patients at that Asclepion, their diseases, and their curing dreams (see Papadakis, *op. cit.*, p. 23). Similar stelae were discovered at other temple sites. Researchers conclude from these stone records that the curing dreams changed in pattern over the years (see Raymond De Becker, *The Understanding of Dreams* [London: Allen & Unwin, 1968], p. 166). Dreams early in the temples' operations were miraculous cures in which restoration of health was *simultaneous* with the therapeutic dream—for example, a lice-ridden pilgrim dreamed that the god undressed him and swept him with a broom; the next morning he was free of vermin. Dreams later in the temples' operations seemed to *provide remedies that were followed by immediate cure*. For example, one pilgrim suffering from pleurisy was ordered in a dream to take ashes from the altar, mix them with wine, and apply the mixture to his painful side, followed, of course, by a cure. Dreams from the latest period of the temples' operations were more like a medical consultation in which a *treatment was prescribed and a cure would take place at a later date*. The change in pattern was concurrent with a decline in faith.

6. De Becker, *op. cit.*, p. 149.

7. As quoted in *ibid.*, p. 170. (Words in brackets added by this author.)

8. Prodromic dreams are also referred to as prophetic, prognostic, proleptic, or theorematic, according to Havelock Ellis, *The World of Dreams* (Boston: Houghton Mifflin, 1911), p. 157.

9. The Middle East civilization comprises the peoples of the fertile valley of the Tigris and Euphrates rivers: Sumerians (in Mesopotamia), Babylonians, Hebrews, Chaldeans, Phoenicians, and Assyrians.

10. For instance, from the Middle East there is *The Epic of Gilgamesh*, a Babylonian poem reflecting the importance of dreams in that time; from Egypt, "The Chester Beatty papyrus III" (now in the British Museum), a papyrus interpreting good and bad dreams written around 1350 B.C. and incorporating material back to 2000 B.C.; from India, the text *Brihadarmyaka-Upanishad* (about 1000 B.C.), which describes philosophical implications of the dream state; from China, records of the sage Chuang-tzu (about 350 B.C.), who raised the question of whether life itself is a dream state. See MacKenzie, *op. cit.*, chap. 2.

11. As quoted in Diamond, *op. cit.* p. 17.

12. Also transliterated as *istikhara*.

13. Johannes Schultz and Wolfgang Luthe, *Autogenic Therapy* (New York: Grune & Stratton), Vol. 1, p. 142.

14. For example, Laurance Sparks, *Self-Hypnosis, A Conditioned Response Technique* (New York: Grune & Stratton, 1962), p. 55.

15. Joseph Murphy, *The Power of Your Subconscious Mind* (Englewood Cliffs, N.J.: Prentice-Hall, 1963), p. 80.

16. This is the basis of Albert Ellis' rational-emotive therapy.

17. For example, see Ann Faraday, *Dream Power* (New York: Coward, McCann & Geoghegan, 1972).

18. Ernest Rossi, *Dreams and the Growth of Personality* (New York: Pergamon Press, 1972).

19. Ira S. Wile, "Auto-Suggested Dreams as a Factor in Therapy," *American Journal of Orthopsychiatry*, 4 (1934), pp. 449–463.

CHAPTER THREE

1. Personal dream record, 3/9/72.

2. As described in Elizabeth Hall, "A Conversation with Arthur Koestler," *Psychology Today*, Vol. 4, No. 1 (June 1970), p. 65.

3. John Livingston Lowes (*The Road to Xanadu* [Boston: Houghton Mifflin, 1927], p. 325) asserted that 1797 was erroneously reported by Coleridge as the year of his "Kubla Khan" dream; it was actually 1798.

4. As quoted in M. H. Abrams, *The Milk of Paradise* (New York: Harper & Row, 1970), p. 46.

5. A more recent authority on Coleridge than Lowes attempts to refute both Coleridge's account of the dream derivation of his poem and Lowes' acceptance of it (Elisabeth Schneider, *Coleridge, Opium, and "Kubla Khan"* [Chicago: University of Chicago Press, 1953]). Schneider seems to regard dream poems as an impossible miracle and prefers the explanation of literary device. Obviously, it is possible to fabricate the origin of a poem. My own experience in dreaming poems, however, convinces me that dream poems are indeed real.

6. Lowes, *op. cit.*, p. 369.

7. Thomas De Quincey, *Confessions of an English Opium Eater* (Baltimore: Penguin Books, 1971), p. 103.

8. *Ibid.*, p. 113.

9. Socrates is reported to have stated that he had had recurrent dreams urging him to "make and cultivate music." He had interpreted these dreams to be encouragement to continue his study of philosophy, but, under the sentence of death, he composed a hymn to Apollo and put Aesop's fables into verse, in case the dreams should have meant music

in the ordinary sense. See Plato, *The Apology, Phaedo and Crito of Plato,* translated by B. Jowett in C. Eliot (ed.), *The Harvard Classics* (New York: Collier, 1937), p. 48.

10. Another ancient Greek, Synesius (c. A.D. 373–414), who was bishop of the Greek colony Cyrene in North Africa, left an autobiographical account of how dreams helped him to write and solve problems. The French philosopher and essayist Voltaire (1694–1778) is said to have composed a whole canto of "La Henriade" in a dream; American poet and short story writer Edgar Allan Poe (1809–1849) is said to have drawn heavily on his dreams for the mood and theme of his stories. The poem "The Phoenix" by English essayist A. C. Benson is said to have been dream-inspired. A Siamese writer, Luong-vichivathlen, had never planned to become an author until his deceased spiritual teacher appeared to him in a dream, handed him a pair of spectacles, and told him to use them for writing books. Other English writers had experiences similar to De Quincey's when they became addicted to opium. George Crabbe (1754–1832), English poet, reported that he was troubled by dreams of "misery and degradation" as he became addicted; these dreams are believed to have strongly influenced his poems "Sir Eustace Grey" and "The World of Dreams." Francis Thompson (1859–1907), English poet, experienced the usual opium dreams, too, according to his letters, ". . . dreams having been in part the worst realities of my life." They are believed to have influenced his work "Finis Coronat Opus." As with De Quincey, Crabbe and Thompson found their opium-related dreams marked by greatly expanded space and time during which they endured suffering, paranoid elements increased, and the element of color became emphasized. There are many such examples.

11. Kathleen Raine, *William Blake* (New York: Praeger, 1971), p. 43.

12. As quoted in Havelock Ellis, *The World of Dreams* (Boston: Houghton Mifflin, 1911), p. 276.

13. Cuneiform writing, invented by the Sumerians about 3000 B.C., is one of the first forms of writing, consisting in making wedge-shaped signs with a stylus in soft clay tablets that were later hardened (*World Book Encyclopedia*).

14. As quoted in Robert L. Van de Castle, *The Psychology of Dreaming* (New York: General Learning Press, 1971), p. 1.

15. As quoted in Norman MacKenzie, *Dreams and Dreaming* (London: Aldus Books, 1965), p. 135.

16. *Ibid.*

17. Otto Loewi, "An Autobiographic Sketch," *Perspectives in Biol-*

ogy and Medicine (Autumn 1960), as quoted in Edwin Diamond, *The Science of Dreams* (New York: MacFadden Books, 1963), p. 155.

18. Offenkrantz and Rechtschaffen, as reported in Diamond, *ibid.*, p. 157.

19. *Ibid.*

20. Robert Louis Stevenson, "A Chapter on Dreams," *Memories and Portraits, Random Memories, Memories of Himself* (New York: Scribner, 1925). Stevenson describes this in the third person at the outset because he does not reveal until later in the chapter that he is the dreamer being described.

21. *Ibid.*, p. 163.

22. *Ibid.*, p. 167.

23. De Quincey, *op. cit.*, p. 113.

24. Stevenson, *op. cit.*, p. 171.

25. *Ibid.*, p. 172.

26. *Ibid.*

27. As quoted in Diamond, *op. cit.*, p. 159.

28. B. Laufer, "Inspirational Dreams in Eastern Asia," *Journal of American Folk-lore*, 44 (1931), 208–216.

29. *Ibid.* Laufer reports the dream of Wu Ting (1324–1266 B.C.), a ruler of the Yin or Shang dynasty. The emperor's aged teacher had died so he induced a dream to show him his new teacher. He had a portrait made of the man he saw in his dream and found a common workman who matched it, whom he raised to the post of prime minister. Another Chinese dream painting, "A Dream Journey to the Other World," was made by Hui Tsung, according to his dream. The Buddhist monk Kwan Hiu (832–912 A.D.) specialized in portraits of the "Arhats," a group of advanced disciples of the Buddha. Because they were Indian, they appeared strange to the Chinese. Most artists portrayed them naturalistically, but Kwan Hiu's portraits were dramatically different, with exaggerated features, with strange hill-shaped heads, long eyebrows, and so on. Kwan Hiu explained that he followed a ritual of a prayer prior to sleep in which he received a dream of the desired saint, awakened with the dream image in mind, and proceeded to paint it. Reproductions of his famous paintings have been preserved.

30. As reported in William Dement, *Some Must Watch While Some Must Sleep* (Stanford, Calif.: Stanford Alumni Association, 1972), p. 101.

31. As reported in Don Fabun, *Three Roads to Awareness* (Beverly Hills, Calif.: Glencoe Press, 1970), p. 49. According to Fabun, most

researchers agree that the creative process consists of the following steps:

> *Motivation.* A person must desire to create something original. He may be curious, he may want to express himself, he may want more money, he may need to respond to a problem confronting him, but he always has a reason.
>
> *Preparation.* Information relevant to the problem is gathered by experiments, research, or experience.
>
> *Manipulation.* After the information is gathered, the creative person shifts it around in his mind or on paper or in concrete objects. He attempts to synthesize it into a new pattern.
>
> *Incubation.* Usually the solution does not appear at once. The person drops attempts and does something else. The subconscious mind seems to continue to wrestle with the original problem, to further manipulate it.
>
> *Intimation.* There is the sudden feeling that the solution is about to be found.
>
> *Illumination.* The solution is revealed. The flash of insight, the "Ah-ha!," the "Eureka!" experience, which has been likened to a "mental orgasm."
>
> *Verification.* At this stage of the process, the new pattern is examined, tested, proved, or found to be personally satisfying.

32. Term used by Mary Arnold-Forster, *Studies in Dreams* (New York: Macmillan, 1921), p. 83.

33. Fabun, *op. cit.*, p. 45.

Chapter Four

1. According to *The World Book Encyclopedia* (Chicago: Field, 1968), Vol. 10, p. 137.

2. This imaginary account is based on several works about the Ojibwa, including:

> Victor Barnouw, "Acculturation and Personality Among the Wisconsin Chippewa," *America Anthropologist*, Vol. 52, No. 4, Pt. 2 (October 1950).
>
> John M. Cooper, *The Gros Ventres of Montana*, Pt. II, Religion and Ritual (Washington: Catholic University of

America Press, 1957). This deals with Plains Indians rather than the Ojibwa. Frances Densmore, *Chippewa Customs* (Washington: Smithsonian Institution Bureau of American Ethnology, Bulletin No. 86, 1929). ———, *Chippewa Music–II* (Washington: Smithsonian Institution Bureau of American Ethnology, Bulletin No. 53, 1913). R. W. Dunning, *Social and Economic Change Among the Northern Ojibwa* (Toronto: University of Toronto Press, 1959).

A. I. Hallowell, *Culture and Experience* (Philadelphia: University of Pennsylvania Press, 1955).

———, *The Role of Conjuring in Saulteaux Society* (Philadelphia: University of Pennsylvania Press, 1942).

Sister M. Inez Hilgar, *Chippewa Child Life and Its Cultural Background* (Washington: Smithsonian Institution Bureau of American Ethnology, Bulletin No. 146, 1951).

Diamond Jenness, *The Ojibwa Indians of Parry Island, Their Social and Religious Life* (Ottawa: National Museum of Canada, Bulletin No. 78, 1935).

W. Vernon Kinietz, *Chippewa Village, the Story of Katikitegon* (Bloomfield Hills, Mich.: Cranbrook Institute of Science, Bulletin No. 25, 1947).

Ruth Landes, *Ojibwa Sociology* (New York: Columbia University Press, 1937).

3. Jackson S. Lincoln, *The Dream in Primitive Cultures* (Baltimore: Williams & Wilkins, 1935).

4. For example, Paul Radin and Arden King, as described in Roy D'Andrade, "Anthropological Studies of Dreams," in F. Hsu (ed.), *Psychological Anthropology* (Homewood, Ill.: Dorsey Press, 1961).

5. George Devereux, as described in *ibid.*

6. Hallowell, *The Role of Conjuring in Saulteaux Society, op. cit.*

7. Landes, *op. cit.*

8. Densmore, *Chippewa Music II, op. cit.*

9. *Ibid.*

10. Paul Wood, "Dreaming and Social Isolation," unpublished Ph.D. dissertation, University of North Carolina, 1962, described in David Foulkes, *The Psychology of Sleep* (New York: Scribner's, 1966).

11. As described in William Dember, *The Psychology of Perception* (New York: Holt, Rinehart and Winston, 1961), p. 368.

12. Patricia Garfield, "Keeping a Longitudinal Dream Record," *Psychotherapy: Theory, Research and Practice*, Vol. 10, No. 3 (Fall 1973).

13. See Ernest Hartmann, *The Functions of Sleep* (New Haven: Yale University Press, 1973), p. 81; and William Fishbein and Chris Kastaniotis, "Augmentation of REM Sleep After Learning," *Sleep Research* (Los Angeles: Brain Information Service, 1973), Vol. 2, p. 94.
14. D'Andrade, *op. cit.*
15. Carolyn Winget and Frederic Kapp, "The Relationship of the Manifest Content of Dreams to Duration of Childbirth in Primiparae," *Psychosomatic Medicine*, Vol. 34, No. 2 (July–August 1972), 313–320.
16. Landes, *op. cit.*
17. Arthur McDonald, Montana State University, personal communication, 1974.

CHAPTER FIVE

1. The Senoi divide into two groups: the Temiar and the Semai. Properly speaking, the Temiar is the more dream-directed culture; it is the one under discussion. However, to preserve unity with the literature, the more general term "Senoi" is used. An alternative term for Senoi is "Sakai," which means "slave" in their language and is, accordingly, unpopular with them; it is also used in literature describing these people. Estimates of Senoi population vary widely.
2. Richard Noone, with Dennis Holman, *In Search of the Dream People* (New York: Morrow, 1972), p. 32.
3. Herbert Noone, British anthropologist, gathered the basic anthropological data on the Senoi, which he used for his Ph.D. dissertation at Cambridge in 1939. Kilton Stewart later joined Herbert Noone in observing the Senoi use of dreams. Stewart wrote extensively on his observations, later founding a system of therapy based on them. Herbert Noone's younger brother, Richard, recently related the story of his journey to untangle the mystery of his brother's death in the jungle (*ibid.*).
4. Calvin Hall and Vernon Nordby, *The Individual and His Dreams* (New York: Signet Books, 1972), p. 19.
5. *Ibid.*, p. 21.
6. Paraphrase from Kilton Stewart, "Dream Theory in Malaya," in C. Tart (ed.), *Altered States of Consciousness* (New York: Doubleday, 1972), p. 164.
7. For example, see Max Hammer, "The Directed Daydream Technique," *Psychotherapy: Theory, Research, and Practice*, Vol. 4, No. 4 (1967), 173–181.

8. Joseph T. Hart, "Dreams in the Classroom," *Experiment and Innovation: New Directions in Education at the University of California*, 4 (1971), 51–66.

9. There is some disagreement on this point between Stewart's writings and Noone's. Stewart says the Senoi accept incestuous love in a dream; Richard Noone describes his brother Herbert's statement that a taboo love relationship—for example, with a mother or sister—in a dream should be assaulted and destroyed. I favor acceptance on the basis that all dream images are parts of the dreamer that need to be integrated.

10. Geoffrey Benjamin, author of *Temiar Religion*, University of Singapore, personal communication, 1972.

11. Reinforcement is the technical psychological term for strengthening the probability of a response occurring in the future by giving a reward after the response occurs in the present. For example, if the child remembers and tells his dream and his parents praise him for this behavior (and he likes their praise), he will probably recall and tell his dreams more often in the future.

12. Nathaniel Kleitman, "Patterns of Dreaming," *Scientific American*, November 1960, *Scientific American* Reprint No. 460, p. 5.

13. Hall and Nordby, *op. cit.*, p. 86.

14. Term used to describe positive interaction used by Harold Anderson and Gladys Anderson in *An Introduction to Projective Techniques* (Englewood Cliffs, N.J.: Prentice-Hall, 1951), p. 15.

15. Kilton Stewart, "Mental Hygiene and World Peace," *Mental Hygiene*, Vol. 38, No. 3 (July 1954), p. 403.

16. Kilton Stewart, *The Mental Age of the Sleep Mind* (article distributed by the Stewart Foundation for Creative Psychology, New York, undated).

17. Alfred Kinsey, *et al.*, *Sexual Behavior in the Human Male* (Philadelphia: Saunders, 1948), p. 519. Kinsey found that at younger ages, males experienced an average of 4–11 nocturnal sex dreams ("wet dreams") a year, while the older ages had 3–5 per year. Some 5 percent of the sample had nocturnal sex dreams more than once a week. The incidence of orgasms in dreams in the various age groups ranged from 28–81 percent, with the peak of activity in the teens and twenties.

18. Alfred Kinsey, *et al.*, *Sexual Behavior in the Human Female* (Philadelphia: Saunders, 1953), p. 196. Kinsey found that at both younger and older ages, the females experienced an average of 3–4 nocturnal sex dreams (to orgasm) per year, with 1 percent of the sample having more than one per week. The range of incidence of

dream orgasm was 2–38 percent in the various age groups, with the peak of activity in the forties. (*Ibid.*, p. 215)

19. G. Winokur, S. B. Guze, and E. Pfeiffer, "Nocturnal Orgasm in Women," *AMA Archives of General Psychiarty*, 1 (1959), 180–184. They report nocturnal orgasm observed in 36 percent of the neurotic subjects, 42 percent of the psychotic subjects, and 6 percent of the control subjects. I speculate that this research team was measuring lack of general inhibition in the disturbed group. Their data are also possibly confounded by their inclusion in the study of women who were temporarily sexually deprived—they found increased nocturnal orgasm among both normal and disturbed subjects who were sexually deprived. Another puzzling aspect of this study is the uncertainty as to whether or not the women experienced a dream in association with their nocturnal orgasms. Of women who reported a nocturnal orgasm, 58 percent said there was an associated dream. In my opinion, all subjects experienced associated dreams but only some subjects recalled them.

20. A. H. Maslow, "Self-Esteem (Dominance-Feeling) and Sexuality in Women," in M. F. De Martino (ed.), *Sexual Behavior and Personality Characteristics* (New York: Grove Press, 1963).

21. Joseph Adelson, "Creativity and the Dream," *Merrill Palmer Quarterly*, 6 (1960), 92–97.

Chapter Six

1. Ernest Rossi, *Dreams and the Growth of Personality* (New York: Pergamon Press, 1972), p. 161.

2. Refers to the operation of autonomous complexes—Carl Jung's term for the psychic contents of the personal unconscious that become twisted together into forms that seem to function independently of the ego—including the shadow, the animus, and the anima.

3. Celia Green, *Lucid Dreams* (London: Hamilton, 1968).

4. Mary Arnold-Forster, *Studies in Dreams* (New York: Macmillan, 1921), p. 28.

5. *Ibid.*, p. 29.

6. Oliver Fox, *Astral Projection* (New York: University Books, 1962).

7. *Ibid.*

8. P. D. Ouspensky, "On the Study of Dreams and on Hypnotism," in *A New Model of the Universe* (New York: Vintage Books, 1971), p. 244.

9. *Ibid.*

10. Frederik van Eeden, "A Study of Dreams," *Proceedings of the Society for Psychical Research*, XXVI (1913), 431–461.

11. Interestingly, all three of the lucid dreams discussed here occurred in the predicted time range (5:00 A.M. to 8:30 A.M.): "Looking at Myself" occurred between 7:30 A.M. and 8:30; "Big, Black Woman" was between 6:15 A.M. and 8:00; "Carving My Name" was just before 7:00 A.M. The first two were final dreams of the night, the third was followed by another, ordinary dream.

12. Van Eeden, *op. cit.*, p. 448.

13. Green, *op. cit.*, p. 90.

14. *Ibid.*, p. 99.

15. See Raymond De Becker's discussion of Chuang-tzu, Karl-Phillipe Moritz, and André Breton in *The Understanding of Dreams* (London: Allen & Unwin, 1968), p. 405.

16. See description of Oliver Fox's and Ernst Mach's experiences in Green, *op. cit.*

17. R. Griffith, O. Miyagi, and A. Tago, "The Universality of Typical Dreams: Japanese vs. Americans," *American Anthropologist*, Vol. 60 (1958), 1173–1179. A questionnaire listing 34 different dream happenings was administered to 250 students in Kentucky and 223 students in Tokyo; about 39.3 percent reported flying dreams in both groups. It is interesting that the researchers found greater differences in dream themes between American men and American women (and between Japanese men and Japanese women) than between American men and Japanese men, suggesting that sex-role training may be more powerful than cultural influence. There were some dream differences between cultures. Dreams of falling, incidentally, were even more common: About 80 percent of the Japanese and American students reported falling dreams.

18. C. Ward, A. Beck, and E. Rascoe, "Typical Dreams: Incidence Among Psychiatric Patients," *Archives of General Psychiatry*, 5 (1961), 606–615.

19. Green, *op. cit.*, p. 55.

20. Van Eeden, *op. cit.*, p. 449.

21. Arnold-Forster, *op. cit.*, p. 38.

22. Generalization: A psychological term for the situation in which a subject, after having learned to make a certain response (flying) to a certain stimulus (fear), finds that other previously ineffective stimuli will elicit the same response.

23. Arnold-Forster, *op. cit.*, p. 51.

24. *Ibid.*, p. 39.

25. *Ibid.*, p. 40.

26. *Ibid.*

27. *Ibid.*, p. 43.

28. I disagree with Green's judgment (Green, *op. cit.*, p. 81) that Arnold-Forster's dreams were dreams that "might have been regarded as extremely 'memorable,' but which were not lucid."

29. As described in *ibid.*, p. 104.

30. Oliver Fox, *Astral Projection* (New York: University Books, 1962), p. 80.

31. My flying dreams are occasionally the first dream of a series (eight times in the last year), the second dream (five times), the third (three times), the fourth (four times), or the fifth dream of a series (once). However, the most common position for the flying dream is the final dream of the night.

32. Havelock Ellis, British researcher of sex life and dream life, reviewed the hypotheses regarding flying dreams in 1911 (*The World of Dreams* [Boston: Houghton Mifflin, 1911], p. 133). They included: (1) Freud's view that the wish to fly "signifies in dreaming nothing else but the desire to be capable of sexual activities"; (2) the suggestion of Stanley Hall, American psychologist, that flying dreams are a kind of remembrance of our life in the primeval sea, that they are "psychic vestigial remains comparable to the rudimentary gill-slits not uncommonly found in man and other mammals—taking us back to the far past when man's ancestors needed no feet to swim or float"; (3) the notion that flying dreams are excursions of the astral body; and (4) his own view, supported, he believed, by later findings of other researchers, that flying dreams result from changes in the respiratory process combined with lack of tactile pressure on the feet.

33. As described in Edwin Diamond, *The Science of Dreams* (New York: MacFadden Books, 1963), p. 39.

34. Ellis, *op. cit.*, p. 144.

35. See Green's description of Subject B (an unidentified lucid dreamer), *op. cit.*, p. 105.

36. *Ibid.*, p. 106.

37. Ouspensky, *op. cit.*, p. 249.

38. Ouspensky claimed that "A man can never pronounce his own name in sleep. If I pronounced my name in sleep, I immediately woke up." He has theoretical reasons for believing that calling one's name is impossible (see Green, *op. cit.*, p. 157). Lucid dreamers have attempted to check this point, with varying degrees of success. For example, Subject C, an unidentified lucid dreamer (see Green, *op. cit.*, p. 85) states: "Another experiment I tried was the following: I thought

of Ouspensky's criterion of repeating one's own name. I achieved a sort of gap-in-consciousness of two words: but it seemed to have some effect; made me 'giddy,' perhaps; at any rate I stopped. (Perhaps at that point I was already losing the lucidity.)"

39. *Ibid.*, p. 103.

40. According to De Becker, *op. cit.*, p. 158.

41. Conclusions on limits to dream control by various lucid dreamers: Arnold-Forster (*op. cit.*, p. 50) states:

> . . . beyond the power of eliminating or ending bad dreams, which has been a great gain, the measure of control that I have been able to acquire is limited, amounting to a certain power of making a favorite dream recur more or less at will, and of being able greatly to increase its pleasurable features. Beyond this I have not gone, and perhaps if our success were greater, if our control were to become more perfect, our pleasure in dreaming would be lessened . . . [our dreams] would cease to have the charm which their unexpectedness gives them, and with the loss of freedom they would lose one of their greatest attractions.

Delage (quoted in Green, op. cit., p. 144) comments:

> . . . in conscious dreams, the awareness of the fact that I am dreaming, is the only point of contact with reality. Everything else belongs to the dream which, although more or less directed by my will in certain respects, still contains a very considerable degree of scope for the operation of the unforeseen, independently of my will and controlled by factors outside my consciousness. Everything appears vividly objective and as convincing as the events of real life, in a way which is quite different from the feeble impressions of daydreams.

Hervey de Saint-Denys reached similar conclusions. He reported in his book *Les rêves et les moyens des les diriger (Dreams and Ways of Directing Them)* his experiments on his dreams over a period of many years. He stated that he first thought that if he practiced enough he could extract from his unconscious only dream images that suited him. However, he found that he couldn't keep his attention continually on the fact that dreams were an illusion: "I have never managed to follow and master all the phases of a dream, I have never even attempted it" (quoted in De Becker, *op. cit.*, p. 158). On the basis of experiments with his own dreams, De Becker also concludes that "the unconscious has considerable autonomy in relation to the will" (*ibid.*, p. 159).

42. Carlos Castaneda, *Journey to Ixtlan* (New York: Simon and Schuster, 1972).
43. Charles Tart, "Toward the Experimental Control of Dreaming: A Review of the Literature," *Psychological Bulletin*, 64 (August 1965), 88.

CHAPTER SEVEN

1. W. Y. Evans-Wentz, *The Tibetan Book of the Dead* (New York: Oxford University Press, 1960), p. 147.
2. For brevity, all references to Yogis in this chapter refer to practitioners of the Tibetan Yoga sect who engage in dream control (Mahayanic Buddhism or Lamaism). Comments do not apply to all Yogis in general.
3. W. Y. Evans-Wentz, *Tibetan Yoga and Secret Doctrines* (New York: Oxford University Press, 1958), p. 221.
4. The information was transmitted orally because it could be dangerous if practiced without the guidance of a teacher and would be, moreover, incomprehensible without explanation, according to Ralph Metzner in *Maps of Consciousness* (New York: Collier, 1971), p. 31.
5. This imaginary account is based almost totally on the writings of Evans-Wentz (*The Tibetan Book of the Dead, op. cit.*, and *Tibetan Yoga and Secret Doctrines, op. cit.*), as I understand them.
6. The generally accepted meaning of the Sanskrit word "Yoga" is "to join." "It implies a joining, or yoking, of the unenlightened human nature to the enlightened divine nature in such manner as to allow the higher to guide and transmute the lower" (Evans-Wentz, *Tibetan Yoga, op. cit.*, p. 21). It also implies a disciplining (harnessing, uniting, yoking) of the mind by diverting the senses from the external world and concentrating thought within. There are various types of Yoga, each forming a path to "Completeness of Knowledge" (see *ibid.*, p. 33).
7. "One-pointedness" can be defined as intense focusing of attention.
8. The original Tibetan manuscript called *The Epitome of the Abridged Six Doctrines* was compiled by Padma-Karpo at the mountain hermitage, Summit of the Essence of Perfection, in Kuri, Tibet,

sometime, it is believed, during the seventeenth century (*ibid.*, p. 250).
9. The climate in Tibet is harsh. In July temperatures average about
58°, while January temperatures average 24°. Blizzards and snow-
storms are common. Violent winds sweep the land all year long.
("Tibet," *The World Book Encyclopedia* [Chicago: Field, 1968], Vol.
18.) The test of ability to generate psychic heat is carried out under
rugged conditions.
10. This state of the *Bardo* is called "Rmi-Lam Bardo" (pronounced
"Mi-lam Bardo"), the "Intermediate State," or "State of Uncertainty
of the Dream-State" (Evans-Wentz, *The Tibetan Book of the Dead,*
op. cit., p. 102).
11. I have taken the liberty of liberally paraphrasing and slightly re-
arranging the doctrine, according to my understanding of it, so as to
make it more applicable for the Western reader.
12. "Pot-shaped breathing" is defined as breathing in which one ex-
hales the dead air three times, then presses down the inhalation to the
bottom of the lungs, raises the diaphragm slightly so as to make the
distended chest similar to the shape of a closed vessel or earthen pot,
and holds it as long as possible (Evans-Wentz, *Tibetan Yoga, op. cit.,*
p. 177).
13. If the disciple is of "plethoric temperament," he is to visualize the
dot as red. The English meaning of "plethoric" as "too full, swollen,"
is puzzling in this context; no definition is given in the text. If he is
of "nervous temperament," he is to visualize it as green. Again no
definition is given, but we might assume the meaning to be "jittery,
excitable" (see *ibid.,* p. 218).
14. *Ibid.,* p. 219.
15. *Ibid.,* p. 220.
16. Yoga philosophy postulates the existence of several levels of
heavens or paradises, known as Buddha realms.
17. Evans-Wentz, *Tibetan Yoga, op. cit.,* p. 221.
18. Evans-Wentz, *The Tibetan Book of the Dead, op. cit.,* p. xxxvi.
(Date in brackets inserted by this author.)
19. The *Bardo Thödol* is described fully by Evans-Wentz in his book
The Tibetan Book of the Dead and briefly in his book *Tibetan Yoga
and Secret Doctrines.* Evans-Wentz believes that the *Bardo Thödol*
text was first committed to writing in the eighth century A.D. (*Tibetan
Book of the Dead,* p. 73). He thinks the manuscript that he used
(about 200 years old) was compiled by a Tibetan from unknown
Sanskrit originals. The author of the manuscript is not known, as he
"—faithful to the old *lamaic* teaching that human personality should

be self-abased and the Scriptures alone exalted before the gaze of sentient creatures—has not recorded his name" (*Tibetan Book of the Dead*, p. 209).

20. Evans-Wentz, *The Tibetan Book of the Dead, op. cit.*, p. 147.

21. *Ibid.*, p. 162.

22. *Ibid.*, p. 168.

23. *Ibid.*, p. 167.

24. The *deva*-world (gods), the *asura*-world (titans), the human-world, the brute-world (animals), the *preta*-world (unhappy ghosts), and the hell-world, *ibid.*, p. 24

25. *Ibid.*, p. 175.

26. Raymond De Becker, *The Understanding of Dreams* (London: Allen & Unwin, 1968), p. 153.

27. Ralph Metzner, *Maps of Consciousness* (New York: Collier, 1971), p. 50.

28. Evans-Wentz, *The Tibetan Book of the Dead, op. cit.*, p. 141.

CHAPTER EIGHT

1. Certain authors (for example, Ann Faraday, *Dream Power* [New York: Coward, McCann & Geoghegan, 1972], or Tony Crisp, *Do You Dream?* [London: Neville Spearman, 1971]) suggest wakening oneself with an alarm clock periodically throughout the night to catch a dream. This method disrupts sleep and/or ongoing dream stories. I recommend it only if other methods are not effective.

2. Hermann Rorschach, in 1942, set down rules for catching a dream, as described by Edwin Diamond in *The Science of Dreams* (New York: MacFadden Books, 1963), p. 89.

3. Henry Reed, *The Art of Remembering Dreams*, unpublished manuscript, Princeton University, 1971.

4. *Ibid.* This comment obviously assumes right-handedness.

5. Edward Wolpert and Harry Trosman, *AMA Archives of Neurology and Psychiatry*, described in Diamond, *op. cit.*, p. 90.

6. Patricia L. (Darwin) Garfield, "Effect of Greater Subject Activity and Increased Scene Duration on Rate of Desensitization," Ph.D. dissertation, Temple University, Philadelphia, 1968.

7. Patricia L. Garfield, "Keeping a Longitudinal Dream Record," *Psychotherapy: Theory, Research, and Practice*, Vol. 10, No. 3 (Fall 1973), 223–228.

8. H. Silberer, "Report on a Method of Eliciting and Observing Cer-

tain Symbolic and Hallucination Phenomena," in D. Rapaport (ed.), *Organization and Pathology of Thought* (New York: Columbia University Press, 1951), 195–207.

9. Hervey de Saint-Denys, *Les rêves et les moyens de les diriger* (*Dreams and Ways of Directing Them*) (Paris: Tchou, 1964; original version published by Amyot in 1867).

10. David Foulkes, *The Psychology of Sleep* (New York: Scribner's, 1966), p. 57.

11. M. Hiscock and D. Cohen, "Visual Imagery and Dream Recall," *Journal of Research in Personality*, Vol. 7, No. 2 (1973), 179–188.

12. David Cohen, "Presleep Mood and Dream Recall," paper presented to Association for the Psychophysiological Study of Sleep, 13th Annual Meeting, San Diego, May 3–6, 1973, in abstract of meeting. High dream recallers seem to remember their dreams regardless of their mood on the preceding day; low dream recallers seem more likely to remember their dreams when they have been in a negative mood prior to sleep.

13. Robert Van de Castle, *The Psychology of Dreaming* (New York: General Learning Corporation, 1971), p. 37. Also, Diamond, *op. cit.*, p. 58, cites a study of 3394 school children indicating that girls report *more* dreams.

14. Cohen, "Motivation and Dream Recall," in *op. cit.*

15. Cohen, "Sex Role Orientation and Dream Recall," in *ibid.*

16. Werner Karle, *et al.*, "The Occurrence of Dreams and Its Relation to REM Periods," paper presented to the 11th Annual Meeting of the Association for the Psychophysiological Study of Sleep, Bruges, Belgium, June 19–23, 1971, in abstract of meeting, *Psychophysiology*, Vol. 9, No. 1, p. 119.

17. See Henry Reed, "Learning to Remember Dreams," *Journal of Humanistic Psychology*, 13 (Summer 1973), 33–48; and David Cohen and Peter MacNeilage, "Dreams and Dream Recall in Frequent and Infrequent Dream Recallers," paper presented to 13th Annual Meeting of the Association for the Psychophysiological Study of Sleep, San Diego, May 3–6, 1973, in abstract of meeting.

In Cohen's study, eight frequent dream recallers and eight infrequent dream recallers kept dream journals for four nights and slept in the dream lab. The difference between the two groups for recall measured by dream journals was 78 percent (high dream recallers) vs. 41 percent (low dream recallers); the difference for dream recall after being awakened from REM periods was 96 percent vs. 75 percent. High dream recallers had more vivid, bizarre, and emotional dreams.

In Reed's study, seventeen students kept a dream journal for eighty-four consecutive days and met three hours a week for twelve weeks to discuss dreams. Their daily observations, totaling 1,428, yielded 77 percent days of awareness of dreaming, 64 percent of the observations yielded recall of a single dream, 21 percent yielded recall of two dreams, 10 percent yielded recall of three dreams, and 5 percent yielded recall of four dreams or more. This contrasts to my method of recording following self-awakening from REM periods, which yields almost 100 percent dream recall with an average of 3.12 dreams per night.

18. G. Devereux, *Reality and Dream: Psychotherapy of a Plains Indian* (Garden City, N.Y.: Anchor Books, 1969).

Chapter Nine

1. For example, L. Caligor and R. May, *Dreams and Symbols—Man's Unconscious Language* (New York: Basic Books, 1968). Caligor and May present a series of dreams from a single patient.

2. For example, Ann Faraday (in *Dream Power* [New York: Coward, McCann and Geoghegan, 1972], p. 58) states that she abandoned her dream diary, which contained over 200 dreams during the first year, because ". . . neither I nor my analyst could cope with so much material."

3. As described in Edwin Diamond, *The Science of Dreams* (New York: MacFadden Books, 1963), p. 32.

4. Carl G. Jung, *Memories, Dreams, Reflections,* Aniela Jaffé (ed.) (New York: Vintage, 1963).

5. A mandala is a design, usually circular, intended as an instrument to hold attention during meditation and support efforts to maintain concentration. The mandala serves as a map in a series of visualization exercises by which wholeness and unity are achieved. In Sanskrit, "mandala" means "circle and center." There is always a center in a mandala design, but its outer shape may not necessarily be circular. The mandala often has symmetry and cardinal points, but they are not invariable. (José and Miriam Argüelles, *Mandala* [Berkeley, Calif.: Shambala, 1972.) To Jung, the mandala was a magic circle symbolically representing the striving of self for total unity (Horace and Ava English, *A Comprehensive Dictionary of Psychological and Psychoanalytical Terms* [New York: McKay, 1958]).

6. Jung, *op. cit.*, p. 192.

7. Julius Nelson, "A Study of Dreams," *American Journal of Psychology*, Vol. 1, No. 3, pp. 367–401.

8. Patricia L. Garfield, "Keeping a Longitudinal Dream Record," *Psychotherapy: Theory, Research, and Practice*, Vol. 10, No. 3 (Fall, 1973), 223–228. Time asleep was controlled since more sleep would result in more REM and therefore greater recall. Peak dream recall is often between days 9 and 16.

9. Ernest Hartmann, *The Biology of Dreaming* (Springfield, Ill.: Charles C Thomas, 1967), pp. 60–62 and 111–113.

10. Ernest Rossi, *Dreams and the Growth of Personality* (New York: Pergamon Press, 1972).

11. There may be other earlier images in the record but I only searched back through two years (approximately 2,000 dreams) for branching women images.

12. Rossi, *op. cit.*, p. 148.

13. For example, Zalmon Garfield, *et al.*, "Effect of 'In Vivo' Training on Experimental Desensitization of a Phobia," *Psychological Reports*, 20 (1967), 515–519, and Patricia L. (Darwin) Garfield, "Effect of Greater Subject Activity and Increased Scene Duration on Rate of Desensitization," Ph.D. dissertation, Temple University, 1968. Other "in vivo" studies support this concept.

14. For example, the Russian philosopher P. D. Ouspensky asserts: "Most of our dreams are entirely accidental, entirely chaotic, unconnected with anything and *meaningless*. These dreams depend on accidental associations. There is no consecutiveness in them, no direction, no idea." (*A New Model of the Universe* [New York: Vintage, 1971], p. 252.) He states further that recurrent dreams are connected "simply with the sensation of the posture of the body at the given moment." (*Ibid.*, p. 246.)

15. According to Ira Wile, "Auto-suggested Dreams as a Factor in Therapy," *American Journal of Orthopsychiatry*, 4 (1934), 449–463.

16. Henry Reed, "Learning to Remember Dreams," *Journal of Humanistic Psychology*, 13 (Summer 1973), 46. Reed cites several studies relating to the hypothesis that meditation may increase accessibility to memory for dreams.

17. See reference note 13.

18. Wile, *op. cit.*

19. Hervey de Saint-Denys, *Les rêves et les moyens de les diriger* (*Dreams and Ways of Directing Them* (Paris: Tchou, 1964, original version 1867), p. 376: ". . . penser à une chose, c'est y rever" (my translation).

20. According to my records, color is far more likely to appear in dreams after several hours of sleep. Data supporting this are: I examined one lunar month of dreaming, which contained 58 dreams on 24 nights. I eliminated 8 of these nights from analysis because on 5 nights color did not appear and on 6 nights there was only 1 dream (2 nights fell into both categories). I analyzed the remaining 16 nights containing 48 dreams. I compared initial dreams to final dreams of the same night, looking for the presence or absence of color. I found that on 10 of the 16 nights color was absent in the initial dream while present in the final dream. On 3 nights color appeared in both initial and final dreams but it was equal (once) or greater (twice) in the final dream. On 1 night color appeared in neither initial nor final dreams but in an intervening dream. On only 2 nights did color appear in the initial dream and not in the final dream.

To verify these data I examined another lunar month of 73 dreams on 24 nights. Color was present in every night and only 1 night had to be eliminated because it contained just 1 dream. I analyzed the remaining 72 dreams on 23 nights comparing initial and final dreams. I found, again, that on 10 of the 23 nights color was absent in the first dream while present in the final dream. Color appeared in both initial and final dreams on 6 nights but in 5 cases out of 6 there was equal color (once) or more color (4 times) in the final dream. On 5 nights color was absent in both initial and final dreams while it was present in intervening dreams of the same night. On only 2 nights did color appear in the initial and not the final dream. The color show appears to come on later in the night.

21. Lucid dreams, flying dreams, and Senoi-type confrontation dreams often appear during the same night (although not necessarily in the same dream). This suggests a common cause is activating the several types of dream control.

22. My dream record contains numerous instances of my dream image deciding what will happen next in the dream, how it will turn out, and so on—what I call "dream composing"—long before dream consciousness appeared. "Dream composing" may be a necessary precursor to lucid dreaming.

23. Many investigators have found dream groups valuable. For example: Joseph Hart, "Dreams in the Classroom," *Experiment and Innovation: New Directions in Education at the University of California*, 4 (1971), 51–66; Eric Greenleaf, " 'Senoi' Dream Groups," *Psychotherapy: Theory, Research and Practice*, 10 (Fall 1973), 218–222; Meredith Sabini, "The Dream Group: A Community Mental Health

Proposal," Ph.D. dissertation, California School of Professional Psychology, 1973.
24. Wile, *op. cit.*
25. Hervey de Saint-Denys, *op. cit.*

Index

Meditation, *continued*
  of Yogis, 181, 184–86, 188, 194–95
Memory
  brain storage of, 28–29
  lucid dreams and, 156
Menstruation, 94
  recall of dreams and, 227–28
Metzner, Ralph, 195, 259, 261
Middle East civilization, 247
Midwifery, 94–95
Monsters in nightmares, 17–18
Montalvo, Braulio, 10
"Montevideo," 67
Moritz, Karl-Phillipe, 256
Mountain climbing, 19–20
Murphy, Joseph, 248
Muscles
  activity of, in dreaming, 24
  relaxation of, 41
Music in dreams, 57–58, 69–70, 248–49

Nagle, Mary, 10
"Naked Babies," 170
Name, calling one's own, 170, 257–58
Naming dreams, 79
Navajo, 76, 108
Neck pain, 49
Negativeness, spreading-out into, 185–86
Nelson, Julius, 227, 264
Nervous impulses, 61
Nervous temperament, 260

Nicklaus, Jack, 71
Nightmares, 13–14
  calling for help in, 19–20, 21
  confronting and conquering danger in, 20–21
  dream labs and, 25
  drugs and, 56
  escaping from, 14
  imprisonment in, 18
  lucid dreams and, 148
  monsters in, 17–18
  transformed into pleasant dreams, 62–63
  waking action to eliminate, 19, 21, 236–37
  Yoga and, 196ff.
Night terrors, 56, 245–46
Nocturnal emissions, 25, 127, 254
Nonthought condition of mind, 189
Noone, Herbert, 106, 253, 254
Noone, Richard, 253, 254
Number of dreams, 14, 24
Nursing of babies, 93–94

Ojibwa, 76, 78, 85, 88, 94–95
One-pointedness, 181, 259
Opium addiction, 54–56, 249
Orang-Asli, 103
Orgasm, 112, 127–28, 129, 254–255
  in lucid dreams, 170
Ornstein, Robert, 246